William Mackergo Taylor, William Mackergo Taylor

Peter the apostle

William Mackergo Taylor, William Mackergo Taylor
Peter the apostle
ISBN/EAN: 9783337562946

Printed in Europe, USA, Canada, Australia, Japan

Cover: Foto ©Lupo / pixelio.de

More available books at **www.hansebooks.com**

BY

WILLIAM M. TAYLOR, D.D., LL.D

AUTHOR OF

"ELIJAH THE PROPHET," "MOSES THE LAW-GIVER," "DANIEL THE BELOVED,"
"DAVID, KING OF ISRAEL," "PAUL THE MISSIONARY," &c. &c

LONDON

CHARLES BURNET & CO

5, CHANDOS STREET, STRAND

1894

[*All rights reserved*]

PREFACE.

IN the volume now presented to the public, the author has attempted to do for a prominent New Testament character what he has done in former works for such Old Testament worthies as David and Elijah.

There are many treatises—some of them of surpassing excellence—on the life of Paul; yet few have undertaken to set forth in order the incidents and lessons of the history of Peter; and in looking for a subject from the Christian Scriptures, the author was led mainly by that fact to the selection of the Apostle of the Circumcision.

As he has prosecuted his work, he has grown in his love of the warm-hearted, impulsive, and often mistaken apostle, and in his appreciation of the incalculable service rendered by him to the Church and to the world.

He has looked at Peter as a brother man, having the same infirmities as the rest of us; and he has sought to bring from his errors, as well as from his excellencies, lessons that may be helpful to Christians generally amidst the trials and temptations of modern life.

It has been a joy to him to find that he has had to keep close company with the Master, in order to do justice to the disciple; and his prayer is, that every reader may be stimulated and strengthened by his words.

NEW YORK.

CONTENTS.

		PAGE
I.	The Ministry of John the Baptist	1
II.	Finding and Bringing	14
III.	Fishers of Men	28
IV.	Walking on the Waters	42
V.	The First Confession	55
VI.	The Second Confession	67
VII.	The Rebuke	83
VIII.	On the Holy Mount	96
IX.	The Washing of the Feet	110
X.	Denial	123
XI.	By the Lake of Galilee	137
XII.	Pentecost	153
XIII.	The Lame Man Healed	167
XIV.	Before the Council	182
XV.	Ananias and Sapphira	197
XVI.	Before the Council Again	213
XVII.	Simon Magus	230
XVIII.	Eneas and Dorcas	244
XIX.	Cornelius	258
XX.	Peter Prayed Out of Prison	274
XXI.	Peter Withstood by Paul at Antioch	291
XXII.	Letters and Last Days	304
XXIII.	Simon Peter a Servant and an Apostle of Christ	320
	INDEX	335

PETER, THE APOSTLE.

I.

THE MINISTRY OF JOHN THE BAPTIST.

JOHN i., 19-39.

IT was the dark hour before the dawn, and the pall of ruin seemed to have spread over the Land of Palestine. The sceptre of David had passed out of Jewish hands, and the civil authority had come to be exercised by those who were the puppets of the Roman emperor. Even the office of the high-priest had lost its prestige, and men were promoted to it for no other reason than that they were the favourites of princes or the masters of intrigue. Crime was rampant, and cruelty was common. "Judea," as Josephus says, "was full of robberies;" and the same historian affirms "that at no time of their history, not even after their return from exile, had the nation been more wretched."*

The religion of the people had degenerated, on the one hand, into a cold and dreary formalism, which seemed to consider that a punctilious attention to all traditional requirements secured an indulgence for the commission of every sort of iniquity; and, on the other, into a cynical scepticism, which, by denying or disbelieving the reality of the unseen and the future, destroyed the eternal sanctions of the divine law, and left the man at liberty to indulge in sin without fear of retribution;

---

* "Antiq.," xvii., 10, 7, 2.

while some, disgusted with society, withdrew into the desert, and in the practice of asceticism learned, alas! only to exchange their hatred of the world for the deification of themselves.

Thirty years before, the dying embers of the nation's hope had been stirred for a season by the story which the Bethlehem shepherds told, and the rumour of some singular words uttered by two venerable saints within the temple courts. But these had long since been forgotten by all save that one thoughtful woman of Nazareth, in whose heart they were still cherished; and now, throughout the length and breadth of the land, there was the silence and the darkness of spiritual death. "When the tale of bricks is doubled, then comes Moses;" and it was at this time of deepest national degradation that a voice was heard calling the people to awake, and telling them that the morning was at hand.

Faint at first, and feeble, like the notes of the earliest bird, came to the cities the rumour of the appearance, on the edge of the wilderness of Judea, of a wonderful preacher of righteousness. Then, as the song of the bird is taken up and repeated by all the tenants of the grove, that report was caught up and re-echoed by the people, until, in eager curiosity, they trooped out by thousands to listen to his words. When they reached his encampment, they found no vulgar ascetic, no common Essene, who made a merit of his misery, but indeed a thoughtful man, who had pondered long in solitude over the problems of life; and who, with eyes that God had opened, descried the coming of a kingdom, for which he called on men, with thrilling earnestness, to prepare.

In dress like their favourite prophet Elijah, he had also the grand old Tishbite's peculiar power. He knew neither fear nor fawning. He called things by their right names; and though he had dwelt so long in the desert, he let his hearers feel that he had not forgotten the evils which he had seen practised in the cities. He aimed right at their consciences, and spoke in plain and unmistakable terms of the sins with which they were chargeable. He knew nothing of that simpering propriety, all begloved and sleek, which has chloroformed so many modern preachers; but he exposed, in words as unadorned as his own camlet robe, the iniquities of his hearers, and called on them, there and then, to repent.

Nor in his lips was repentance a mere thing of word profession. He made men feel that, to be genuine, penitence must bring forth appropriate fruits. And among these fruits it is remarkable that he made no mention of his own hermit-like life. He did not say to the crowds that thronged around his tent, "If you would prepare for the coming kingdom of heaven, then leave the busy haunts of men, as I have done, and withdraw from all participation in the engagements of your fellows." But he bade them return to their homes and their callings, to practise there the principles of righteousness which he inculcated. He did not command the Roman soldier to desert his legion, and seek another sphere for serving God; but he exhorted him to remain in the ranks, and conquer there, himself. He did not condemn the publican for gathering taxes, or inveigh against the honour and respectability of his occupation; but he sent him back to his work, to be honest in it, saying, "Exact no more than that which is appointed you." He did not pamper the pride of his fellow-countrymen by alleging that, because they were Abraham's children, there was no fear of them; but he set them all face to face with the law of God, and bade each one measure himself with its requirements. And, though men were thus condemned by his words, and made to tremble under his rebukes, there was such a fascination exerted by him, that they could not stay away from his ministrations. His very fidelity attracted them. He held them by the stern earnestness of his " glittering eye ;" so that wherever he moved along the Jordan, the cities emptied themselves into his audience.

In connection with his withering exposure of prevailing sins, and giving to that much of its power to produce immediate results, he made proclamation of the near approach of that kingdom to which all the prophets of the nation had borne witness; and he seems to have had clearer views of its nature than had been obtained by any of them. He was far, indeed, from having gained such a perception of the character of Messiah's mission as that which was afterward enjoyed by Paul. In this respect, the least in the kingdom of heaven is greater than he. Yet he was as much in advance of the prophets of the Old Testament as the morning star is brighter than the other luminaries in the train of night. To him the Prince of the new kingdom was no mere earthly monarch who was to wield the sword of the world, and outrival all Roman renown, but he was a heavenly visitant, who was to "baptise men with the Holy Ghost and with fire." He was the herald, thus, not of an external revolution, but of an internal and spiritual regeneration, to be accomplished through the mission of the coming deliverer, and the descent of the Holy Spirit into men's hearts.

As a symbol of this purification which the great expected one was to make, and as a pledge that on his coming they would submit themselves to his spiritual ablution, he called upon his hearers to receive baptism by water from his hands. The Lord was at hand! And, as when he went into the Holy of Holies, the high-priest was careful to sanctify himself, so he would have them prepare to meet the Messiah by a change of life and conduct, of which the fitting emblem was the washing of their bodies with water. Hence at Bethabara, the ford of Jordan, where, as was supposed, the tribes had crossed under Joshua, and where the waters were parted by Elijah's mantle, there was a constant stream of penitents seeking to observe this new and striking ordinance.

But among these there were some who were drawn into closer fellowship with the preacher than others. Their hearts were stirred more deeply than those of others by his words. New ideals were set before them by his instructions. Their consciences were quickened by his appeals, so that they became almost his constant attendants, and had for him that romantic affection which a youth always conceives for the teacher who has first awakened him to intellectual and spiritual life.

In this inner circle of the Baptist's disciples there were two young men belonging to the fishing village of Bethsaida, on the Lake of Galilee, who had been attracted to him most probably in one of his Galilean tours, and had remained with him so long as the season kept them from their usual labours; and it was while they were with him that he gave, to the official deputation who came to ask him who he was, that remarkable answer which we read in the first chapter of the fourth gospel. "He said, I am the voice of one crying in the wilderness, Make straight the way of the Lord, as said the prophet Esaias." And when they inquired again why he baptized, if he were not the Christ, he replied, "I baptize with water: but there standeth one among you, whom ye know not: he it is, who coming after me, is preferred before me, whose shoe's latchet I am not worthy to unloose."

It seems certain, from these words, that Jesus Christ was at the moment among the crowd that stood around the speaker; but in any case, on the following day, the Baptist seeing Jesus, pointed him out to his disciples, saying, "Behold the Lamb of God, which taketh away the sin of the world!" On the same occasion he told them how, when Jesus presented himself for baptism at his hands, he had the assurance of his identity given to him, by the sight of the Holy Spirit descending with dove-like motion upon him, and remaining with him, and by the hearing of a voice from the excellent glory, which said, "This is my beloved son, in whom I am well pleased." This statement, we may be sure, was full of interest to all who heard it; but it produced a deep impression on the two fishermen to whom we have alluded; for when, the day after, pointing to the same stranger, John said, "Behold the Lamb of God!"

they followed him to his home, and, after spending the night with him, and becoming convinced that he was indeed the promised Messiah, they enrolled themselves among his disciples.

In these two Galilean peasants we see the nucleus of the Christian Church; and John having in them introduced the Bride to the Bridegroom, had virtually fulfilled his course. From that hour onward his brightness waned, but only as the lustre of the morning star is paled by the light of opening day; and so there was not a shade of either envy or jealousy in his heart. "He must increase, but I must decrease"—these were his noble words; "This therefore my joy is fulfilled"—that was his noble sentiment; and when, for his unflinching reproof of iniquity in Herod's household, he was cruelly put to death, his disciples showed that they had imbibed their master's spirit, for they "took up his body and buried it;" and, as the most appropriate thing to do next, "they went and told Jesus."

Such were the main features of the ministry of John the Baptist. The circumstances connected with his birth, and the tragic character of his death, lent a special interest to his history; but it was the character of the man himself that gave him, under God, his power. He was, as one has said, "not merely a prophet; he was ancient prophecy personified in the last of its representatives, and appearing on the threshold of the Gospel history, to own and hail the Messiah, of whom in all ages it had spoken."* He wrote no book; he sung no songs. His book was himself; his sermons were his songs; and he who preached repentance was himself the sincerest penitent, even as he who proclaimed Messiah's approach was the first to recognise him when he came.

Yet, unflinching as he was in courage, and unwavering, for the most part, as he was in his convictions, he was, after all, only a man. Like Elijah in so many other respects, he was like him also in this, that he had his "juniper-tree," beneath

---

* Pressensé, "Jesus Christ: his Life and Times," p. 213.

which he lay in the sadness of despondency. Haply he, too, like his great prototype, expected that immediate regeneration of all things was to follow on the appearance of the Lord, and so, when he discovered that things went on much as before, he was discouraged, and sent to ask Jesus, "Art thou, indeed, he that should come, or must we still look for another?" But that was only a momentary eclipse. In a little time the darkness passed; and though, like Moses, he died within sight of the promised land, he was soon to reap in gladness the harvest of those fields which he had sowed in tears.

The Sabbath-school child of to-day knows really more concerning Jesus and his work than John did. Yet none the less was he the pioneer of the Gospel. He stood on the lookout in the labouring ship, as she crossed the troubled ocean, and was the first to cry "Land ahead!" But he left the continent itself unexplored. Yet it were as absurd to depreciate him for that as it would be to reproach Columbus because he did not add the geography of America to its discovery. Truly has the poet said:

> "John, than which man, a sadder or a greater
>   Not till this day has been of woman born;
> John, like some iron peak, by the Creator
>   Fired with the red glow of the rushing morn.
> This, when the sun shall rise and overcome it,
>   Stands in his shining desolate and bare;
> Yet not the less the inexorable summit
>   Flamed him his signal to the happier air."*

And so his "well done" has been already pronounced by the Judge ere yet he has mounted the judgment-seat; for Jesus said, "He was a burning and a shining light."

But now, ere we turn away from John, to enter upon the history of that wayward and impulsive apostle, whose brother was one of these whom the Baptist introduced to Christ, let us

---

* Frederick W. H. Myers, quoted by H. R. Reynolds, D.D., in "John the Baptist."

see if we can carry with us some lessons from this remarkable ministry, which may be valuable to us in our present circumstances.

We may learn, in the first place, that when Jesus is about to visit a community in his saving power, his coming is generally preceded by loud calls to repentance. It was the special mission of the Baptist to unfold the majesty of the divine law, and call men up to its unerring standard. Thereby they discovered how sinful they had become, and how helpless they were to regenerate themselves. Their attempts at reformation revealed to them their spiritual impotence, and made them ready to welcome that Divine Redeemer whose special gift was the baptism of the Holy Ghost. The law went before the Gospel; for the knowledge of sin must precede the appreciation of salvation; and as it was in the case of the two dispensations, so is it yet in those instances of genuine revival which at intervals have come to nations or to neighbourhoods.

In some form or other still, John the Baptist comes always to foreherald Christ. Now, he takes the form of a Luther, a Latimer, or a Knox, and with scathing eloquence, or plain, blunt sense or dauntless courage, he exposes prevalent evils both in Church and State, until men's hearts fail them for fear, and they cry, "What must we do to be saved?" Again, he comes in no human shape, but takes the form of some terrible calamity—a money panic, like that which swept over this city in 1857; an epidemic of cholera or yellow fever; or some destructive dispensation of Providence, that throws men out of themselves, and sets them, all uncovered and open, before the eyes of Him with whom they have to do. I may misread greatly the signs of the times, yet I think I recognize John the Baptist among us now. We cannot take up a respectable newspaper without reading in it some call to repentance. The demand it makes is for honesty, for truth, for righteousness. Its most pungent political articles read only like so many variations of John's sermons to the soldiers, to the tax-gatherers, and to the Scribes and Pharisees. Nay, even the political orator is calling upon the occupants of our pulpits to speak plainly to their fellow-men about the duties of every day, that they may become the conservators of the republic. What does it all mean? It surely means that John the Baptist is abroad, and that he is anew the herald of a coming Christian revival. Let it go on, then; for this cry for reformation is an aspiration inspired by God himself, and is the assurance that regeneration is at hand.

We may learn, in the second place, that when Jesus comes to a place in saving power, his presence is recognized by the descent of the Holy Spirit. John knew that Jesus was the coming deliverer when he saw the Holy Ghost like a dove coming down upon him, and remaining with him. Nor was this all: the Saviour himself was, so far, at least, as his human nature was concerned, prepared for his ministry of service and of sacrifice by the reception of the Spirit. As Neander says, "The quiet flight and the resting dove betokened no sudden seizure of the Spirit, but a uniform unfolding of the life of God; the loftiness, yet the calm repose of a nature itself divine; the indwelling of the Spirit, so that he could impart it to others, and fill them completely with it, not as a prophet merely, but as a Creator."*

Now, as the descent of the Spirit upon the body of Christ was the token that he was the Messiah, so the sight of his body, the Church, revived by the power and effusion of the Spirit, will be the sign to the world that its wished-for regeneration is to come through its instrumentality. Revival in the Church must precede the regeneration of the world. Men are crying out for a return to uprightness and truth; but they will not acknowledge that this is to be effected through the Church until they behold a revival of these same qualities in professedly Christian people. That which is needed to leaven the nation

---

* Neander's "Life of Christ," Bohn's edition, p. 71.

is not the pseudo principle, which is, alas! too common in the Church, but the real Spirit of Christ living and working in the believer.

I think it would be easy to make it appear that in all times, when scepticism has been rampant, and morality low outside of the Church, there has been little else than a cold, negative orthodoxy within the Church itself. It was so in England just before the Wesleys came forth preaching repentance; and if to-day there is a revival of scepticism and an increase of iniquity, one cause may be found in the Phariseeism and formality that are so prevalent among those who "profess and call themselves Christians." So, if we wish a blessing for the nation, we must cry for a fresh descent of the Holy Ghost upon the Church. Oh, for that baptism of fire, which shall impart to our hearts its own flaming energy, and consume within them every particle of sinful chaff, while it consecrates all their powers to the service of the Lord! Let the Church rise to its highest tidal mark in purity, in prayer, in self-sacrifice, and in devotion, and the blessing will overflow the nation too.

When revival is mentioned, we who believe ourselves to be Christians are too apt to think of others, and to look for the appearance of quickening in them. But that is beginning at the wrong end. When Christ himself went forth to his ministry of salvation, the first thing he did was to open his soul for the reception of the descending Spirit. Pentecost began by the descent of the Holy Ghost on the disciples in the upper room; and if we are to have a revival now, it will come only when you, and I, and all the members of our churches, are willing to be ourselves revived by the acceptance of this burning baptism. Ay, this burning baptism; for it burns wherever it purifies: it brings a discipline, as well as imparts an energy; and he who would possess its power must submit himself to its scorching flame. Are you willing, my brother? That is the question which for you lies at the root of all revival.

We may learn, in the third place, that they who would experience Christ's saving power must accept him as a sacrifice for sin. When John saw Jesus, he said, "Behold the Lamb of God, which taketh away the sin of the world!" and as he was not only a Jew brought up under the Mosaic law, but a priest, or at least the son of a priest who officiated at the altar, this language in his lips could have but one meaning. It indicated that Jesus Christ was to be the great antitype of the lamb of sacrifice; and that what was only figurative in the case of the animal was real and true in his offering of himself for human sin. This is the distinctive doctrine of the Gospel; this is the grand significance of the cross of Christ; and he who would really experience the salvation which is in Jesus with exceeding joy, must regard him as the great voluntary victim who took upon himself the burden of the world's sin, and nailed it to his cross.

If we are to have revival, this is what our ministers must preach, and this is what the people must believe; for the secret of evangelical success is not so much in the qualities of the preacher as in the matter which he preaches. Doubtless Luther was a great man. Yet, in his day there were other men as largely dowered with intellectual gifts as he; but none of them performed the work he did, because none of them preached the sacrificial character of the death of Christ as he proclaimed it. Read his "Lectures on the Galatians," and you will find that he sets forth the doctrine of Christ's substitution in the room of the sinner in the most objective form; and iterates and reiterates the truth, that he was made sin for us "who knew no sin, that we might be made the righteousness of God in him."

Glance over the sermons of Whitefield and the Wesleys, and you will be struck with the fact, that they also most emphatically insisted on the sacrificial character of the death of Christ. The same thing is seen in all the discourses of Mr. Spurgeon, and still more recently in the addresses of Mr. Moody. And is not an induction of particulars like these warrant enough for the inference, that in this particular presentation of the cross of Christ lies the secret of its power? It was when Andrew and John heard of Jesus as the lamb of sacrifice that they followed him to his abode; and wherever this aspect of Christ's death is fairly and fully set before men, multitudes yet will be stimulated to become his disciples.

That was a strange confession which an influential Unitarian layman made a few months ago in Liverpool, when, at a meeting of the Domestic Mission of the church to which he belonged, he said, "that though he had little sympathy with the methods they adopted, disliked the bad taste which they evinced, and could not at all agree with the doctrines which they preached, yet he felt bound to confess that Mr. Moody and Mr. Sankey had in one short month effected more among the masses of that town, in the way of reclaiming drunkards and reforming prodigals, than he and those who laboured with him had accomplished in all the years during which they had been at work." Alas! he did not see that the secret of the power of these men was their preaching of Christ and him crucified, in that very sense in which he and those who acted with him had repudiated the doctrine. Let us be assured, therefore, that if we wish revival we must obtain it, not by the ventilation of novelties in religion, but by the rebrightening of the old truth, that "Jesus died, the just for the unjust, that he might bring us to God."

Let us learn, finally, that wherever Christ is present in his saving power, there will be a disposition among men to merge themselves in him. John would not let any one put him into the Master's place; and even when some came to him seeking to make him jealous by telling him of the popularity of Christ, he said, "He must increase, but I must decrease." He was quite willing to be put into the shade by Jesus. Nay, that is far from being a right way of expressing it. His one desire was to give prominence to Christ, and to point him out to others. And in this respect he was like-minded with the Christian apostles; for Paul's ambition was that Christ should be magnified, no matter what became of him.

Brethren, wherever Christ is faithfully preached thus, revival is sure to come, sooner or later; and when our ministers shall cease to strive after eloquence as an end in itself and determine only to hold up Christ before men's eyes, then they shall be both eloquent and successful; for true oratory comes when self is forgotten in the eager desire of the heart to bring souls to salvation.

The perfection of John's wish was secured when thus he succeeded in destroying self. That is the lesson of John's ministry for the pulpit of to-day; and as we rise from the study of his career, we cannot forbear joining Keble, in his exclamation:

> "Where is the lore the Baptist taught—
>   The soul unswerving, and the fearless tongue?
> The much enduring wisdom sought,
>   By lonely prayer the haunted rocks among?
> Who counts it gain his light should wane,
>   So the whole world to Jesus throng.
>
> "Thou Spirit, who the Church didst lend
>   Her eagle wings, to shelter in the wild,
> We pray thee, ere the Judge descend
>   With flames like these, all bright and undefiled,
> Her watch-fires light, to guide aright
>   Our weary souls, by earth beguiled.
>
> "So glorious let thy pastors shine,
>   That by their speaking lives the world may learn
> First filial duty, then divine;
>   That sons to parents, all to thee, may turn:
> And ready prove, in fires of love
>   At sight of thee, for aye to burn!"

II.

FINDING AND BRINGING.

John i., 38-42.

GREAT things, alike in nature and in history, have come out of very small beginnings. In the Mariposa grove, the traveller looks on trees three hundred feet in height, yet each of these sprung from a seed no bigger than a grain of wheat; and the noble river, which at its union with the sea is broad enough and deep enough to float the navy of a nation on its waters, is at its source a tiny rivulet over which a child might stride. Similarly, the germs of some of those movements which have been mightiest for good or evil among men have been wrapped up in some apparently trivial thing. What, for example, in the view of most men of that day, could have been more unimportant than the interview which two fishermen from the Lake of Galilee had with one who for years had been known as a carpenter at Nazareth? Yet in that conference we have the earthly origin of the Christian Church. Here is the seed of that tree which has filled the nations with its branches, and which is destined yet to bless the world with its beneficial fruits. Nor need we wonder at the proportions to which it has attained, for one of these three was the "Word" who "was God," and became "flesh," that he might deliver men from the curse and power of sin.

The other two were John, the son of Zebedee, and Andrew, the son of Jonas, who belonged to the city of Bethsaida, which was situated on the northern shore of the Galilean lake, near the entrance of the river Jordan into its waters. There they had been brought up along with James, the brother of John, and Simon, the brother of Andrew, like other Jewish boys, receiving no better education than that which was common among the great body of the people. As they grew up, they gave themselves to the work of fishing, which was indeed, as its name (literally, *the house of fish*) implies, the great industry of the place. It is probable, too, that by their industry and economy they had built up a very considerable business; for Zebedee had hired servants, and James and John were partners with Simon, and presumably also with Andrew.* Hence, though they were by no means wealthy, in the modern sense of that word, they were yet in comfortable circumstances, and had, by the diligence and frugality of their lives, raised themselves somewhat above the precarious and proverbial uncertainty of the fisherman's lot.

As we saw in our last lecture, Andrew and John followed with deep interest the stranger whom John the Baptist had pointed out to them as "the Lamb of God." Their master's words had created longings in their hearts which he himself could not satisfy. He was constantly calling on them to make ready for the appearance of another who was greater than himself; and it seemed to them, from the description he had given them, that this was he. So they went after him, until, his attention being directed to them by their evident purpose to follow him, he turned and said to them, "What seek ye?" They replied, "Rabbi, where dwellest thou?" and as he cordially answered, "Come and see," they went with him, and remained beside him until the following morning.

We have no record of the conversation of that night. Doubtless John remembered it well; for even in the narrative which he has given there are minute details, such as the mention of the hour, which indicate that the whole particulars of the interview were present to his recollection; but, under the guidance of the inspiring Spirit, he has withheld the

---

* Mark i., 20; Luke v., 10.

account of what Jesus said to them, and has told us only the result. Was it because, in Christ's dealings with individual souls, there are always passages that never can be fully unfolded to others? Was it that in this incidental way the Author of the sacred Scriptures would discourage the attempt, so often made in these days without discrimination, to tell all the confidences that pass between the seeking sinner and his Saviour? We cannot tell; but just as Paul has given us no description of what occurred between him and the Master during those three days of darkness in Damascus, so John here has said no syllable of all that Jesus spake to him and Andrew on that ever-memorable night.

But in the words of Andrew to his brother we have the decided expression of the conviction at which they had both arrived. They had "found the Messiah." Now their longing was satisfied. Now their search was ended. Now the discord of their hearts was hushed to peace, and joy unutterable and divine had filled their souls. This, of course, they could not keep to themselves; for joy is ever diffusive in its nature. So Andrew's first care was to "find his own brother Simon;" and when he introduced him to Jesus, the Lord met him with these words, wherein cordiality and prophecy were combined, "Thou art Simon the son of Jonas: thou shalt be called Cephas."

There can be little doubt that the Evangelist, in recording this statement, designs to give us the impression that Jesus knew by divine insight the character of Peter, even as, at the close of the chapter in which this history is recorded, he gives us the same idea in regard to the Saviour's words to Nathanael; and the substitution of Cephas for the commoner name of Simon not only betokened what Jesus would yet make of the son of Jonas, but also indicated that he clearly understood wherein the weakness of Simon's character lay. There was, therefore, in his words a meaning which would go right to the heart of Simon, and reveal to him, as by a lightning-flash, the great want of his nature. Physically strong, he was yet not strong enough spiritually to control himself; and so, by this change of name, the Saviour indicated to him that, from his attachment to himself, he would partake of those spiritual influences by which he would be enabled, in spite of the vacillations of his impulsive disposition, to hold with persevering grasp the faith which he now embraced.* Every true believer is a stone to be built into the living Temple, which is in process of erection through the ages, for "an habitation of God through the Spirit;" but Simon, naturally unstable, was, by the grace of God, to become so conspicuous for his steadfastness, that he would be at length the stone nearest to, and resting on, the foundation whereon the Church is built.

Such was the first interview between the Master and him who was to be the Apostle of the Circumcision. And taken with its surroundings in this beautiful history, it is fraught with most valuable lessons for our modern life. We shall pick up only the more prominent and suggestive.

Notice, then, in the first place, the attitude of the Saviour to the inquirer. When Jesus turned and saw Andrew and John following him, he said, "What seek ye?" And again, when they asked him, "Where dwellest thou?" he replied, "Come and see." The Lord had nothing to conceal. He was willing to receive every one who came to him, and ready to submit his claims and his salvation to the investigation of the sincere examiner. And he is so still. True, he is now upon the throne of the universe, head over his Church, and head over all things to his Church, but he is still as tender and loving toward seeking souls as he was that day to John and Andrew by the banks of the Jordan. Exaltation has changed many men's hearts, and turned many men's heads; so that full often the chief butler in the day of his prosperity forgets the Joseph to whom, in the season of his adversity, he had been deeply indebted. But what Jesus was

---

* See Fairbairn's "Imperial Bible Dictionary," article PETER.

on earth to inquiring sinners, that is he still in heaven. Still does he say, "Come unto me all ye that labour and are heavy laden, and I will give you rest." Still does he invite the timid seeker to "come and see" the rich provision which he has made for every soul's necessity. Still does he call upon the needy everywhere, "Oh, taste and see that the Lord is good; blessed is the man that trusteth in him."

Nay, we may widen the application of this principle, and say that we have here the attitude of the Gospel toward all. It has nothing to fear from the fullest investigation. It submits all its claims to the test of experiment. It says, "Come and see." This is what Philip said to the prejudiced Nathanael; this is what the woman of Samaria said to the men of her city, who knew not whether she had not become insane; this is what the Christian of to-day says to the men of learning, who are continually speaking of difficulties in the way of their believing in Jesus: I know nothing of your scientific discoveries; your perplexities about the supernatural; your hesitancies concerning the authenticity of these sacred books; but I do know that Jesus Christ has given peace to my conscience, happiness to my heart, purity to my life, and the elasticity of inspiration to my whole being. Come and see if he will not do the same for you as he has done for me. Come; for it may be that there is a learning above your lore, and a science above your earthly philosophy. The test is in the trial. You are always talking of experiments; why refuse to make this one?

"Oh, make but trial of his love:
Experience will decide.
How blest are they, and only they,
Who in his truth confide."

Notice, in the second place, that it is a great thing when a man "finds" Christ. Now, in working out this thought, we must have a clear idea of what we mean by "finding" Christ. Andrew and John were in visible and bodily contact with Jesus, and it might seem, therefore, that it was an easier thing to come to Christ when he was on earth than it is now, when he is enthroned in heaven. But that is a mistake. Many came to converse with him when he lived in the world who yet failed to find the Saviour in him. Multitudes might be pushed into contact with him that day when the poor woman timidly sought a cure by touching his clothes; but it was to her alone that he referred when he said, "Somebody hath touched me." Therefore, the contact in her case must have been something more than physical, and could be nothing else than the application of her soul to him in simple faith for healing.

In like manner, the finding of the Messiah by Andrew and John must have been something else than their coming into conversation with him, and could be nothing less than a description of the fact that they were intellectually convinced that Jesus of Nazareth was the promised Messiah, and were sincerely willing to accept him as their Saviour and guide.

But the presence of Jesus in actual humanity before us is not essential to the exercise of such confidence as that; and so soon as a man becomes convinced that Jesus Christ came into the world to save sinners, and is willing to accept salvation at his hands, he "finds" Christ just as truly as he was found by Andrew and John, as recorded in this section of the sacred narrative. Now, when a man "finds" Christ thus, it is for him the greatest event of his life, dominating and directing every after-circumstance in his career.

How much the history of the world has been affected by the discoveries which men have made! Take a few. The discovery of America; the invention of printing; the discovery of the power of steam, and the manifold application of the steam-engine; the invention of the telegraph: who shall say how much all these have done for the progress of civilization? But put them all together, they have not done so great things for the world at large as the discovery of Christ does for every soul that "finds" him. It opens up a whole new world for his exploration; it enstamps a new name and nature upon his heart; it brings him under the influence of a motive principle which "laughs at impossibilities," and removes mountains; and it gives him a means of communication with the unseen as real, as mysterious, and as immediate as that hidden cable whereon the messages of two hemispheres vibrate in response to each other. It relieves his conscience from the weight of guilt; it elevates his intellect; it purifies his affections; it forms his character; it gives a new aim to his life and a new centre to his heart, and brings him so under the constraining influence of the love of Christ, that, while retaining the great outstanding marks of his individuality, he may yet truly be said to be a new man. See how this comes out in Paul. Converted or unconverted, the man of Tarsus would still have been a leader of his fellows. But mark how, after he has found Christ, his whole being goes into a new direction, and becomes transfigured and ennobled by the change. His energy becomes sublimed, his ambition purified, his nature elevated. Behold, also, how it appears in Peter! What a contrast between the fisherman and the Apostle! And how much this discovery of Christ made by him, through Andrew's guidance, did to give him character and influence among men! Had he never found the Messiah, who had ever heard his name? But from this hour he begins to be illustrious! Said I not truly, therefore, that it is a great thing when a man finds Christ? It is indeed the very greatest thing for safety, for happiness, for usefulness, for honour, that can be said of any man, when it is affirmed of him that he has found Christ. My hearer, can it be truly said of you?

Notice, thirdly, that when a man has found Christ, he ought to bring others to Jesus. The first thing Andrew did was to tell to another the good news which had already thrilled his own heart. So Philip, as recorded in this same chapter, found Nathanael, and repeated the same news to him. Indeed, it is quite worthy of note how often this "finding" occurs in this delightful narrative. Andrew "findeth" Messiah, then he "findeth" his brother. Jesus "findeth" Philip; and Philip "findeth" Nathanael. So that, as Trench has beautifully said, in allusion to the well-known exclamation of Archimedes in connexion with one of his discoveries, this "is the chapter of the Eurekas."* "I have found him! I have found him!" Indeed, the promptings of one's own nature here are in perfect accordance with the commands of the Lord; for we cannot but tell to others the tidings which have made us glad; and in proportion to the happiness which they have produced in us will be our eagerness to make others sharers with us in our delight. As Matthew Henry says here, "True grace hates all monopolies, and loves not to eat its morsels alone." The woman of Samaria ran to tell her townspeople of the great Messiah, and the disciples who were scattered abroad by the first persecution "went everywhere preaching the Word." The command is, "Let him that heareth say, Come!" and every Christian should become thus a missionary of the Cross. Indeed, we have not rightly heard, if there is not within us an impulse to say "Come." If there be no enthusiasm within us for the diffusion of the Gospel, or the conversion of sinners, we make it only too apparent that we have not the Spirit of Christ; but if our souls are stirred at the sight of our perishing fellow-men, and our hearts prompt us to make efforts for their salvation, we prove that we are in sympathy with those celestial beings among whom there is "joy over one sinner that repenteth," and that the same mind is in us which was in him who died that men might be redeemed.

"As ye go, preach." "Go into all the world, and preach the Gospel to every creature." These are what the Great Duke once styled "the marching orders" of believers; and it is at our peril if we refuse to carry them out. But when the word "preach" is used, let us beware of supposing that we need all the outward accessories of a crowded congregation and a modern church, in order to obey this command. The meaning simply is, that we should tell the good news as we have

---

* "Studies in the Gospels," p. 67.

opportunity. We may "preach" by conversing with our friend as we walk down with him to business in the morning, or by an incidental remark introduced, not obtrusively or impertinently, but naturally and lovingly, as we talk with our fellow-traveller in the steamboat or in the railway car; or by the giving of an interesting volume that contains the truth to some ingenuous youth upon his birthday; or by repeating at the couch of some sick one the leading portions of a sermon which we have just heard in the sanctuary; or by teaching a class in the Sabbath-school; or by bringing a friend with us to the church where we know that the faithful preacher will be sure to have some word that will point out the way to the Cross; or even, without a word at all, we may preach the most eloquent and powerful of all sermons, by simply living for Jesus where we are. There is a sphere for every one; and none can claim exemption from this great Gospel law, "As ye go, preach."

But who would desire exemption when there is so great need for the exertions of all? See how earnest the apostles of evil are to allure men to destruction, through one or other of the several avenues that lead to death; and shall we be less eager to labour for their salvation? Behold how indefatigable are the endeavours of those who live to spread abroad the news of every day! What telegraphic agencies they use to bring to this one centre the record of important occurrences the world over! What magnificent machinery they employ to multiply the number of impressions of their journals! And how eager they are to send forth their messengers in the gray morning twilight, to leave at every door their daily photographs of God's providence as it reveals itself to their eyes—alas! not always clear enough to read it right. Shall they be so enthusiastic about the news of earth, and we be inactive with the better news of the Gospel? It is told of the commentator Thomas Scott that, as he went to preach at a church in Lothbury at six o'clock in the morning, he used to observe that if at any time in his early walk he was tempted to complain, the sight of the newsmen, equally alert, and for a very different object, changed his repining into thanksgiving. So, every time we take up a newspaper, let us feel reproved for our remissness in telling the good news of God's salvation to our fellow-men; let us be stirred up to self-sacrifice and devotion in this glorious cause, and let us resolve to do our utmost in bringing others to the Saviour whom we have found for ourselves.

Notice, in the fourth place, that, in seeking to bring others to Jesus, we should begin with those most intimately connected with us. Andrew went first to find Simon, his "own brother." In like manner, Philip sought his friend Nathanael. And the Lord Jesus himself laid down the same general law when he commissioned his disciples to preach repentance and the remission of sins "among all nations, beginning at Jerusalem." Now, this is a point of pre-eminent importance; for among those who really desire to be useful in the world the idea is too common, that they must go somewhere else than where they are in order to find their proper and peculiar work. They look so far away, and so high up, for a mission-field, that they overlook the work that is already waiting for them just at their feet. Thus, while professing to be eager for labour, they are standing in the market-place, "all the day idle."

In spiritual activity, as in all other matters, it is a good rule to begin at the beginning. How many, in trying to learn some of the sciences—say geology, for example—have disdained the use of hand-books for the mastering of the elements, and, plunging at once into some elaborate treatise, which presupposed familiar acquaintance with the rudiments, have felt themselves unable to understand it, and have thrown up the whole study in disgust! Now, it is just thus many do in Christian work. They begin at the wrong place, and so they speedily become discouraged. Work from the centre out, and the radii of your influence will go out to every point of the circumference; but if, leaving your own proper centre, you take your station somewhere on the circumference, your labour will produce very little result. Now, home is the centre of every man's sphere; and it is there he must begin to work for Jesus. Let the husband begin with the wife, and the wife with the husband; the parents with the children; and the children, where need is, lovingly and humbly, with the parents; the brother with his sister; and the sister with her brother. Then, when the home sphere is filled up, let your life's influence flow over, and seek to benefit those with whom you are coming into daily business contact. Thus the branches of your vine will "run over the wall," and your sphere will widen ever with your endeavours.

"Oh yes!" you will say to me, "that may be all very true. But it is far more difficult thus to begin at home than to commence abroad. I would rather teach a class in the mission-school than speak to my own family about Jesus. I would almost sooner address a meeting than make a private appeal to my brother or my sister." But why is that? Surely it cannot be because you love those who are nearest to you less than you do those who are farther away! Can it be because you would get more prominence and honour among men, by working abroad, than you could secure by labouring at home? Or is it because you are conscious that your home conduct would destroy the influence of any teachings on which you might venture there? You know best. But whatever be its cause, let me beseech you to revise your whole procedure, and make home the head-quarters of your effort. Can it be that there are here a wife and husband who have never had one hour of heart communion with each other on this all-important matter? If there be, may God himself in some way break that silence that has sealed their tongues; and let us all rest assured that the truest revival of religion will be gained when our church members are resolved to test what shall be the result of beginning to labour thus for Christ at home.

We are making far too little in these days of the Church in the house. We are waiting for our children to be converted by outside influences, when, if we were to look at the matter rightly, it should be our ambition to be ourselves the leaders of our sons and daughters to the Lord. Some years ago I read an account of the manner in which a cold church was stirred into warmth and vitality; and as it bears directly on the point to which I am now referring, I will take the liberty of introducing it here. At one of the conference meetings, a simple man, not remarkable for fluency or correctness of speech, made an appeal something to the following effect: " I feel, brethren, real bad about the people who don't love the Lord Jesus Christ here in our own neighbourhood. We're not as we ought to be, that's very certain, but it's hard work rowing against the stream. We find that out when we talk to men about religion on Sunday who haven't any religion all the week. They don't mind us. And just so with the young folks. Their minds all seem running one way. Now, what's to be done? Not much with the grown folks, for they aren't controlled by us, and we can only drop a word now and then, and pray for them. But here's our own children. I have four boys, and only one of them comes to the communion with his mother and me. And I don't think I have done my duty to those younger boys. They love me, and God knows I love them; but I kind o' hate to speak to them about religion. But rather than see them go farther without my Jesus for their Jesus, I'm going to ask them to join him. I'm going to pray with them; and if I can't tell them all they want to know, why, our minister can. Brethren, I'm going to try to turn the stream for my boys. Home is the head of the river. I mean to begin to-night. Won't some father do like me with his boys, and give me his word out?" Scarcely had he seated himself, when, one after another, some thirty people pledged themselves, saying, "I'll do the same at my house;" and the pledge was kept. In a short time the minister's labours began to tell as they had never done before. The influence spread, but there was no excitement. On the occasion of the communion-service, from family after family, one and another came to enroll themselves among the followers of Jesus, and nearly every one that came was under twenty-five years of age. So, through revived home effort, the work of God was stimulated both in the church and in the neighbourhood. My friends, this witness is true, "Home is the head of the river." Is there no one here to-night who will join in the resolution made by that earnest man, and say, "By the grace of God, I'll do the same at my house?"

Notice, finally, that in following this plan of working for Christ we may, all unconsciously to ourselves, be the means of introducing to Jesus one who will be of far more service than ever we could have been. It was Simon Peter whom Andrew brought to Christ. We do not hear much in the New Testament of Andrew's after-history, but if he had never done anything else than lead his brother to the Lord, it was worth living for just to do that; and when we get to heaven, we shall see that the lustre of Peter's crown casts special radiance on Andrew's face. When we read of the conversions on the Day of Pentecost; of the heroic protest before the council; of the conversion of Cornelius; and above all, when we peruse those two precious letters which Peter has indited, let us not forget that, humanly speaking, but for Andrew, Peter would not have been himself a Christian. Doubtless, God could have called him by some other instrumentality, but he made use of Andrew to teach us the lesson that, in doing the good that lies at our hands, we may at length really do more for the Church than we could have effected by more ostentatious effort in other places. Let the lowly and timid, therefore, take courage. They may not have shining talents or commanding position, yet by working where they are they may be honoured in bringing to Jesus some who shall take foremost places in the Church, or become leaders in some missionary or evangelistic movement.

Many of the greatest men the Church has known have been converted through the agency of individuals all but unknown.

Some of the greatest theologians the Church has ever seen, and some of the most useful ministers who have ever lived, have been made and moulded by so common a thing as a mother's influence. Robert Pollok, whose "Course of Time" used to be a household book throughout Scotland, said once of his poem, "It has my mother's divinity in it." Mother, will you take note of that? Many a time you have regretted that you could not take part in any public work for Christ, by reason of the bond that held you to your boy. Regret no more, but bring that boy to Christ, and he will live to do his own work and his mother's too; and when the crown is placed upon his head its diamonds will flash new glory upon your countenance.

The sum of what we have been saying, then, is this: that each of us should begin to do all that he can, where he is, for Christ. But if we would succeed in that effort, we must be sure that we have already found him for ourselves. A minister had preached a simple sermon upon the text, "He brought him to Jesus;" and as he was going home, his daughter, walking by his side, began to speak of what she had been hearing. She said, "I did so like that sermon." "Well," inquired her father, "whom are you going to bring to Jesus?" A thoughtful expression came upon her countenance as she replied, "I think, papa, that I will just bring myself to him." "Capital!" said her father; "that will do admirably for a beginning." This, brethren, is the true starting-point. We must be good, if we would do good. Bring yourselves to Jesus, therefore; and, as iron by being rubbed with a magnet, becomes itself magnetic, so you, being united to Christ, will become partakers in his attractive power, and will draw men with "the cords of a man," which are also "the bands of love."

III.

FISHERS OF MEN.

Luke v., 1-11; Matthew iv., 18-22; Mark ii., 16-20.

MANY things in the ministry of Jesus had occurred between that day on which Simon Peter had been introduced to him by Andrew, and this on which, from his boat-pulpit on the Lake of Galilee, he addressed the multitudes that lined its banks. From the scene of John's baptism on the river Jordan, the Master, accompanied by some of those who had cast in their lot with him, repaired to Galilee, where he signalized his entrance upon public life by performing the miracle of turning water into wine. Thence he went up to Jerusalem to keep the Passover, and while there he drove the traders from the Temple, and wrought many marvellous works. It was at this time, also, that he received Nicodemus by night, and had with him that important interview described by the fourth Evangelist.

From Jerusalem, the Lord passed into the rural districts of Judea; but learning there that the faithful Baptist had been cast into prison by Herod, he returned to Galilee, taking Samaria on his way, and meeting thus the woman to whom he spoke so faithfully, yet so lovingly, at the well of Jacob. From Galilee, after having performed a second miracle at Cana, he went to Nazareth, where he entered into the synagogue on the Sabbath, and expounded one of Isaiah's predictions with immediate reference to himself. But his townsmen were filled with enmity against him, and even sought to put him to death, so that he withdrew to Capernaum, where he fixed his residence for the time; and it was during the first weeks of his sojourn there that those events occurred to which our attention is now to be directed.

I have been thus particular in enumerating these incidents, that you may have clearly before you the fact that Peter and his partners had returned to their ordinary pursuits after their first fellowship with Jesus. It is impossible, indeed, to fix at what particular point they left him and went back to their business. Probably, on his return from Jerusalem, instead of accompanying him to Nazareth, they went back to their homes. But, however that may have been, they were once more in their boats and with their nets.

Nor let that seem strange. They had become disciples. But they had not yet been called to the apostleship. Now, to be a disciple, it is not necessary that we should leave our secular calling and spend all our time in preaching Christ. All that is needed is, that we serve him in our business; and so, if before this time they had left all their common pursuits, they might have been chargeable with presumption, and with running before they had been sent. Only here and there a Matthew, sitting at the receipt of custom, is commanded to leave his desk and give himself to the ministry of the Gospel; the great majority of men are called to follow Jesus while they remain at "the receipt of custom;" and the ministry of such a life, maintained in holiness and integrity for Jesus' sake, may be only less powerful, if indeed it be less powerful, than that of the consecrated preacher.

The scene which is painted for us by the Evangelist here is one of the most fascinating description. It is morning by the Lake of Gennesaret, and the cities and villages around its banks have awaked to the activities of life. The hills on its eastern shore are baring their heads to greet the day; and the waters rippling under the early breeze are reflecting, in myriad flashes, the gay sunbeams. To the right, as we look across the lake, lies the city of Capernaum, so near us that we may hear almost the hum of its inhabitants; and to the left, the fleet of fishing-boats, which have been out all night, are standing in toward Bethsaida. Far away long the shining beach the eye catches a glimpse of Magdala and Tiberias, while everywhere there are indications of stirring energy among the people. Here was no place of solitude, like that which one finds by the shore of a Scottish Highland lake, or on the margin of a hidden sea in the depths of our own wilderness; but, instead, a centre of teeming, earnest life. "It was," as Stanley has remarked, "to the Roman Palestine almost what the manufacturing districts are to England. Nowhere, except in the capital itself, could the Lord Jesus have found such a sphere for his works and words of mercy; from no other centre could his fame have so gone throughout all Syria; nowhere else could he have drawn round him the vast multitudes that hung upon his lips."*

See how they throng him now! He has but just made his appearance, coming either from his mountain closet or his city home; yet, as he moves along the shore, a constantly increasing multitude follows him, until the pressure becomes inconveniently great; and then, that he may the more easily and effectively address the people, he goes into Simon's boat, and getting him to push off a few yards, "he sat down and taught the people out of the ship." Some parable from the scene that was around him; some tender appeal, or some solemn warning, or some far-reaching and impressive enforcement of a spiritual principle— we are not told what—was the subject of his discourse. But whatever it was, it would gather in upon him the eager attention of the listeners, while the fishermen by his side, forgetting their nets, would cease their work for the time, as they listened to his words.

But now the discourse is ended, and the Lord, turning to Simon, bids him "Launch out into the deep, and let down your nets for a draught." The fisherman is astonished, and replies, not in unbelief, but in amazement, "Master, we have

---

* Stanley's "Sinai and Palestine," p. 368.

toiled all night, and have taken nothing; nevertheless, at thy word, I will let down the net." He did not mean to say that it would be useless, because the night was always the most favourable time for fishing; and since they had been unsuccessful then, there was no probability that they would get anything now. But his answer was an acknowledgment of failure, and an expression of faith triumphant in failure: "I should not have thought of doing anything of the kind; but if thou sayest it, I will let down the net, and look yet for success!" And his faith was amply rewarded, for they inclosed such a multitude of fishes that the net began to break, and only by the help of James and John, his partners, could Simon secure his haul. Even as it was, both of their boats were filled with the finny freight, so that they were all startled.

But the effect on Simon was electric. With that quick insight, and that prompt yielding to the impulse of the moment, which, as we proceed in his history, we shall discover were characteristic of him, he saw the glory of Messiah's Godhead streaming through the miracle,* and fell at his knees, saying, "Depart from me; for I am a sinful man, O Lord."

But Christ was better to him than his words besought, for he said, "Fear not; from henceforth thou shalt catch men;" and, looking round upon the others, he said to them, "Follow me, and I will make you fishers of men." Nor did they hesitate as to their response, for, "when they had brought their ships to land, they forsook all, and followed him."

This scene marks another stage in Peter's history. Let us see what we may learn from it for our direction and encouragement.

---

* For miracle it was, betokening that "Jesus as the Lord of nature, the ideal man, the second Adam, in whom is fulfilled the words of David, 'thou hast put all things under his feet, the fowl of the air, and the fish of the sea,' did, by the secret yet mighty magic of his will, wield and guide the unconscious creatures so as to make them subserve the higher interests of his kingdom."—*Trench on the Miracles*, p. 131.

We may, in the first place, be reminded that discipleship comes before apostleship. Peter had been, for at least some months, a docile learner in the school of Christ before he was called here to forsake all, and follow him as an apostle. They who would teach others about the Lord must first be acquainted with him themselves. It is, indeed, true that God may sometimes employ the agency of one who is himself unconverted as a means of leading others to the knowledge of the Lord Jesus. Thus it is not at all improbable that the title which Pilate, himself a time-serving trimmer, placed over the cross of Christ to this effect, "This is Jesus of Nazareth, the King of the Jews," was one of the means used by the Spirit in leading the penitent thief to present the prayer, "Lord, remember me, when thou comest into thy kingdom." But that is not his ordinary method. Usually he employs one who is already a disciple to bring others to himself.

Now, this is a most important matter for those of us who, as preachers, or missionaries, or Sabbath-school teachers, or parents, are striving to commend Christ to others. Do we know him ourselves? My brethren and fellow-labourers, that is for us the question of questions! One may be like a lightship, guiding others into the harbour, and yet himself so anchored that he cannot enter it! Like Noah's carpenters, we may help to build an ark for the salvation of others, and yet perish ourselves. What a fearful possibility! Let us take care that it be not actualized in us!

We complain sometimes that we cannot interest those whom we are trying to instruct. We are discouraged because we see small results from our exertions. May not the reason be that we are not truly converted ourselves? That was a wise advice which an aged minister gave to a young clergyman: "Whatever goes wrong, always blame yourself." And we may almost always conclude that, if we are not successful in winning souls, the reason is either because our own souls are not yet won, or because they are cold and destitute of the highest energy. It is only light that can enlighten; it is only fire that can kindle flame; hence, if we would illuminate others, we must have within ourselves the true light; and if we would set the hearts of others in a blaze, we must take the live coal with which we do so from off the burning altar of our own spirits. Disciples first, my hearers! It is good to work for Christ; but the first thing is to let him work in us! "Freely have ye received, freely give"—that was his charge to those whom he first sent out. They could not give until they had received. So, if there be one here to-night, himself unconverted, who is a Sabbath-school teacher, or a worker in some Christian enterprise, let me beseech him, now and here, to open his own heart for the reception of the blessing of Christ's salvation; and that will give his lessons a power, and his labour a success which he has never known before.

We may be reminded, in the second place, that the knowledge of self, obtained through the discovery of Christ, is one of the main elements of power in seeking to benefit others. It is not a little remarkable, that when God has called some of his greatest servants to signal service, he has begun by giving them a thorough revelation of themselves, through the unveiling to them of himself. Thus, when he appeared to Moses at the bush, the first effect was that "Moses trembled, and durst not behold;"* and the ultimate issue was that he cried, "O my Lord, I am not eloquent; but I am slow of speech, and of a slow tongue." Forty years before, he had been ready enough to trust in himself, and stand forth as the deliverer of his people. But that very self-confidence betokened his unfitness for the work which he assumed, and now his self-distrust, albeit he let it go too far, was an indication of his preparation for the enterprise which Jehovah set before him. So, again, when Gideon at his threshing-floor was visited by the angel of the Lord, who summoned him to go forth and

---

* Exodus iv., 10; Acts vii., 31.

deliver his people from the hand of the Midianites, the exclamation of his heart was,* "O my Lord, wherewith shall I save Israel? behold, my family is poor in Manasseh, and I am the least in my father's house." In the same manner, when Isaiah† saw God's glory in the temple, the result was that he cried out, "Woe is me! for I am undone; because I am a man of unclean lips, and I dwell in the midst of a people of unclean lips: for mine eyes have seen the King, the Lord of Hosts;" and this, together with the purifying of his lips, was the fitting prelude to his reception of the great commission to speak to men in Jehovah's name.

Now, we see precisely the same thing in the case of Peter here. He recognized the deity of Jesus through the miracle, but the light of that Godhead did at the same time flash into his own heart, and reveal him unto himself as he had never had himself revealed unto him before. Nay, the contrast between the holy God and the unholy self was so terrible, and the recoil of the one from the other so tremendous, that he cried out, " Depart from me; for I am a sinful man, O Lord!" Then came the Master's "Fear not," with its soothing influence; and thus, through his discovery of himself and his knowledge of his Lord, he was prepared for his apostolic service.

A knowledge of his own heart, and an experimental acquaintance with Christ—these are, next to the accompanying agency of the Holy Ghost, the mightiest elements of the preacher's power; and by the preacher here, I mean, not the minister only, but anyone who seeks to witness for Christ. Those with whom you have to do are men like yourselves; and that which has found its way to your heart will find its way to theirs. They are environed with the same besetments as those which surround you. They have to do battle with the same temptations as those with which you have to contend. The help which supported you will sustain them; and the Saviour who delivered you can deliver them.

---

* Judges vi., 11-15. † Isaiah vi., 1-8.

I have seen a housemaid in one of our great hotels take a skeleton-key and pass into every chamber of a spacious corridor, laying open the contents of each, and setting to work in its purification. Now, such a skeleton-key is the knowledge of his own heart to the minister of Christ. It enables him to unlock the hearts of others, and enter into them and turn out their hidden things, so that, as he proceeds, his hearers cry "Who told him all that? He seems to be reading the very innermost secrets of my soul." Who told him? I will answer. It was Jesus, when, in the hour of his discovery of the Saviour, the light of the Godhead gleamed in upon his own heart, and let him see *himself*. But mere self-knowledge is not enough: it must be combined with, nay, consequent upon, the knowledge of the Lord. Oh, how far Peter saw into the heart of Christ through that "Fear not!" It showed him that bad as he had found out that he was, the Lord was willing to receive him still, and so it gave him the assurance that he was able to save others as vile as himself. Doubtless, therefore, the remembrance of this "Fear not" was one of the factors of his power on the Day of Pentecost, when, even to "Jerusalem sinners," he could say, "Repent and be converted, that your sins may be blotted out."

Nor is Peter's case singular here. You have an instance of the same thing in Bunyan, although in his experience the discipline spread over years, instead of being, as here, concentrated into a moment. How he loathed himself for long before he heard the Lord's gracious "Fear not!" and yet, terrible as the ordeal was, if he had not gone through it, he had never written his immortal allegory, or told his thrilling story of "grace abounding to the chief of sinners."

So, too, John Newton passed through the same terrible tunnel to his destination in the pulpit. William Jay, of Bath, tells the following story of an interview with him. "When I, one day, called upon him, he said, 'I am glad to see you, for I have just received a letter from Bath, and you may know something of the writer,' mentioning his name. I told him I did, and that he had been for years a hearer of mine, but he was a most awful character, and 'almost in all evil.' 'But,' said he, 'he writes now as a penitent.' I said, 'He may be such; but if he be, I shall never despair of the conversion of anyone again.' 'Oh,' said he, 'I never did, since God saved me.'" That confidence in Christ's almightiness to save! Who can tell how much it added to John Newton's power? "Since he saved me!" Who can doubt that the memory of that gave tenderness to his heart for sinners such as he had been? On the wall of his study at Olney, over the place where his desk stood, he had written, in very large letters, these words, "Remember that thou wast a bondsman in the land of Egypt, and the Lord thy God redeemed thee;"* and every reader of his letters feels that the memory of that experience is throbbing through all these heart utterances. Read thyself thoroughly in the light of the manifestation to thee of the glory of Christ, and that will give thee power in dealing with other men for him. Go to thy work in self-abasement and self-distrust, but with confidence in him, and to thee, too, O humble teacher, Christ will say as unto Peter, "Fear not; from henceforth thou shalt catch men."

We are reminded, in the third place, that the work of the Christian ministry demands the concentration of the whole man upon it. These first apostles "forsook all, and followed Christ." This was their response to the call to active and official service by the Lord. Their ordination came later; but their acceptance of the call was now, and was signalized by their withdrawal from their ordinary pursuits. "They forsook all." It was a poor "all," some have said—"two boats and a few nets;" but it was not so poor, after all; for, as we saw in our last lecture, there is good reason for believing, that though very far from being wealthy in the modern sense of that word, Peter and his partners were in circum-

---

* "Autobiography of Rev. William Jay," pp. 275, 277.

stances of comfort; and, in any case, what they did leave was their all.

Now, let no one suppose that Jesus, by requiring this sacrifice from them, has branded ordinary secular labour so called with dishonour. On the contrary, he whose own hands had been hardened by the carpenter's hammer has thereby given dignity—I had almost said divinity—to manual toil. But he wished these men to know, and his ministers of every after age to learn, that the work of seeking after, and caring for souls was enough for all the energies of their natures, and all the ambition of their hearts. And so, though occasionally they reverted to their original calling, they did, from this time forward in the main, and, so far as appears, from the day of Pentecost, wholly keep themselves for their apostolic labours. It may be said, indeed, that Paul, after entering upon his public work, is found both at Ephesus and at Corinth making tents in the workshop of Aquila; but that case, as the apostle himself is very careful to explain, was quite exceptional; and his exhortation to Timothy, "Give thyself wholly to them," indicates what his judgment, in all ordinary cases, was.

He who would be a minister of Christ must be content to turn away from all other avenues to eminence, however inviting they may appear. The gains of the merchant, the fame of the philosopher, the influence of the statesman, the glory of the discoverer, are not for him. Into the field of authorship he can enter properly only when he is on his Master's business, and when he is seeking either to save souls or to educate them in the knowledge of the oracles of God. His work is simply and only to seek and to save that which is lost; and on that he must focus his whole time and force. Very beautifully, in connection with his own department of foreign missionary enterprise, did Robert Moffat, the father-in-law of Livingstone, and himself for fifty years a Christian apostle in South Africa, express this thought, when, being asked to write in a lady's album, he penned the following lines :—

> "My album is in savage breasts,
>   Where passion reigns and darkness rests,
>   Without one ray of light:
>   To write the name of Jesus there,
>   To point to worlds both bright and fair,
>   And see the pagan bow in prayer,
>   Is all my soul's delight."

And every true minister of the Gospel feels in a similar way in reference to his work. It must have him all. He casts no lingering look of regret over the pursuits he used to love, or the studies in which he once was interested. All these things he lays, with Peter's boats and nets, and Paul's political ambitions, upon the altar for Christ; and he has his reward in the joy of his work and in the peculiar delight, the purest allotted to mortals, of bringing sinners to the knowledge of their Saviour. His old fellow-students may be met by him in places of honour and emolument; and though he may have stood higher than they in their classes, and might have looked, had he entered upon other departments of labour, to have still kept ahead of them, he is content to be as he is. Content! oh, how much more than content! He is enthusiastically devoted to his calling, and would not give the joy of being instrumental in the saving of one soul for all the glittering prizes which all other pursuits have in their offer.

Let no one seek the ministry who is not ready for this sacrifice; but when it is made, it will cease to be a sacrifice, and become a joy; and he who made it will enter into the fellowship of the Redeemer's delight, as he sees the fruit of his soul travail, and will cheer himself with this holy song:—

> "'Tis not a cause of small import
>   The pastor's care demands;
> 'Tis what might fill an angel's heart,
>   And filled the Saviour's hands."

If a man can stay in any other calling, he is not yet designated for the ministry. His true call to that noble work is when necessity is laid upon him, and he feels he must leave all to enter upon it. Hence, though it was quaintly expressed, and a little apt, at first, to be misunderstood, that was a wise advice which a professor gave to a young man who came to consult him about the propriety of his becoming a preacher of the Gospel: "Don't be a minister if you can help it." He who can not help being a minister is the really Christ-called man; and before such a one there is a career of honour and usefulness, ay, and of such happiness too, as rarely falls to the lot of other men. Is there no youth before me, to-night, who hears now the Saviour's call, "Follow me, and from henceforth thou shalt catch men?"

We are reminded, in the fourth place, that the higher life of the ministry lifts into itself and utilizes all the experiences of the lower life that preceded it. We see, in tracing the history of Paul, how his residence in the Greek city of Tarsus, and his training under the tutorship of Gamaliel, were, all unconsciously to him at the time, real preparations for his apostolic work, and every successful preacher in the present day will acknowledge that the observations which he made, and the lessons which he learned, in the store, or the office, or the editorial chair, have been of signal service to him in his public ministrations. The curriculum at college, and the course at the seminary, have been, indeed, unspeakably valuable; but the university of daily life was his first "alma mater," and now that he has attained the field of his proper and peculiar possession, his early experiences come back upon him, to his signal advantage.

In the case of Peter here, the very words which the Lord addressed to him would be sufficient to send him back continually in thought to his own life by the shores of Gennesaret. "Follow me, and I will make you fishers of men." Fishers of men! What a light did our Lord throw for Peter over his new occupation by that phrase! Look at it for a moment or two; for it has lessons for all Christian workers as well as for ministers of the Gospel.

For one thing, it tells us that, if we would catch men, we must use the right kind of net. Is it not the case that the meshes of the nets we commonly employ are so wide that they let every body through? We speak of the Gospel as if it were something far away from our hearers. We dwell upon it as a history eighteen hundred years old, but fail to make men feel that they have a present and pressing duty in regard to it. "When I hear Dr. —— preach," said one, 'he makes me think a great deal of him; but when I listen to Mr. ——, he sends me away with a very poor opinion of myself." Depend upon it, the latter minister had a net with narrow meshes! We may marvel at the skill of a man who is throwing stones at a mark; but when another comes and commences to throw stones at us, ah! that is a different affair. So, in all our pulpits, I fear we have too much aiming at marks, out of and away from the people, and too little aiming at men's hearts! When, here and there and everywhere in the audience, individuals are saying within themselves, "*That means me*," the preacher is working with a proper net; but when there is nothing but a hush of admiration of *his* words, he might as well have held his peace.

For another thing, this phrase tells us that we must follow men to their haunts if we would catch them for Christ. Three years ago, I was living during the summer months on the beautiful Bay of Northport, on the Long Island coast, and one morning there was a great and unusual stir upon the waters. A number of boats came in whose crews began at once to cast and haul their nets. They had never been there before during all the weeks I had lived in that neighbourhood. Why did they come then? They were following the fish, for they had seen a shoal pass in before them. So we must go where men congregate, if we would win them for Christ. As Archbishop Leighton once said, "We must follow sinners to their houses, aye, even to their ale-houses." If men will not come into our churches, let us go out of our churches after them. Let us organize, if need be, a visitation from house to house; let us go to the halls they frequent, and the streets and lanes they inhabit, and then we may have the delight of seeing this "a city of truth."

Finally, this phrase teaches us that we ought to improve special seasons of opportunity. There are times when, in the fisherman's boat, one may toil all night, and for many nights together, and catch nothing; and there are other occasions when every cast of the net is rewarded by an enormous draught: and you never find the fisherman idle when the "take" is large. So it is also in the experience of the Christian worker. Sometimes, let him be ever so earnest, he seems to be doing no good, and is made to cry constantly, "Who hath believed my report?" But then, again, he has periods of success. These are the days of revival, when multitudes on every hand are "seeking for Jesus." Such seasons he ought to improve to the utmost, and if he cannot draw in the net alone, let him beckon to his fellow-labourers to help him. Blessed times of refreshing! oh, how we long for their enjoyment! Send them to us, thou quickening Spirit! And send with them the energy, the strength, and the enthusiasm to make the best of them, for the glory of Christ in the salvation of men.

But there may be those among our Christian workers who may be crying, "How can I become thus skilful in winning souls?" And to them, as to myself, I would reply, Obey the Master's command. He said, "Follow me, and I will make you fishers of men." Follow him, then, brethren. Keep close to him; the nearer, the better. You can not be too near him, and your very proximity to him will give you success. "That man preaches," said one, concerning John Brown, of Haddington, "as if the Lord Jesus were at his elbow." It was his nearness to his Lord that gave him power. Keep close to him, therefore, and, whether you preach from the pulpit or the Sabbath-school, in the home or in the shop, your words and your lives will catch men for Christ.*

---

* In the preceding discourse the reader will discover some similarity of thought and expression to one of the author's lectures on the "Ministry of the Word;" but he has preferred to let the passages remain, rather than destroy the unity of the exposition here by removing them.

IV

WALKING ON THE WATERS.

MATTHEW xiv., 22-33.

ACCORDING to the commonly received chronology of the gospels, a full year elapsed between the incidents which were reviewed in our last lecture and those which are recorded in the narrative to which I now invite your attention. Much had occurred in that interval which it would be important for us to consider, if we were engaged in the investigation of the public ministry of our Lord; but only two things were done in it, so far, at least, as the evangelists have given us information, which had any special bearing upon Peter. Of these, the first was the healing of his wife's mother, who was lying at Capernaum sick of a "great fever." This was in itself considered a comparatively unimportant miracle; yet, from the record of its performance, we learn, to the confusion of all those who would insist upon the celibacy of the clergy as essential, that Peter was a married man; and also, to the rebuke of those who are continually sneering at mothers-in-law, that Peter had a heart large enough to love, and a house big enough to receive, the mother of her whom he had chosen as the companion of his life.

The second was Peter's ordination to the apostolic office along with the eleven whom Christ had chosen to be his specially commissioned witnesses. This solemn act was performed by Jesus, after a night of prayer upon the mountain; and, in connection with it, he addressed to them that discourse upon the plain which has so much in common with his Sermon on the Mount. In all this Peter was concerned no more than the other eleven; but it is remarkable that in all the lists of the twelve, varying though they do in other respects, his name stands first.* Now, this is not merely accidental. There was a certain primacy given to Peter among the twelve, and because the Papists have perverted that into a sanction of their claim of supremacy for the pope, we must not be withheld from recognising it. Whether on the score of age, or, as is most likely, on that of character and ability, he was, by common consent—nay, as we shall see in a later stage of his history, by the appointment of Christ himself—the first of the twelve. He was their spokesman on all great occasions; he was the eager confessor for the company when any expression of their faith was asked. But, then, he had no official prerogative over them. His position was one of honour, and not of power; one of influence, and not of authority; and even if it were to be granted that the Bishop of Rome is his successor, that would form no foundation for the claim which the pope makes to the most absolute supremacy over the souls and the most unlimited authority over the lives of men.

But now we turn to the contemplation of that night-scene on the Lake of Galilee which is described in the narrative of Matthew. The apostles had just returned from their first ministry through Galilee; and as, in the exuberance of their joy, they were telling Jesus "all things, both what they had done and what they had taught," the disciples of John came to cast a gloom over their gladness by the information that Herod had beheaded their master, to gratify Herodias. This news at once revived in Jesus the remembrance of the nobleness of John, and awakened within him the presentiment of his own crucifixion, so that he longed for quietude and retirement. He saw that matters with him, too, were hastening to a crisis. Twice had he gone round the towns and cities of Galilee; and though the multitudes crowded round him and "heard him gladly," he knew that they were looking

---

* See Luke vi., 14-16; Matt. x., 2-4; Mark iii., 16-19; John xxi., 2.

for a Messiah of another sort than he was, and he foresaw that very soon they would have to choose between him and the idol which their own imagination had set up. Hence, that he might prepare himself for the coming ordeal, and fortify his followers against the temptation that was in store for them, as well as secure for them a season of needed rest after their toil, he took them with him to the eastern shore of the lake.

But the inconsiderate selfishness of the people utterly defeated his plan. Seeing him setting out in the boat which he had secured and retained for his convenience,* they walked round the head of Gennesaret in great numbers, and, immediately upon his landing, they flocked around him. They were cruel, but he was compassionate. So he did not send them away, but preached to them during a great portion of the day; and when the evening drew on, he gave them a feast, miraculously provided for them from the five loaves and two fishes which a lad had brought with him in his sachel. The effect was great. The enthusiasm of the multitude was roused to the highest pitch. They cried out,† "This is of a truth that Prophet that should come into the world," and they wished to "take him by force, to make him a king." His own immediate followers, too, had some sympathy with this desire, and so the fellowship of the multitude at such a time was no safe thing for them. Therefore he sent them away to cross the lake by themselves, and, after dismissing the multitude to their homes, he went up alone into the mountain to soothe and refresh his spirit by fellowship with his Father.

While he was thus engaged, however, his disciples were contending with a furious storm, which had arisen with such force that, after toiling for nine hours, they made no more than "five and twenty or thirty furlongs." Nor need this surprise us; for such hurricanes are by no means uncommon on an inland sea like that of Tiberias. Dr. Thomson tells us that he

---

* Mark iii., 9. † John vi., 14.

spent a night in the Wady Shukaiyif, which enabled him to sympathize with the disciples in the case before us. He says: "The sun had scarcely set when the wind began to rush down toward the lake, and it continued all night long with constantly increasing violence, so that, when we reached the shore next morning, the face of the lake was like a huge boiling caldron. In a wind like that, the disciples must have been driven quite across to Gennesaret, as we know they were. To understand the causes of these sudden and violent tempests, we must remember that the lake lies low—six hundred feet lower than the ocean; that the vast and naked plateaus of the Jaulan rise to a great height, spreading backward to the wilds of the Hauran, and upward to snowy Hermon; that the water-courses have cut out profound ravines and wild gorges, converging to the head of this lake; and that these act like gigantic funnels to draw down the cold winds from the mountains. On the occasion referred to, we subsequently pitched our tents at the shore, and remained for three days and nights exposed to this tremendous wind. We had to double pin all the tent-ropes, and frequently were obliged to hang with our whole weight upon them to keep the quivering tabernacle from being carried up bodily into the air. No wonder the disciples toiled and rowed hard all that night."*

At length, as the dawn was drawing near, they beheld one moving majestically toward them, walking over the foaming waves; but the sight only aggravated their misery, for with the superstition of their times strong within them, they supposed it was a phantom from the other world, and they cried out for fear. But immediately the answer to their exclamation came in the Master's well-known voice, "I am! be not afraid." I am! What a singular announcement if he were only a man! what a natural utterance if he were truly God! For how can God reveal himself, except by the assertion of his existence?

---

* "The Land and the Book," English edition, p. 374.

Is not this another of those I AMS which were so often on the Saviour's lips, as the fourth Evangelist has testified? And is not the assertion here corroborated and confirmed by his miraculous march over the waters? There was one, at any rate, in the boat to whom the words and the action were alike significant, and he, not, as we might have imagined, the intuitional and keen-eyed John, but the warm-hearted and impulsive Peter, who replied, "Lord, if it be thou, bid me come unto thee on the water."

Nor were these words of doubt, as if still he hesitated whether the stranger were the Christ or not. Rather they were the utterance of faith: "Since thou art, let me be sharer with thee in the calm self-poise which can move thus, unaffected by the storm around thee, and unsubmerged by the waves beneath thee." It was not forwardness, as some would have us believe, but it was faith quickened by affection; and therefore the Lord said to him, "Come.. And when Peter was come down out of the ship, he walked on the water to go to Jesus." So for a time all was well. But, taking his eyes from the Master's face, and looking down upon the yawning billows, he was afraid, and began to sink, and cried, "Lord, save me!" The appeal was not in vain, for "immediately Jesus stretched forth his hand and caught him, and said unto him, O thou of little faith, wherefore didst thou doubt?" Then, when this singular episode was over, Jesus went into the boat with his followers; the storm ceased; and as they reached their destination "they that were in the ship came and worshiped him, saying, Of a truth thou art the Son of God."

Now, it is not difficult to discover the characteristics of Peter as they come out here. He wore no mask. Whatever he felt for the moment was sure to be expressed either by his words or his actions. He carried his heart upon his sleeve, and was ever unsophisticated and genuine. The cunning duplicity of the traitor was foreign to his nature, and even the caution of the prudent man was wanting in his disposition. He never forecast the future, or attempted to count the cost; and so we account for the fact that, with a certain generous and eager impetuosity, there was combined in him an occasional infirmity of purpose or weakness of character. He easily "slopped over" on one side, and that was invariably followed by a similar occurrence on the other. In the case before us, the ardour of his love to the Lord led him to make this singular proposal—so far ahead of any thing that any of the others in the boat had thought of—that he should be permitted to walk upon the waters. But no sooner is his wish granted to him than the reaction comes, and he sinks into a weaker faith than that which the least of his brethren exercised.

Now, it is easy to blame here, and to say that either Peter should not have been so eager to meet his Lord, or he should have maintained his faith unto the last. But we must not forget that the very height to which, for the moment, his faith had attained exposed him, more than others, to the temptation to unbelief. They who have never walked on the waters, but who sit securely in their boats, are not so liable to sink, as is the Peter who goes marching over the waves. The men of even temperament who are rarely, if ever, discomposed, can not understand an experience such as this. They know nothing either of ups or downs. They are never down, because they are never up; and so they are apt to regard such spiritual alternations as this as either a mystery or a lie. When they read the sighings and cryings of David at one time, and his ecstatic utterances at another, they declare that they are either exaggerations or untruths. But all this springs from their own commonplace natures. Where the hills are highest, the ravines are deepest; and when, by an outburst of faith, one rises to fellowship with Jesus in his walk over the waves, the very elevation places him in new peril. Peter, therefore, must not be unduly blamed for his sinking. At least they who have never tried his dangerous walk upon the deep ought to be the last to ridicule his lack of faith when he began to be afraid; and if we hint at a fault at all, it is that he did not learn the lesson which this self-revelation might have taught him, and so save himself from that greater jeopardy in which he placed himself when he entered the palace of the high-priest, and of which this was a faint rehearsal and parabolic warning.

But now, leaving the impulsive apostle for the time, let us see what lessons of admonition and of cheer we may learn for ourselves, from the consideration of this interesting episode.

And, first, we learn that when his disciples are in danger of being carried away by earthly influences, Christ sends them into trial. Matthew tells us that the Lord "constrained" his disciples to get into the boat. The word is very strong. It might even be rendered he "forced" them, or he "compelled" them, to embark, and it indicates that it was only by the exercise of his authority that he prevailed upon them to set out. Now, why this constraint? Some answer, because he desired that they should become accustomed to act for themselves without his presence. As Trench has said, "He will not have them to be clinging only to the sense of his bodily presence: they must not be as ivy, needing always an outward support, but as hardy forest-trees which can brave a blast; and this time he puts them forth into the danger alone, even as some loving mother-bird thrusts her fledglings from the nest, that they may find their own wings and learn to use them."* And, no doubt, something of this may have entered into his design; yet that was not so likely to have been the reason for his procedure, as it would have been if the circumstance had occurred at a date nearer to the close of his ministry, when he was just about to withdraw from them altogether. Hence, I cannot quite accept that as an explanation of the course which he here adopted. But when I open the Gospel of John, I find a suf-

---

* "Notes on the Miracles," p. 277.

ficient reason suggested in a moment, for we are there informed that the multitude wished to "take Jesus by force and make him a king." Now, in cherishing this desire and seeking to act upon it, the people were adopting a thoroughly false idea of the royalty of the Messiah. They thought that the long-expected deliverer of whom their prophets had spoken was to be a temporal potentate, and that, gathering earthly forces around him, he would break the yoke of the Roman oppressor, set up his throne in Jerusalem, and distribute among his adherents the rewards of place and preferment. But of a kingdom founded upon truth and love, or of a royalty over the hearts and consciences and lives of men, they had not the very faintest conception. In seeking, therefore, to make Christ a king, though it seemed that they were conferring honour upon him, they were really doing their best to wreck the cause of which he was the head. They were repeating only in their own way, and, in a sense too, with love and loyalty to him, the temptation which Satan had set before him on the mountain when he offered him the crown without the cross; and so he could not listen to their proposal.

But the disciples, just at this stage in their development, were more in sympathy with the multitude than with their Master in this matter. They, too, desired to see him a king, as the request of James and John presented through their mother attests, and as even the question put to their Lord long afterward, on the very eve of his ascension, fully corroborates. So it was dangerous to let them remain in the company of the crowd while this frenzy was upon them. Something else must be found, which, for the time, will take their minds entirely from this seductive dream. Therefore, even by the exercise of constraint, he sent them away; and, very soon, they had enough to do to keep their boat from sinking, and had no thought to spare for the kingdom that a few hours ago seemed to be so near.

Now, if this be a correct explanation of the case, does it not throw light on many of the trials that come upon God's people still? Our afflictions are not merely chastisements to mark God's displeasure at sins of which we have been guilty, or restoratives to bring us back to the life from which we have partially fallen; but they are frequently also preventives, and come to occupy our hearts, our energies, and our prayers, so that some temptation which we were courting or coquetting with shall lose its power to harm us. If we are bent on something which shall endanger our spirituality, God may send upon us a serious affliction just to keep us out of mischief. Can not you look back on many occasions in your own history when it was just thus with you? The world was too much with you; you were becoming enamoured of its pleasures and its pursuits; you were just on the outer rim of the vortex, and were beginning to feel the fatal fascination of the whirlpool, wherein so many are ingulfed, when, lo! your beloved child was stricken with dangerous illness, or your business became dreadfully involved, or your life-companion was taken from your side, or you were yourself made the target at which the unscrupulous and the vicious shot the arrows of their scorn, and, in the pressure of the terrible calamity, you were delivered from the spell by which the world was holding you. Let us be thankful, brethren, that the arrangement of our lives is in the hand of One who sees the end from the beginning, and who makes thus our very buffeting with trial the means of holding us back from folly, and delivering us from the influence of evil.

In the second place, we learn that while our trial lasts, the Lord prays for us. All during the night, the Saviour was on the mountain, and his eye was on that little boat, while his supplications ascended to his Father on behalf of those who were exposed to danger in it. These were weary hours to the disciples, and there was in their hearts, in spite of all their toil, an ever-present sense of danger; yet, had they only known it, the prayers of Jesus were between them and shipwreck, and, trusting in him, they might have been at rest, even in spite of the waves by which their boat was rocked. "Now all this happened unto them for an ensample," and the record of it is preserved here for us, that we may learn even under trial to be calm, trusting in the intercession of our great High-priest.

Nor is this a solitary instance. The Church of Christ, as a whole, has often been like that little skiff on the boiling waters of Gennesaret; but her Lord's prayers for her in the heavenly temple have prevailed on her behalf. And for martyrs, confessors, reformers, his intercession has availed, so that, amidst the fiercest antagonism of ungodly men, they have been enabled to possess their souls in patience. Cheer up, therefore, my afflicted brother! I know that you are toiling in rowing, and that you seem to yourself to be in danger of being submerged; but, though you can not see him, Jesus is praying for you, and his intercession is always efficacious. I fear we all make too little of the intercession of the Lord! Our prayer-meetings are famous for the presentation of multitudinous requests that the petitions of the brethren should be offered for those who send them in, and I find no fault with that, for I believe in intercessory prayer; but do we ever seek to have Jesus himself pray for us? Have we not too largely forgotten " that he ever liveth to make intercession for us?" We are apt to imagine that, as on earth, the man who would intercede for a multitude must make his petitions so general that they descend not to the individual wants of each, so it must be with Jesus. But that is a mistake; for the omniscience of his deity makes him acquainted with our undermost necessities, and the love and sympathy of his humanity dispose him to plead on our behalf. Is any among you afflicted? then let him remember that "we have an advocate with the Father, Jesus Christ the righteous;" and let the consciousness that he is interceding for him fill his heart with that peace which passeth understanding.

In the third place, we learn that when Christ comes to us in our trials, we are enabled to rise with him above them. You observe how, as the Lord approached and spoke to them, Peter was strengthened to overcome his fear, and was even enabled to walk upon the waters. But concerning this coming of our Lord to us in trouble, the narrative before us is very suggestive; and I must name two or three things that can not fail to strike the thoughtful reader as he meditates upon it.

For one thing, the Lord did not come at once. He let the night wear on until the fourth watch, and then he went to their relief. Now, so it has frequently been with us; our deliverances have not always come at the moment when the peril appeared. The Lord has left us to ourselves, that we might test our strength and discover our weakness. He has waited till the object of his discipline has been accomplished in us, and then he has approached us with his help.

Again, the Lord came to these disciples over the very waves which constituted their trial. So he frequently makes his pathway into our hearts over the affliction which is at the moment distressing us. No one else can do that. For in every one of our distresses there are elements which we must keep hidden from our fellow-men. But these are entirely known to Christ, and it is just through these secret door-ways that he enters into our souls and brings with him his cheer and succour. Brother, is there no comfort for you here? The Lord makes your trial his very avenue into your spirit. Look out for his coming, then, and see that you give him a right royal welcome when he does appear.

Still farther, the disciples did not know Christ when he came and aggravated their misery for themselves by supposing that he was a ghost. But let us not laugh at their superstition, lest we should be found also making merry at our own expense. Have we never mistaken Christ for a ghost, or perhaps, worse still, for an evil spirit? We have been in trouble, and matters, as we think, have come to a crisis, when something happens which at first we judge will surely bring ruin upon us, and we cry out for fear. We are undone! the Lord hath forsaken us! we are utterly overwhelmed! But we wait a little, and, in a wonderful way, we see that what at first sight seemed our undoing has actually become our salvation. Have you never had an experience like that? And as you heard the Master's voice saying to you, "It is I; be not afraid," have you not had your fears put to shame and reproved by his favour? Brethren, this night-scene on the Galilean lake was the rehearsal of much which is happening every day to the people of God; and if we studied it more closely we should have far fewer difficulties about what we call the mysteries of Providence.

Once more: when Christ comes, and is recognized, he brings relief. The very recognition of him is a relief; for there is no real distress and no formidable danger to the Christian while his Lord is nigh. The presence of the Master may not immediately still the tempest, but it will enable us to walk upon the waves. The man who can see Jesus in his troubles always keeps them under him; it is when he fails to keep his eye upon the Lord that they threaten to overwhelm him. So long as Peter was "looking unto Jesus," there was an influence beneath him that held him up above the waters; but when he saw the wind boisterous, he began to sink. Ah! how many of us are like him there! We see the wind boisterous; there is a likelihood that we shall lose money, or forfeit the good opinion of our fellows, or perhaps lose life itself; and so we let that which is immediately before our eyes shut out from our hearts the remembrance of the glorious promise, "I will never leave thee nor forsake thee." Who can help being reminded by this whole history of that great reformer whose career has so recently been introduced into his drama by the English poet-laureate? I mean Archbishop Cranmer. In his life, generally, there was not much of the time-server; but when the storm arose, and the wind was contrary, and he, Peter-like, essayed to walk over the waves, he began to sink, and unworthily signed that recantation which he so nobly cancelled by his speech at his trial and his conduct at the stake. Brethren, let us be at once warned and encouraged by such experiences as these: warned, when we are in trouble, to preserve our faith in Christ; and encouraged, even when we have lost our faith in part, and have begun to sink, to cry most earnestly for succour to him, who is a present help in time of trouble. Lord, save me! I perish! What short, sharp, agonizing cries are these! When the soul is in anguish and in earnest, its prayers are telegram-like, both in their swiftness and in their brevity, and, thank God, Christ's answers are as prompt and as pointed as our prayers can be. Is there one here to-night who feels like Peter weltering in the waters? Let him send up Peter's prayer, and he will have the same answer which the Lord vouchsafed to his impulsive apostle. He who "stilled the rolling waves of Galilee" can hush the tempest that is howling around thee. Make thy prayer, then, to him.

> "When the mighty storm is surging,
>   Stars are hid, and wind is shrill,
> Satan striving, passion urging—
>   Saviour, whisper, 'Peace, be still.'
>
> "When the waves of doubt and terror
>   Toss me at their own wild will,
> Light seems dark, and truth seems error—
>   Saviour, whisper, 'Peace, be still.'
>
> "When affliction's storms are howling,
>   And its voice my soul doth thrill,
> Earth is black, and heaven is scowling—
>   Saviour, whisper, 'Peace, be still.'
>
> "When the tide of Death's cold river
>   Shocks me with its icy chill,
> Body quakes and billows quiver—
>   Saviour, whisper, 'Peace, be still.'"*

---

* "Poems by the late William Leighton," p. 77.

V.

THE FIRST CONFESSION.

JOHN vi., 66-71.

ON the morning after their perilous night upon Gennesaret, and Peter's attempt to walk upon the waters, the disciples, having received Jesus into the boat with them, landed at Capernaum, where our Lord had his temporary home, and Peter his permanent abode. It is probable that they still contemplated the taking of a season of rest. At all events, if they were needing relaxation before they visited the eastern side of the lake, they would all require it much more after the fatigues of the day, and the vigils, the toil, and the dangers of the night. But there was little hope of retirement for them now; for as soon as the people who had been with them on the previous day discovered that Jesus was no longer in their neighbourhood, they also took boats, and crossed to Capernaum, seeking for him. Nor did he seclude himself from them. Inquirers are ever welcomed by the Lord, whether, like Nicodemus, they come to him by night; or, like Zaccheus, they are moved to approach him by the merest curiosity; or, like the multitudes in the present instance, they are impelled to follow him by some earthly consideration. He receiveth all alike, and gives to each the special instruction which he needs. To the Pharisee he speaks of the necessity of the new birth; to the publican he discourses of his mission to seek and to save that which was lost; and to those eager companies who lived upon the sensationalism of great miracles, and sought from him only such worldly advantage as they could make out of him, he addresses one of the most spiritual and searching sermons that he ever preached.

Rising from the miracle of the loaves, for a repetition of which on a larger scale, and in a different form, they were looking, he bids them become more earnest for the meat which endureth unto everlasting life than they were for the bread that perisheth, and he proclaims himself to be the Bread of Life, saying, "He that cometh to me shall never hunger; and he that believeth on me shall never thirst." Nay, going further still, he affirms that "except they eat the flesh of the Son of man and drink his blood, they have no life in them."

Now, these words implied that he was not the sort of Messiah whom they were expecting. They looked for a king, who should surround himself with all the glitter of earthly royalty, and restore to the tribes the splendour which they associated with the throne of David; but, instead, he speaks of himself as the author of all spiritual life, and declares that unless they received him by a faith which should appropriate him to themselves, as thoroughly as one makes bread his own by eating it, they could not have everlasting life. This was to Jews like them a "hard saying." They had been accustomed to plume themselves on being Abraham's children. They supposed that, as the descendants of the Father of the Faithful, they already had everlasting life; and when they spake the day before of making him a king, they regarded themselves rather as his patrons than his beneficiaries. They thought more of giving honour to him than of being dependent upon him for their eternal salvation. No doubt they had an eye to their own interests. But they were looking only at their temporal advantage, and even that they were seeking to promote through their condescending to support him. They would carry him to his throne, and then, of course, they would expect their reward in the distribution of his favours. That was the programme which they had made out for themselves. But when they heard him claim as his own, by right of his inherent deity, a loftier greatness than any which they could confer, they said, "Is not this Jesus, the son of Joseph, whose father and mother we know? How is it then that he saith, I came down from heaven?" And when he asserted that faith in himself was indispensable to everlasting life, they were offended at him; so that even they who had up till this time numbered themselves among his disciples murmured at his words.

Thus, by the full revelation of his divine dignity and spiritual mission, the Lord brought matters to a crisis; and now, with that winnowing fan whereof the Baptist spake, he begins to separate the chaff from the wheat. He does not alter his teachings to suit the changing disposition of his hearers, but he reiterates the truth, only in a stronger form than ever, saying, "Doth this offend you? What and if ye shall see the Son of man ascend up where he was before? It is the Spirit that quickeneth; the flesh profiteth nothing: the words that I speak unto you, they are spirit, and they are life."

This uncompromising firmness of his put an end to indecision among them, and so from that time "many of his disciples went back, and walked no more with him." Nay, even in the chosen circle of his own twelve, there were some signs of defection. On the preceding day, as we saw in our last lecture, he had sent them away from the crowd, just that they might be removed from the influence of the seductive error by which the multitude was possessed; and one might have imagined that the experiences of the night might have cured them of their devotion to earthly concerns. But, no! they were still in some measure under the spell by which the people were charmed. Therefore, turning upon them a look of intense affection, he said, "Will ye also go away?"

It was a critical moment, like that when a general, seeing his troops about to break before the enemy, tries to rally them with the lightning of his eye and the inspiration of his appeal, and the effect was remarkable; for Peter, speaking for them all, exclaimed, "Lord, to whom shall we go? Thou hast the words of eternal life: and we believe and are sure that thou art that Christ, the Son of the living God."

It was nobly spoken, and we can forgive the son of Jonas for many acts of indiscretion, in consideration of the hearty emphasis of this well-timed utterance. When the banner is raised, the storm of opposition only unfolds it more fully to the gaze of men; and when true decision is in the heart, a time of prevalent apostasy only makes it more conspicuous. Nor need we wonder that this noble and magnanimous response came from Peter. He had been prepared to give it by the glimpses of the deity of Jesus which he had caught through the miracle of the fishes and the walking on the sea; and, believing that his brethren were ready to indorse his confession, he made himself for the moment the spokesman of the band.

But he went farther than the facts, had he been fully acquainted with them, would have warranted; for by his side was standing one who bitterly, though silently, dissented from his words. For this was the Rubicon with Judas also, and he refused to cross it. He was one of those who were looking for a mere worldly Messiah; and as he heard the solemn and searching words of Jesus at this time, he gave up all hope of remaining permanently in his service. Now, for the first time, the pang of disappointment pierces his soul. He feels that he has made a great mistake. He sees that he will never gain that which he fancied he would obtain when he joined the company of the twelve. But he will not leave just yet. He will remain a while, and see if he can make any thing out of the enterprise. He will watch his opportunity, and continue an outward adherent, that he may the better carry with him, when he goes, something tangible as his portion of the spoil.

Thus the crisis which evoked the honest enthusiasm of Peter struck out of the flinty heart of Judas the spark which, after smouldering for months in secret dishonesty, was at length to burst forth into the blaze of uttermost treachery, in his betrayal of the Lord. All this was not hidden from the Master's eye.

So, noting what was passing at the very moment in the soul of Iscariot, Jesus said to Peter, " Have not I chosen you twelve, and one of you is a devil?" Dreadful words, which must have shot through the hearts of those who heard them as with the suddenness and the shock of an electric stroke, and yet, while in their definiteness they were full of warning to them all, in their indefiniteness they were full of mercy to Judas. He said "*one* of you;" so that no one could tell which, and Judas, if he chose, might repent, and return, all unsuspected, to his allegiance. He said " one of *you*," so that each of the twelve might be sent in upon himself with the inquiry, " Is it I ?"

Now, in connection with this narrative many practical lessons suggest themselves. I select only the following:

We are reminded by this history of the fluctuating character of human applause. The day before this defection of his disciples, the popularity of Jesus might be said to be at its height. The multitudes followed him all the way round by the head of the lake, and forgot their food as they listened to his discourses; so that, in compassion for their hunger, he made for them a repast out of the loaves and fishes which the sachel of a lad supplied; and then they were eager to proclaim him king. But he discouraged them from such a course, and sent them away; and when, the next day, they renewed their efforts with that object in view, he not only would not sanction their proceeding, but gave such an exposition of his purpose and ministry as showed them that he had no sympathy whatever with their aims and ambitions. Then they left him forthwith, and were changed from admiring followers into murmurers against him, and ultimately into open antagonists. Behold what a revolution a single day may produce! And in the light of such a history, who would be so foolish as to cater for popularity?

No doubt there is a certain satisfaction in having what one might call the indorsement of a multitude; and while the attraction lasts, it furnishes a larger field of usefulness than could perhaps be otherwise attained. But it has a snare as well; for it is apt to put the pleasing of the people uppermost in the aim of the teacher or the preacher, and so to bring him under the operation of the histrionic maxim that "they who live to please must please to live." Of course it will be said here that, in a certain sense, it is necessary that you should please, in order to benefit or to persuade; and so much as that will be at once admitted. He who shocks every well-bred person with his coarseness, and violates every canon of wisdom by his folly, does not deserve to succeed, and has already closed against him every avenue into his hearer's souls. There is a propriety to be observed in this as in every thing else; and they who set that at defiance are certainly not in that the followers of the Lord Jesus Christ; for no teacher was ever so wise, so watchful, so tender, so illustrative, and so persuasive as he. If, therefore, we would imitate him, we must cultivate these characteristics. That they are elements of popularity does not in the least matter, for they are so only in the sense of being the pre-requisites to the gaining of the ear of the community.

But when it comes to this, that we must either be guilty of treason to that which we know and believe to be the truth, or lose the allegiance of the crowd, then I should hope there are few among us who would prefer the huzza of a multitude to the approbation of conscience and of God. Herein lies the great difference between the true popular leader, whether in the pulpit or on the political platform, and the vulgar demagogue. The one seeks to guide the throng; the other is guided by it. If, under the one, some epidemic of misdirected enthusiasm manifests itself, as in the case before us, he seeks to subdue it, and will rather forfeit the popularity of the hour than be guilty of the permanent folly of giving his sanction to what he knows to be wrong. But if a similar outburst of zeal without knowledge takes place under the other, it carries him away with it. He seems to be directing that which is in reality directing him. He mistakes the empty glory of being the figure-head of the ship for the substantial honour of being its captain; and when the whole argosy comes to grief by striking against a rock, it is he who is first destroyed. Thus disastrous in his case is the issue of that which once seemed for him so prosperous. But the wiser teacher bides his time; and, in their calmer moments, men will come round to him again, and place him on a still loftier altitude than that which formerly he occupied.

It comes, then, just to this, that if one means to serve his generation, he must not care for applause. His heart's devotion must be one and undivided to the truth, and to him who is the Lord of truth. Let him ever hold aloft that which he knows and believes to be right; and though such a course may diminish the number of his followers at first; though it may provoke the blind rage of his adversaries, and lead them to nail him to a cross; yet, from the grave of such reproach he will rise at length to a throne of power on which no living man could ever sit, and from which the very mention of his name will move men's spirits as with some potent spell. The temporary withdrawal of popular favour is nothing; but this permanent enthronement of personal influence is real greatness. Let us live, therefore, not for the applause of the hour—the merest clap-trap can get that—but for the advancement of the truth; and sooner or later we shall share in the glory of its final triumph.

We are shown, in this history, the tap-root from which all apostasy springs. It has been to me a very striking discovery, that the first indications of the estrangement of Judas from Jesus were connected with the discourse which caused the open withdrawal of so many others. This indicates that apostasy may exist in the heart a long while before it is manifested in the life. From this point on, the traitor was out of sympathy with Christ. Yet no one of the twelve apparently suspected him. On the very night of the last supper, just before he went out to do his villainous work, he had apparently the perfect confidence of his companions, for they supposed that he had gone out after some necessary business, and never dreamed of the false-heartedness of his after-conduct. Yet for all these months the leaven had been working within him; and apostle though he was, it accomplished his perdition.

I presume not to be able to resolve the question why, with his prescience of the future, Jesus selected the traitor for one of the twelve. I can see that a very valuable element was added to the evidence of his Messiahship by the fact that he had one among his followers who proved false, and who yet could lay nothing whatever to his charge, and was constrained by remorse, after confessing his guilt, to take away his life.

But I am more concerned now to say, that at least one reason for this singular selection by our Lord might be to put every minister, office-bearer, and member of his Church upon his guard, by showing him that even the holding of the highest office in that Church will not keep a man from falling away. The member has dropped out of the ranks; the Sabbath-school teacher has disappeared from the head of his class; the elder, or deacon, has gone ignominiously back; the minister has fallen from the pulpit; yea, even the apostle from one of the very pinnacles of the Temple. Who, then, dares to think of himself as absolutely secure? Blessed Jesus! our safety is in thee alone. "Hold thou up our goings in thy paths, that our footsteps may not slip!"

But how shall we account for the apostasy of Judas, and of those who openly went back at this time? I think the cause of it is not far to seek. Look at the discourse which preceded this defection. From beginning to end it is addressed to those who put the things of time and sense above those which are eternal and spiritual. Their concern was for the bread that perishes; and they thought little of that which endureth unto everlasting life. They came to Christ for the advancement of their earthly interests; and the very moment that he urges them to subordinate these to the things of eternity they turn against him. So with Judas. Men marvel at his doing such a foul deed as that which he perpetrated for thirty pieces of silver; but I do not wonder at it at all. This world was his God. He put temporal interests uppermost; and the man who is seeking only and always that which he can make for himself is fit for "treasons, stratagems, and spoils;" for anything, in short, which promises him gain. These apostates, therefore, were all wedded to the world. In fact, they had never let go the world all the while they were following Christ. They went after him as the ship at anchor drifts with the tide, because the current was flowing in his direction, and because they hoped to obtain some individual benefit, or some national deliverance, at his hands. They had never given themselves to him in hearty consecration; and as for everlasting life, they had not thought of that. So, when he bids them receive him by faith as the Son of God, and their Redeemer, they are offended at him.

Now, is not this too often yet the source from which apostasy springs? One says, "Put me into the priest's office, that I may eat a piece of bread;" and it is not wonderful, therefore, that if he can get a larger piece elsewhere, he leaves his office, and his professed faith also, behind him, and goes for that. Another joins the Church in order that he may get into good society, or improve his business connection, or obtain some worldly advantage. Of course, if by leaving it he can obtain a greater temporal advantage, the very motive which took him into the Church at first will take him out of it again. For in the one case and in the other, the entering of pulpit and the joining of the Church was only a part of the man's worship of Mammon. He who, in the ranks of the Church, puts any thing above salvation through Jesus Christ and obedience to him, is already an apostate, and is only waiting, like Judas, for a favourable opportunity of making thirty pieces of silver by betraying the Lord. How is it with you in this regard? I have spoken strongly, but surely not more strongly than the subject warrants for oh! what must have been the agony of the Saviour's heart, when there were crushed out of him such awful words as these: "Have not I chosen you twelve? and one of you is a devil."

We have here, finally, the elements of Christian steadfastness. It is pleasant to turn from the contemplation of the apostasy of the many, to look at the magnanimous response which Peter made to the Master's question, "Will ye also go away?" It not only reveals to us the generous character of Peter's impulses—that we knew before—but it also shows us what are the best antidotes against falling away, when apostasy becomes, as it was here, epidemic. They are these two things:

1. The setting of spiritual things above temporal. Peter said, "We are seeking eternal life, and there is no one who can give us that but thee. If we forsake thee, to whom can we go? The Pharisees will mock us with the husks of formalism, while we are wishing the kernel of truth. The Sadducees will chill us with the cold negation of unbelief, and bid us be still, for that there is no spirit and no hereafter. Our souls protest against them both alike, and we must come to thee, for thou hast the words of eternal life." So, by keeping uppermost in his thoughts eternal life as the prime necessity of the human spirit, Peter was saved from falling away. And is it not in the same way that we are to keep ourselves steadfast in our allegiance to Christ to-day?

There may be many who would seek to persuade us that science and philosophy are sufficient for human guidance, and would estrange us from the Gospel of Christ. And if there were no spiritual nature within us, and no future life before us, we might be disposed to listen to their entreaties. But so long as we give the foremost place to the necessities of our souls, we shall be constrained to keep very close to Jesus, for only he can meet and satisfy these. Amidst the apotheosis of science by its followers, and the exaltation of philosophy by its votaries, we should never allow it to be forgotten that there are deep, solemn, all-important experiences in the human heart, which only Christ's words can meet. There is the sense of sin, the poison of the arrow of conviction, which no earthly antidote can neutralize, and which can be counteracted only by the blood of the Redeemer's cross. There is the dark sorrow of bereavement, which can be removed only by the vision of the angel at the door of the sepulchre, and the hearing of his soothing words, "Why seek ye the living among the dead? He is not here; for he is risen, as he said. Come, see the place where the Lord lay." There is the sense of lonesomeness stealing over the heart, even in the midst of bustle and of business, which can be dispelled alone by the consciousness of the Saviour's presence. There is the spirit-shudder at the thought of death, which only faith in Christ can change into "the desire to depart and to be with him." For these things science has no remedy, and philosophy no solace; and so the thoughtful Christian can still say, amidst the conflicting claims of the various forms of scepticism, "To whom shall we go? Christ has the words of eternal life."

2. But the second element of steadfastness suggested by Peter's words is the experimental knowledge of Christ's salvation. He adds, "We have believed, and know that thou art the Christ, the Son of God." He had before him at the moment the various revelations which he had received from Jesus of his personal glory and his saving might. So he knew whereof he spoke. He had seen the majesty of Godhead streaming through the miracles of the Master, and he had felt in the depths of his nature the stirrings of that new life which Christ had awakened in him. No man could reason him out of these things. He might be affected by a sudden panic, as, indeed, at a later date he was, but he could not be permanently persuaded to dishonour Christ.

So it always is. The experience of the Christian is his strongest shield against unbelief. He knows that Jesus has given him peace. He has felt that Christ has quickened him into new and nobler life. He has received a new nature from his Lord. He has by him been enabled to overcome appetite, and to put the tempter to flight. No one else has ever been to him what Jesus is, or done to him what Jesus has done; and you may as well attempt to persuade a man at noonday that the sun is not shining overhead, as seek to shake the Christian's confidence in his Lord. Every argument is met by the old assertion of him who was cured of blindness, "One thing I know, that, whereas I was blind, now I see." Get this experience, and it will give you steadfastness.

This is the impregnable inner citadel of the Christian's faith. This has given strength to those who have been opposed by the most specious and insidious argument; this nerved apostles and martyrs to go to death for Jesus' sake; this has upheld confessors before kings and councils, before diets and tribunals of the earth; this has enabled many a man amidst the vain philosophies of earth to preserve his faith in Jesus and his work. Get this, my friends, and you may stand unmoved amidst the assaults of modern unbelief, as you say to those who are its apostles, "I know Jesus Christ. I have experienced what he has done for me, and have long rejoiced in his salvation. For whom, or for what, am I to leave him now? Find me a better Saviour than he is, before I forsake him. Find me one who shall tell me more about sin and salvation, about heaven and hell, than he has told me, before I give him up. Till then, cease all your efforts, for I will have none but Christ."

VI.

THE SECOND CONFESSION.

MATTHEW xvi., 13-19.

AFTER the defection of the multitude, which furnished the occasion for Peter's first confession of his belief in the Messiahship of Jesus, our Lord went to the region of Tyre and Sidon,* where, in answer to her believing importunity, he healed the daughter of the Syrophenician woman. Thence he returned to the shore of Gennesaret and crossed into the district of Decapolis,† where he healed one "who was deaf and had an impediment in his speech," and where he fed the four thousand with the seven loaves. From Decapolis he crossed to Magdala,‡ on the western side of the lake, and thence§ he went northward to Bethsaida, where he opened the eyes of one who was blind. From Bethsaida he passed up, probably along the bank of the Jordan, until he came "into the coasts of Cesarea Philippi,"‖ which were beyond the boundary of Galilee.

Thus, just at this crisis of his ministry, the Lord spent his time, for the most part, in districts which were outside the limits of the land of Israel.

Where the evangelistic narratives are silent, it is not for us to assert, with anything like certainty, that we know what his motive was for adopting this course. But we may conjecture that he was induced to take it, by one or other, or

---

* Matt. xv., 21-28. † Matt. xv., 39.
‡ Ibid. xv., 29-38 ; Mark vii., 31-37.
§ Mark viii., 22. ‖ Matt. xvi., 13.

all, of the following considerations; he may have desired in this practical way to administer a reproof to the Galileans, by showing them and the Jews generally that their rejection of him would be immediately followed by the calling of the Gentiles; or, perceiving the influences that were at work among the people, he may have determined to withdraw his chosen apostles, for the time, from the sphere of their operation, and to secure leisure and opportunity for instructing them in the things of the kingdom; or, as Dr. Robinson has suggested,* he may have chosen these localities because they were all beyond the limit of the jurisdiction of Herod, whose attention had been directed to him after the death of John the Baptist, and perhaps, also, because the temporary presence of Herod in that province might, at the moment, have increased his personal danger.

But, however his movements may be accounted for, he came at length to Cesarea Philippi. This place is to be carefully distinguished from the sea-port on the Mediterranean which formed the Roman capital of Palestine. That had been only recently built, under the auspices of Herod called the Great. This was one of the ancient centres of heathenism, and but a few miles beyond Dan, which was the most northern point in the land of promise. It was originally called Paneas, probably from some connection with the Greek deity named Pan;† and that his worship was at some time practised in the neighbourhood seems to be attested by inscriptions yet visible in the face of the rock.

When Augustus Cesar visited Palestine in the year B.C. 20, he gave to Herod the Great the province of Paneas, and, in recognition of the imperial kindness, the Jewish king built there, in honour of Cesar, a splendid temple of white marble. At a later period the city formed part of the territory of Philip,

---

* "Harmony of the Gospels," English edition, p. 76, note.
† See Stanley's "Sinai and Palestine," pp. 390, 391.

who rebuilt it, or enlarged it, and gave it the name of Cesarea, in honour of the Emperor Tiberius, adding to it Philippi, ostensibly to distinguish it from the other Cesarea, but really to glorify himself. But now these names have both disappeared, and the ancient appellation has revived in the modern Baneas.

The town itself was situated just at the most easterly source of the river Jordan, where the water flows from the base of a high limestone rock in several rivulets, which presently unite into a considerable stream.* All travellers speak in terms of glowing admiration of the beauty of the place. Stanley affirms that "in its situation, in its exuberance of water, its olive groves, and its view over the distant plains," it is "almost a Syrian Tivoli;" and Porter has thus graphically described it: "Baneas occupies one of the most picturesque sites in Syria. A broad terrace on the mountain-side looks out over the rich plain of Huleh, westward to the castellated heights of Hunim. Behind it rises, in bold and rugged peaks, the southern ridge of Hermon, wooded to the summit. Two sublime ravines descend from the ridge, having between them a conical hill, more than a thousand feet in height, and crowned by the ruins of the ancient castle of Subeibeh. On the terrace at the base of this cone lie the ruins of Cesarea Philippi. The terrace is covered with groves of evergreen, oak, and olive trees, with intervening glades of the richest green turf, and clumps of hawthorn and myrtle here and there. A cliff of ruddy limestone, nearly one hundred feet high, rises on the north side of the ruins. At its base is a cave, whose mouth is now almost choked up with the *débris* of ancient buildings and fragments of the overhanging cliff. From the midst of these ruins, and from numerous chinks in the surrounding rocks, the waters of the great fountain gush forth. They collect a short distance below

---

* See Fairbairn's "Imperial Dictionary," *sub voce*; Stanley's "Sinai and Palestine." p. 389.

and form a rapid torrent, which leaps in sheets of foam down a rocky bed, now scattering its spray over thickets of oleanders, and now fretting against fallen columns."*

Here, then, at the base of Hermon, where to-day there is such a startling contrast between the transitory glory of man's proudest works and the permanent outflowing of that life-giving fountain that feeds the sparkling river, Jesus spake those words which described the indestructible character and enduring influence of that Church which he came to earth to found.

All heathen temples will one day moulder, as that of Paneas has crumbled into dust; but even then God's people will sing, "There is a river, the streams whereof shall make glad the city of God, the holy place of the tabernacles of the Most High. God is in the midst of her; she shall not be moved. God shall help her, and that right early."†

At this time, and in this place, the Lord, not for the purpose of eliciting information, but in order that he might have an opportunity of giving emphasis to the truth about himself, said unto his followers, "Whom do men say that I, the Son of man, am?" The question, by incorporating in it the title "Son of man," by which the prophet Daniel undeniably designated the Messiah, contained an implied claim that he was the Christ, and drew different answers from different individuals among them. Some had heard the opinion expressed that he was John the Baptist risen from the dead; others had been told that he was Elijah; and others had been informed that he was Jeremiah, or one of the prophets.

It is remarkable that, in reporting what they had gathered of the general sentiment of the community regarding him, none of them should have said, "We have heard it affirmed that thou art the Christ." Some twelve or eighteen months before, while yet the testimony of John the Baptist was vividly remem-

---

* Alexander's "Kitto's Cyclopædia," *sub voce.*
† Psa. xlvi., 4, 5.

bered by them, there might have been found not a few who would have said, "Thou art the Messiah." But now the influence of his antagonists was in the ascendant, and even those who believed in the rectitude of his character were not prepared to go farther than to suggest that he was the prophet whom they expected as the forerunner of the Christ. The tide had begun to ebb toward the Crucifixion. There was even danger, as we saw in our last discourse, that some of his chosen apostles might be carried away with it. So, once again, he put to them the pointed inquiry, "Whom say ye that I am?" to which, with his accustomed promptitude, Simon Peter made reply, "Thou art the Christ, the Son of the living God."

Thus again, as the spokesman of the twelve, Simon gave utterance, without hesitation or misgiving, to the sentiments of their hearts regarding Jesus, intimating that they received him, not simply in the sense in which the Jews of their day were prepared to receive the Messiah when he came, but as, in deed and in truth, a sharer in the deity of the Godhead. For the idea of the Messiah then current among even pious Jews, was that he was to be a divinely commissioned man, of exalted virtue and noble character, but still a man, who, like Daniel, or Ezra, or Nehemiah, or David, would be of signal service to their nation. But Peter shows that he had risen above this low and earthly conception of the great deliverer, and that he, and presumably also his brethren with him, believed Jesus to be "the Son of the living God."

Now, as we know that on another occasion, when Jesus spoke of God as his Father, the Jews accused him of blasphemy, on the ground that, by such a mode of expressing himself, he made himself equal with God,* we have no hesitation in affirming that Peter here, in his own name, and in the name of his fellow-apostles, expresses his conviction of the truth, not only of the Messiahship, but also of the Deity of Jesus.

---

* John v., 18.

Many things had led Peter to this conclusion. He had been deeply impressed by some of the miracles which he had seen, and some of the discourses which he had heard; and he could not be insensible to the matchless beauty of that perfect life which was daily unfolding itself, like a flower, before his eyes. But at this particular moment all these were brightened and vivified to him by the influence of God himself upon his soul, so that, carried out of himself, or at least lifted above himself, he spoke with a fervour and an earnestness which were perfectly unlike any former manifestations of his attachment to the Lord, and which therefore drew most naturally from his lips the warm commendation, " Blessed art thou, Simon Bar-jona; for flesh and blood hath not revealed it unto thee, but my Father which is in heaven. And I say also unto thee, that thou art Peter, and upon this rock I will build my church; and the gates of hell shall not prevail against it. And I will give unto thee the keys of the kingdom of heaven: and whatsoever thou shalt bind on earth shall be bound in heaven; and whatsoever thou shalt loose on earth shall be loosed in heaven."

There have been endless discussions among controversial theologians over the meaning of these words; and even to give a summary of the various opinions which have been advanced, with the arguments by which they are enforced, would require more time than that which is allotted to a single discourse, and call for more patience than that which is commonly manifested by modern sermon-hearers. I shall content myself, therefore, with setting before you as clearly as possible the interpretation which, after much careful investigation, I have adopted as, all things considered, the most natural and obvious.

Let me say, in the outset, that it is, in my opinion, undeniable that our Lord here wished to confer a special honour upon Peter. The other apostles, indeed, agreed with Simon in the matter of his confession; but the promptitude with which it was made, and the earnestness which glowed through his manner when he made it, were all his own; and it was very plainly in recognition of these that the Lord thus singled him out for commendation and reward. The words "Thou art Peter," and the frequent recurrence of the second personal pronoun throughout the sentence, clearly indicate that the Saviour's design was to confess Peter before the apostles even as Peter had confessed him, according to that word of his own, "Whosoever confesseth me before men, him will I also confess before my Father who is in heaven."

This is not to be disputed; and though the advocates of the Papacy have built upon it a superstructure of arrogance and intolerance which has outraged humanity, we shall gain little, and may lose much, by denying the modicum of truth which is in their treatment of this subject. Truth is truth, no matter how much men may have sought to pervert it to their own selfish ends; and as it is the truth we are in search of here, we must come to look for it without controversial bias.

Now, if it be granted, as I think it must be, that the Lord's design throughout was to honour Peter, it will follow that the rock on which he affirms that he will build his Church is neither the confession which Peter made, nor the Lord Jesus himself, to whom he made it, but Peter, to whom the Master is at the moment speaking. "By this confession of me"—as if the Lord had said, "Thou art the first who, as a living stone, has laid himself upon me; and so on thee, the stone nearest to, and resting first upon, the foundation-stone, I will build my Church."

What can be simpler or more beautiful than that? The words thus understood do not make Peter the foundation of the Church any more than the expression of Paul does, when he says that we "are built upon the foundation of the apostles and prophets, Jesus Christ himself being the chief corner-stone;"* or the language of John in the Apocalypse does, when he declares "that the wall of the city had twelve foundations, and

---

* Eph. ii., 20.

in them the names of the twelve apostles of the Lamb."* The whole purpose of the Lord is to confer an honour on Peter consequent upon, and indeed in some sort resulting from, the priority of this earnest confession publicly made by him. The first member of the visible Church upon the earth, in its Christian form, was Peter. By this open expression of his faith, he first laid himself on Christ; and so, naturally and of course, the others were built above him; but all still rested on Christ.

Now, if this interpretation be accepted, see how gradually the other things said by the Lord are developed out of it. "And the gates of hell" (*i.e.*, of Hades, which may mean here the grave) "shall not prevail against it." As if he had said, "I shall never lack in the future noble confessors, after thy type. One generation after another shall pass away, but the Church, consisting of all those who truly believe in me, and openly confess me before men, shall forever remain. Death shall not destroy it, for evermore new and enthusiastic ones will enter to take the places of those who are removed from earth. Persecution shall not abolish it, for the blood of the martyrs will be the seed from which new confessors shall spring up; and still, all through the ages, there will be those who shall avouch me to be their God, and accept me as their Redeemer."

"And I will give unto thee the keys of the kingdom of heaven." The kingdom of heaven here is not the kingdom of glory; and so this passage gives no countenance to the absurd idea that Peter is the porter who is stationed at the gates of the celestial city. The kingdom, as we gather from the many passages in which this mode of speech is employed, is that system of things of which Christ is the head, which he came to earth to introduce, and which, in its issues, stretches into the realm of glory. It is not, perhaps, entirely synonymous with the phrases "the Gospel dispensation" and "the Christian

---

* Rev. xxi., 14.

Church," but these come the nearest to it, in our common and ordinary speech.

Now, "the keys" of this kingdom must have something to do with its doors; and the gift of them to Peter signifies that, as the first confessor of his Lord, he was to have the honour of opening the dispensation of the Gospel, or the Church of Christ, to men. And how remarkably was this prediction verified! It was Peter who was prominent on the Day of Pentecost. He it was who opened the Church to the Jews; and as the result of his appeals and those of his brethren on that ever-memorable day, three thousand were converted to the Lord, and "added to the Church."

That was remarkable enough, considering the backsliding experience out of which Peter had so lately come; but, in a way that was even more striking, he opened also "the Gospel dispensation," or "the Christian Church," unto the Gentiles. Humanly speaking, he was indeed about the last man who might have been excepted to do anything of that kind; for he was all through his life a devoted Jew, and was as pre-eminently the apostle of the circumcision as Paul was that of the uncircumcision. But he was prepared for the work by a vision from heaven; and so, when the servants of Cornelius came to Joppa for him, he was ready to return with them to Cesarea, where, as he preached to a congregation of Gentiles, a new Pentecostal baptism came down, and he admitted those who had received it into the ranks of the infant Church. Thus, with his "keys," he opened the Gospel door alike to Jews and Gentiles.

But the Saviour adds, "And whatsoever thou shalt bind on earth shall be bound in heaven; and whatsoever thou shalt loose on earth shall be loosed in heaven." The key was sometimes of old a symbol of office and authority, and so, very naturally, the Lord passes into the thought which these last words express. "To bind" and "to loose" are modes of speech having reference to organization. They refer here to the authority which was vested in Peter, and, as we shall by-and-by see, in the other apostles, for the regulation of the government and affairs of the Church. He was to be one of the first and greatest of its office-bearers; and, as such, he would have delicate and difficult work to do. But so long as he sought to perform that work in the spirit which had dictated the noble confession which he had just made, he might rest assured that all his deeds would be approved and ratified on high.

All this, but nothing more than this, seems to be implied in these words. And doubtless in those days of weighty responsibility, when Peter stood before the Council, when he called for judgment on Ananias and Sapphira, when he rebuked Simon Magus, and preached to the household of Cornelius, he would be sustained by the remembrance of his Master's words on this never-to-be-forgotten occasion.

Such is the interpretation of this vexed passage, which commends itself to me as the most simple and natural. But lest any should suppose that the Lord here gave to Peter any such primacy as that which is claimed for the Pope in his name, I would remind them of the following things:

1. The sole thing that is specially given to Peter above the rest is that which is thus described, "I will give thee the keys of the kingdom;" for when we turn to Matthew xviii., 18, we find that the power of binding and loosing is conferred on the other apostles as well as on him; and when we read John xx., 23, we discover that a similar privilege seems to be conferred, in its collective capacity, upon the Church itself. In so far as that is concerned, therefore, the primacy of Peter consisted in the fact that to him first, as a recognition of his confession, was the intimation made that such a power would be conferred upon him. In the same way we have seen that the other apostles, as well as he, are spoken of as foundation-stones; but the honour of the keys he possessed alone; and that, therefore, represents the whole difference which Christ here put between him and them.

2. It is clear that the other apostles had no idea whatever that Christ, by these words, intended to set Peter over them as their visible head; for, at a later date, Salome, instigated by her two sons, requested that they should obtain the foremost place in his kingdom; and even at the Last Supper there was an unseemly dispute among the twelve as to which of them should be the greatest. Now, all these requests by them, and discussions among them, would have been as unnecessary as they were unsavoury, if the Lord had by this utterance already decided that Peter was to be their head.

3. Even if the words addressed to Peter conveyed in them all that Roman Catholic interpreters allege, there would still be wanting evidence that he was ever Bishop of Rome, or that, even if he ever occupied that position, he could transmit his personal prerogative to any successor. The questions raised by this remark are too large to be considered here, in anything like fulness. Let it be only observed that all the honour conferred by these words on Peter was given to him, not as an apostle, but as a prompt and enthusiastic confessor of the Lord; and the succession to that honour, if there be any succession in the case, must come only to those who are endowed with the characteristic which evoked it from the Saviour at the first.

As a matter of order, it may be true enough that a bishop may ordain a bishop, and a presbyter a presbyter, and the ordination may indicate the fact, that, by the consent of the Church, the individual ordained shall discharge the functions belonging to his office.

But apostles have no successors: it was a condition of their office, that they should be appointed directly and immediately by the Lord.* Hence, if this honour was given to Peter in his apostolic capacity, he could not transmit it to others. But if Peter could not, as an apostle, impart this honour to others,

---

* See Gal i., *passim*.

neither could he as a bishop; for though a bishop may ordain another bishop, yet he cannot transmit character. Hence, even if it were true, which is far from being universally conceded, that Peter was Bishop of Rome, he could not leave his character as a legacy to those who should come after him in that office; and without his character the honour would be impossible.

It was on Peter the confessor, and himself resting on the Lord Jesus, that the Church was built, and it was to Peter the confessor that the keys were given. Now, it is vain for any man, be he bishop or pontiff, to claim these honours if he is destitute of the character on which the honour was bestowed; while, on the other hand, the humblest believer, who makes a similar sincere and enthusiastic declaration of his faith in Jesus, does in a measure enter into Peter's succession, and share with him his privilege and prestige. He who in the face of a wavering world, and when men, in answer to the question, "What think ye of Christ?" are giving diverse replies, stands forth and says, "He is the Son of the living God," does thereby put himself into the chair of Peter, and will be privileged to open many doors into the Church for sinners converted through his instrumentality; and that is a higher honour than to be the Pope of Rome.

These last sentences have prepared the way for the enforcement of those practical lessons which are very obviously suggested by our interpretation of this interesting passage: For, in the first place, when we take confession of Christ as the central subject of this section of sacred history, we are reminded of the truth that, wherever it is genuine, it is the result of the operation of God upon the soul. There is, indeed, the highest degree of moral evidence attesting the fact that Jesus is the Christ, the Son of the living God. All ancient prophecy converges toward him; and, as Nicodemus said, "No man could do those miracles which Jesus did except God were with him." So, also, the matchless purity of his life, and the sublime originality and authority of his teachings, point to the same conclusion, while his resurrection from the dead, which is the best-attested fact in human history, declares " with power that he is the Son of God according to the spirit of holiness." It is possible, therefore, to construct a compact, well-jointed, and irrefutable argument in favour of the Messiahship and Deity of Jesus of Nazareth.

But while all such reasonings have their value, and must on no account be despised—for they are the outworks of the citadel of the Christian faith—still, it ought to be borne in mind that conversion, and confession like this of Peter, are not the results of any logical process, but of spiritual illumination. "Flesh and blood" doth not reveal this truth to a man, but the Father who is in heaven.

If any proof of this assertion be demanded, you have it on the very surface of the evangelical narratives; for even they who ate the bread of miracle, and saw the Lord bringing the dead to life, were found among his adversaries, though they readily admitted the supernatural character of his works. It is necessary that there be not only a sufficient degree of evidence for the fact that Jesus Christ is the Lord from heaven, and the Saviour of men, but also a soul ready to receive that evidence. For this is a matter of morals as well as a question in history; and the bias of the heart may neutralize the force of the appeal to the head. So, if we are earnestly desirous to see the conversion of our friends, and to have them brought to the point of making an open confession of Christ, we must not only labour with them in the way of setting before them the evidence by which his claims are supported, but we must also fervently appeal to God in their behalf, that he would open their eyes to see the truth, and dispose their minds to accept it.

Conversion to-day is as really the result of a divine illumination as it was when Paul was confronted with Christ on the way to Damascus; and though God works by means, in the preaching of his Gospel, we ought always to accompany our use of these means with earnest supplication unto him, that he would bring home the truth to men's hearts in demonstration of the Spirit, and with power. It is not by syllogisms alone, or by sermons alone, that men are brought to acknowledge Christ, but by the revelation of God through them, and along with them. Is it not written, "Not by might, nor by power, but by my Spirit, saith the Lord of hosts." As, therefore, we contemplate the careless and unconcerned around us, let us offer for them Elisha's prayer, "O Lord, open thou their eyes, that they may see."

But, in the second place, this passage shows us very clearly the connection of the confession of Christ with the permanence and the progress of the Church. "On this rock will I build my church, and the gates of hell shall not prevail against it." What has preserved the Church until to-day? "The faithfulness of God," you answer, "as manifested in its protection," and you are right; but by what means has he specially perpetuated it? Has it not been by the constant addition to it of those who, as they entered it, declared their faith in the Messiahship and Deity of Christ? It is often asked, "Why should a man join the Church? Is it not possible to be a Christian without being connected with any visible society?" And to this we may very frankly reply, that no doubt it is possible for an individual to be a Christian alone.

But, then, where would Christianity have been to-day, if all who have received Jesus as their Lord had acted on that plan? Could there have been, in that case, any such concerted efforts as those which have been put forth in the missionary enterprise? Or would it have been possible for Christianity, under such a system, to have pervaded society as it has done, or to have perpetuated itself at all? You have but to put these questions to yourselves, to see in a moment what their answer must be. Even in national efforts for the overturning of some political evil, men have found that it is hopeless to think of succeeding unless they can secure the combined action of all who agree with them. Hence in England there were anti-corn-law leagues, and in this country there were anti-slavery societies, without which the evils of protection there, and slavery here, could never have been overthrown.

Now, similarly, Christianity can be efficiently promoted only by a visible society; and he who seeks to keep himself isolated is only shrinking from a duty which, if all acted as he is doing, would be discharged by nobody. It is therefore essential to the permanence of Christianity on the earth, that men, through the Church, should make a public confession of their faith in Christ. The guerilla soldier is of small avail in a hotly raging battle. The close-compacted cohorts and well-drilled battalions win the day. And Christianity will conquer the world, not through each individual fighting for his own hand, but through the disciplined exertions of the churches of the saints.

Mark, again, how closely connected this confession is with the progress of the Church. "I will give thee the keys of the kingdom." That was, as we have seen, a special honour to Peter; but it is true yet that Christ puts a key into the hand of every sincere confessor of himself, wherewith he may open a door into the Church for some one else. Each new member does, by his avowal of himself on the Lord's side, influence some one else to take a similar stand.

I question if there are many Sabbaths in our Church history more fruitful in such results than those on which, in connection with the observance of the Lord's Supper, we receive new members into our fellowship. Their very appearance in the midst of us is itself an appeal to the undecided as pointed and earnest as that of Elijah on Carmel, "How long halt ye between two opinions?" And in conversing with applicants for admission to the Church, I have been surprised to find how many have traced their final decision to the sight of the public confession which others were making.

So, still, the Lord gives the keys to his faithful witnesses; and they who enter the Church are able to open a new door for others. But this result of confession must not be restricted to the moment of joining the Church. Wherever a man speaks out for Christ, in business or in society, the Lord puts into his hand a key; and at the end, when he sees the issues of his conduct, he will discover that he has therewith opened up the way of some soul to the Saviour. Enthusiasm is infectious; and the outburst of one may at length sway a multitude. Is there not here an argument why you who have hitherto stood timidly aloof should come with hearty earnestness into the ranks of the Church? How know you that your zeal may not provoke many? For if one Peter, through the baptism of the Holy Ghost, was instrumental in the conversion of thousands in a day, what would be the result if each of us were to be inspired by Peter's enthusiasm, and to copy his example? Come, then, and take your stand for Christ. The question of these times, as of all times, is this: "Who is on the Lord's side?" And if, in your secret souls, you are convinced that his side is the right one, you are doing an injury to yourselves, to the Church, and to the community, by keeping your conviction to yourselves. "Add to your faith courage;" and when others see your valour, they will be animated to follow your example. Hoist your flag! and determine, by God's help, to keep it fluttering in the breeze till your warfare is accomplished. "In the name of our God, let us set up our banners;" and we shall see, in their noble colours, at once the badge of our decision and the pledge of his protection.

VII.

THE REBUKE.

MATTHEW xvi., 21-28.

THE careful reader of the gospels can observe a distinct gradation in the course of instruction through which the Lord Jesus led his disciples. He taught them "as they were able to bear it." At first he was content to reveal himself to them as the Messiah promised to the fathers; and when they had become accustomed to think of him in that character, he carefully abstracted from it all those elements of mere earthly royalty with which in their imaginations it had been associated. Then he made known to them his divine dignity as the incarnate Son of God, and, in immediate connection with this manifestation of his personal greatness, he foretold his sufferings, death and resurrection.

It is remarkable, too, that in connection with each of these stages in the development to his followers of our Lord's character and work, there was what might be called a crisis in his ministry. Thus, his public claim to be regarded as Messiah drew upon him the antagonism of the men of Nazareth, to such an extent that he left the town in which he had been brought up, and took up his abode at Capernaum. So, again, his refusal to become a king, and act the part which popular opinion had allotted to the Messiah, led to the defection of multitudes in the synagogue of Capernaum, and planted in the heart of Judas the seed of that dissatisfaction of which at length his treachery was the fruit. And when, after drawing from the twelve, through Peter, a confession of his Deity, he proceeded to speak of his death, the effect was so staggering that they knew not well what to make of his words, and Peter, presuming somewhat on his lately received honour, actually began to rebuke him.

All this is valuable as an indication of the fact that the Lord Jesus could not have been an impostor. Had he been a pretender to the Messiahship, then he would have sought to work out the Messianic ideas that were current in his day. But, instead of doing that, he deliberately turned from all offers of earthly glory and declared that "the Son of man came not to be ministered unto but to minister, and to give his life a ransom for many." In taking such a course, he fulfilled in the most exact manner the predictions concerning the Messiah in the Old Testament. But while that fact adds an element of great value to the evidence in favour of his claims, it suggests at the same time the question, how it came that the Jews could read the writings of their own prophets without discovering that their Messiah was to be divine, and yet a man of sorrows and acquainted with grief.

On the one hand, it is undeniable that at the time of the advent almost all the people of Israel believed that their Messiah was to be a man, noble and great, but yet only a man, and that his career was to be one of uninterrupted glory. And, on the other, it is equally undeniable that David, Daniel, Isaiah, and Zechariah refer to him as stricken, smitten, and cut off. How, then, shall we account for the fact that the Jews should have made such a mistake? Something may have been due to the facts that the prophecies which refer to Messiah's glory are more numerous than those which describe his sufferings and death, and that even these prophecies are couched in such terms as veil their spiritual significance beneath a material covering.

But more is to be traced to the working of the familiar law, that the eye sees only what it brings the power of seeing. From the first, the Jews had been educated under a system of externalities. Even the sanctions of the moral law, as written in their books, were mainly temporal, and so they were apt to make more of the seen than of the spiritual, and to elevate the earthly above the eternal. Again, the wish is often "father to the thought;" and, as in the days of Herod, the people were groaning under a foreign despotism, they came naturally to think of their Messiah as a deliverer from Roman oppression. The bondage of sin was forgotten by them in the humiliating consciousness of their subjection to the empire. And so we can understand how it came that they could not tolerate the idea of a Messiah who would not consent to be a king, and were positively offended at the thought that he should die upon a cross. It was a stumbling-block unto them.

Now, with all his excellencies, Peter was in this respect no wiser than his fellow-countrymen. He had, indeed, seen and recognised the Deity of his Master, but he was not willing that his Master, being such a one, should be put to death. Hence when he heard the Lord describe how, at Jerusalem, he should "suffer many things of the elders and chief priests and scribes, and be killed, and be raised again the third day," he took him aside, and began to rebuke him, saying, "Be it far from thee, Lord: this shall not be unto thee." It was kindly meant. The loving apostle would spare his Master all trial and affliction. But he knew not what he said; and he must have been startled when the rebuke came, "Get thee behind me, Satan: thou art an offence unto me: for thou savourest not the things that be of God, but those that be of men." These seem strong words, and, apparently, when we think only of the spirit in which Peter spoke, they are harsh words. But when we go beneath the surface, we get at once the key to their interpretation. For what was it that Peter would have placed before the Lord? It was the kingdom without the cross. He saw no necessity for the dying of the Lord Jesus. His suggestion was that he should ascend to his throne in some other way than by that of Calvary. To him there were hardship, disgrace, and agony involved in the endurance of such things as Christ had been describing, and he besought the Redeemer to choose some other means for the attainment of his end. Thus his words were to the Lord a repetition of the temptation which the arch-fiend had put before him when on the mountain-top he showed him "all the kingdoms of the world and the glory of them;" and said, "All these things will I give thee, if thou wilt fall down and worship me;" and, recognizing the source from which the suggestion came, he said, "What! is Satan come again with his old lure? Get thee hence, thou tempter! But a little while ago I called thee rock, but now thou art a stone of stumbling, and a rock of offence unto me, and all because thou mindest not the things which be of God, but those that be of men."

Then, rising from this error of Peter regarding himself, he proceeds to guard them against similar mistakes concerning themselves. "You think it unseemly that Messiah should die upon a cross, but what say you to this, that you, too, must be ready to renounce yourselves, and take up your cross daily, and follow me?" The disposition which places safety uppermost, and makes every thing bend to that, does in reality only court destruction; while he who forgets himself in the service of the Lord is always sure of everlasting life; and when that is in the balance, what is there that will outweigh it? "What is a man profited, if he shall gain the whole world and lose his own soul? or what shall a man give in exchange for his soul?" The full import of these words may not be understood by you now; but in the day when the Son of man shall come in the glory of his Father, with the angels, and shall render to every man according to his works, it shall be clearly perceived by all who stand before the great white throne; and of the certainty of that day you shall have assurance when, by his resurrection from the dead and ascension into glory, you see him coming in his kingdom.

Such is a brief exposition of this interesting section of the sacred narrative. Let us see what we may deduce from it applicable to our present circumstances.

I pass by all reference to the fact, suggestive though it be, that this mistake of Peter followed immediately upon his commendation by the Lord. Every height has a precipice on one side; and when we receive signal honour we ought to be on our guard against falling into some peculiar disgrace.

I dwell not, either, on the bearing of all this on the infallibility, which, as it is alleged, has come through Peter to the Pope; for that is too patent, not to say too ludicrous, to escape the observation even of the most cursory reader. Of all the apostles, one would have thought that Peter was the very last whose history could suggest such a claim. He was constantly getting into trouble, and, if he received higher honour than ever was conferred upon his brethren, he came in also for more trenchant reproofs than any one of them ever called forth. Considering all that was to be built upon the eighteenth verse of this chapter by the Church of Rome, it is certainly not a little remarkable, that almost in the same paragraph Peter should be thus addressed by Christ, "Get thee behind me, Satan;" and every reader of history knows that of this latter sort of infallibility we have had more than enough in the chair of Peter, and elsewhere in the Church.

But I wish at this time to turn your attention more immediately to a matter of doctrinal importance. For there are those among us who, though like Peter, they are perfectly convinced of the Deity of Christ, still stumble at the idea that his death is a true and proper sacrifice for sin; and as, in our estimation, that state of mind proceeds from regarding the things that be of men more than those that be of God, it may be well to embrace this opportunity of meeting, and if possible removing, the prejudice which many thoughtful persons have on this subject.

Thus they tell us that it is positively unjust to compel the innocent to suffer for the guilty. They put the matter familiarly in this way: if the son of a king and the son of a peasant were at school together, and if the peasant-boy were obliged to answer for the misdeeds of the prince, everybody would exclaim against the unrighteousness of such a procedure. Now, we frankly admit that such a thing would be unjust. But, then, we contend that the analogy is false; and perhaps we may best bring out the truth if, taking the case which they suggest, we try to make it in some degree parallel to that of Christ and the sinner. To be so, then, it must be that the prince suffers for the peasant, and not the peasant for the prince. It must be, also, that the suffering of the prince is a purely voluntary thing, not suggested by the master, but accepted by him as sufficient for the ends of justice. It must be, further, that the suffering of the prince in the room of the peasant is the only thing that will avail to soften his heart, and actually does bring him to a sense of duty, so that he craves forgiveness and returns to obedience.* Now, when the case is put thus, who does not see that, so far from exclaiming against the vicarious suffering of the prince as an infliction of injustice upon him, everybody would applaud his generosity and love for submitting to indignity for the benefit of another? Now, this last is the true parallel to the work of Christ. He was no mean one in his Father's house, but, indeed, the fellow of Jehovah himself. He was not compelled to suffer for mankind, for when he came into the world he said, "Lo, I come (in the volume of the book it is written of me), I delight to do thy will, O my God;" and when again he spake of the same matter, he said, "I lay down my life of myself. No one taketh my life from me: I have power to lay it down, and I have power to take it again."

Further, this sacrifice of his was the only thing that could meet man's case, and melt his heart. Hence, when he came forward to give himself for human sinners, the act was one lifted above all legal questionings into the region of moral excellence; and it was only not righteous because it was so much

---

* See this point very strongly made by Archbishop Trench, in "Five Sermons before the University of Cambridge," pp. 30, 31.

higher than righteous as to take rank among those things which are good and merciful and godlike.

Nor can we forbear from saying that they who repudiate the doctrine that Christ's death was a voluntary sacrifice for sin do thereby give to his dying the very character of injustice, which they affirm adheres to it according to the orthodox view. For if, being God, as they admit, and so possessed of perfect moral excellence, he died, then he suffered that which he had not personally deserved. Nor does it better the matter to say that his death was an example. For it must have been more than an example, otherwise its exemplary force will be something more terrible than those with whom I am reasoning can imagine. If Christ's death were not a sacrifice for sin, voluntarily offered by Christ himself, then it was the most unjust thing in the universe, and becomes in the expressive words of Henry Rogers, "an example of this, that the more men obey and love God, the darker may be the divine frown and the greater the liability to suffer, under the incomprehensible mysteries of the divine administration, so that, if we were to become absolutely perfect as Christ was, in that moment we might reach the climax of misery.* Brethren, this witness is true. There is no injustice in the dying of the Lord Jesus, if we regard it as the giving up by him of that which was at his own disposal, in order that he might save sinners. But if it be otherwise, then, so far from alluring us into the paths of righteousness, the example of Christ must ever deter us from entering upon them, since it declares to us that the holiest man endured the heaviest sufferings.

There is no evading the force of such an argument, and so those who consider vicarious atonement, as Peter at this moment did, something derogatory to the character of God, retreat into this other stronghold. They say that the principle of substitution is not admitted in human law; and that, therefore, it can have

---

* The "Greyson Letters," p. 238.

no place in the divine. We accept the premise, but we deny the conclusion; for how comes it that the principle of allowing the innocent voluntarily to suffer for the guilty is not permitted to be exemplified in human law? We answer, for two reasons. First, because no adequate compensation can be given by that law to the substitute himself. In the matter of money, when the law can give to the man who pays another's debt a claim upon him or his property for that debt, no question is raised against substitution. But when one dies for another, he passes by his death beyond the domain of human law, and it is no longer possible for that law to give him adequate recompense. And, second, because by adopting the practice of substitution in human law, injury would be inflicted on the community, inasmuch as a guilty man would be set free from all restraint, while yet his disposition was unchanged, and no guarantee could be given that he would not repeat his former crimes. For these reasons, it is plain that substitution never can be permitted in human criminal jurisprudence. But if, in any way, these objections could be obviated, then I can see no reason, either in the law itself or in the welfare of the community, why it might not be allowed.

Now, in the case of the substitution of Christ for sinners, these objections are both removed. For, first of all, an adequate compensation is given him for his sacrifice. Death did not remove him from the sphere of divine law; nay, rather, it only introduced him into a department where that law could give him higher honour than any which on earth he could enjoy. So there he is exalted "above principalities and powers and thrones and dominions, and every name that is named." There he "sees of the travail of his soul, and is satisfied." There his exaltation is as great as his humiliation here was low. Moreover, in the second place, although the sinner is set free, he is not discharged with a disposition unchanged; for in the very moment of receiving his pardon his heart is renewed, so that he hates his sin, and turns from it to God, seeking ever after "to live soberly, righteously, and godly in this present world.' So by the sacrificial death of Christ, no injury is inflicted on any; the sufferer is compensated; the sinner is regenerated; the law is magnified, and God is glorified.

But, beaten back from this stronghold, they who repudiate the doctrine that Christ's death was a vicarious sacrifice, still minding the things that be of men more than the things that be of God, say, "Is not God a father? Why, then, should he not forgive his children on the simple expression of their penitence, and without an atonement?" To which we answer, God is a father. But he is a poor father who is not at the same time a governor. Every one knows how rebellious children become when their misdeeds are passed over on the mere expression of their sorrow; and if God had acted in this way with his human creatures, the result would have been the dishonour of his administration, and the triumph of evil in the world. It must not be forgotten that God stands to his creatures in the two-fold relation of king and father, and in his fatherly dealings with his children he cannot divest himself of his governmental character While as a ruler he has beneath his royal robes a paternal heart, it is no less true that as a father he has to maintain the administration of the king.

Now, we know how rampant crime becomes when, through carelessness, or partiality, or treachery, the criminal is permitted to go unpunished; and if God were to wipe out guilt on the mere expression of penitence—a thing, by-the-way, which no earthly judge would do—the resultant evil would be tremendous. Hence, we have only to admire the matchless wisdom of that wondrous plan whereby, at the very instant of his receiving forgiveness, the sinner, seeing the foundation of his pardon in the Cross, is led to hate his iniquities, and in every moment of temptation beholds the face of Jesus between him and the enticement, and hears him say, "Oh, do not this abominable thing that I hate. Wilt thou crucify me afresh, and put me to an open shame?"

Thus have I passed under review the most common objections to the doctrine that the death of Christ was a vicarious sacrifice for the sins of men, and shown you that those who entertain them are following mere human analogies, which, after all, are either false or defective, and so are minding, like Peter, "the things that be of men more than those that be of God."

It is time now that I should turn briefly to the practical department of the subject suggested by the instructions which Jesus gave on this occasion. The law of the cross is the law of the kingdom. True, there is not one of us who can endure the cross in the same precise sense as Jesus did, for he suffered, "the just for the unjust," and by his stripes men are "healed." But still the disciple must be as his Lord in so far that he has to lay his account with hardship, and must prepare for antagonism. It is not all plain sailing in the Christian life. He who would cross this ocean also must prepare for storms, for so the law runs: "If any man be willing to come after me, let him deny himself and take up his cross and follow me." What honesty have we here! The Lord will not seek men's allegiance upon false pretences. He is not like the recruiting-sergeant at the country fair, who tries to allure the gaping rustics to join the army by painting in glowing colours the romance of the soldier's life, and telling of this one and that one who rose from the ranks until he bore the star of a duke upon his breast, and carried the baton of a marshal in his hands; while he carefully conceals the discomforts of the barracks, the exhaustion of the march, the hardships of the camp, and the dangers of the battle-field. On the contrary, he sets before them all that they shall have to encounter, saying, "In the world ye shall have tribulation;" but beyond that, and as the result of that, he shows them the crown, promising "to him that overcometh" a seat with him upon his throne. He puts the two together. It is not all cross and no crown; but neither is it all crown and no cross. It is after the cross, the crown; and the heavier the cross, the brighter the crown.

Yet let us be on our guard here against mistaking our Lord's meaning, for we are not to make crosses for ourselves, or to cultivate self-denial merely for its own sake. A false reading of this verse has sent many an ardent spirit into a convent, and tempted many devout souls, like Pascal, to the practice of ascetic austerities, for no other reason than because they were disagreeable to the flesh. But when the Lord said, "Let him deny himself," he did not mean that the disciple was to inflict upon himself flagellations with the scourge, or deny the body its necessary food. He meant something far deeper and more important than that; namely, that he should renounce self as the ruler of his spirit, and that he should take Christ instead. And when he said, "Let him take up his cross daily," his words imply, not that the Christian is to make a cross for himself according to his own fancy, but rather that he should lift and carry that particular cross which the Lord hath laid on him for that day, whether it be the ridicule of his companions, or the loss of his profits, or the persecution of his enemies. And while he is bearing that, he is to think of Jesus, and seek to follow him, who, "when he was reviled, reviled not again; when he suffered, he threatened not, but committed himself to him that judgeth righteously."

Ah! my brethren, we who have begun the Christian life already know what this means; for though, as John Newton used to say, "the first stage of Christian experience is one of joy and peace," it is also true, as the same great and good man was wont to affirm, that "the second is one of conflict." The earnest believer very soon discovers that his life is to be a fight, and Christ here would prepare him beforehand, so that when it comes he may not be tempted to run away. If Jesus "pleased not himself" in order that he might save us, we are to give up self-pleasing and self-seeking in order that we may serve him. If he endured the cross, despising the shame, in order that he might deliver us, we are to take up our cross in order that we may honour him. And when we look upon our trials thus, they are more easily borne.

It is told of Charles Simeon, of Cambridge, that in the early days of his ministry there, he was assailed with such ridicule and scorn by the enemies of evangelical truth, that he was almost tempted to give up his post, and retire to some spot where he could escape their attacks. But just at that time, when walking in the gardens of one of the colleges, he came in his Greek Testament to the verse which reads thus: "They laid hold of one Simeon of Cyrene, and him they compelled to bear his cross." In this Simeon he saw himself, and so with joy he took the after-onsets of his adversaries, for he saw in them the cross he was carrying for Christ. Let us learn from his example, and take with patience, nay, with gladness, these hardships which come upon us for our allegiance to Christ. Only let us see that it is for Christ, and not for our own glory, or self-conceit, or evil temper, that we are called to suffer, and then the nails of our cross lose all their sharpness.

But some one may say, "I will take care of myself. If the following of Christ entails all these things upon me, they may follow him who will; I will take another course." Yes, but then, what will be the issue? The Christian's warfare comes first, and then he has his reward, and that is everlasting. Your enjoyment comes first, and then you have your punishment, and that is eternal. To seek to save yourself from present hardship thus, is to incur at length everlasting misery, for he that loveth his life thus shall lose it; and oh, the dreadful loss! "For what is a man profited, if he shall gain the whole world and lose his own soul?" The world cannot satisfy our infinite spiritual longings, for "God has made us for himself, and our souls are restless, until they rest themselves in him." Nay, even if the world could content the heart, the soul will outlast it, for the day is coming when the world and all that is therein shall be burned up; but even then the spirit of each man shall be immortal as God himself. Woe's me! at that day for him whose only treasure is the world. For then it will be too late to obtain the true riches, and the loss will be irreparable. The loss of the soul! The loss of the soul! It is not the end of being; it is the end of well-being, for it is the eternal severance of the soul from God.

Who that has read can ever forget those weird sentences of Richter which Carlyle has translated in one of his articles, and in which he depicts the utter misery of a soul groping through outer darkness in search of a rest that will not come, sending out its longings ceaselessly, like blazing rockets signalling distress, in the midnight of its despair, and crying evermore, "O God! O God! where is thine infinite bosom that I might rest myself thereon?" And even these sentences to which I have referred, but cannot quote, are but a feeble description of the immortal misery of a soul that is without God. Oh, is it for this that you are buying the world's happiness to-day? I have seen many a foolish bargain made on earth, but none so infinitely foolish as this. To give for a few years of an enjoyment which yields no substantial delight all your felicity for eternity! You are purchasing your earthly comfort and sinful pleasures at too dear a price.

If Jesus gave his blood for your soul, why should you sell it for a darling sin, or put it in jeopardy to save yourself from a little hardship? You talk of self-denial as if it were a dreadful thing; but our self-denial is nothing to yours. You deny yourselves the pleasures of holiness, which are enduring; we deny ourselves the pleasures of sin, which are evanescent. You deny yourselves the approval of conscience and the assurance of God's favour; we deny ourselves remorse with its gnawing anguish, and fear with its horrible forecastings. You deny yourselves that peace at death which springs from the persuasion that to depart is to be with Christ, which is far better; we deny ourselves a thorn-filled pillow on our death-beds. You deny yourselves the glad invitation, "Come, ye blessed; inherit the kingdom prepared for you from the foundation of the world;" we deny ourselves the withering malediction, "Depart, ye cursed, into everlasting fire, prepared for the devil and his angels." The path of Christ for me! Even if it lead through Calvary, it ends in a crown of glory that fadeth not away.

VIII.

ON THE HOLY MOUNT.

MATTHEW xvii., 1-9; MARK ix., 2-10; LUKE ix., 28-36.

ABOUT eight* days after the conversation between Christ and his apostles which formed the subject of our last discourse, and while yet their minds were earnestly engaged with the startling information which he had given them concerning his sufferings and death, the Lord took Peter and James and John apart with himself, and led them up "into a high mountain." To these three of his disciples the Saviour was drawn by a peculiar attraction; so that when he had any special privilege to bestow, he generally chose to confer it upon them. Thus they were selected to be the witnesses of the resurrection of the daughter of Jairus;† and they were honoured to go farthest with him into Gethsemane.‡

It is as vain to ask for the reason of this preference as it is to inquire why, out of these three, one was known as "the disciple whom Jesus loved," and was permitted to lean upon his bosom. There were doubtless good grounds for the selection in both cases; but whether it is to be accounted for by the supposition that these chosen ones had more in them in common with the Master than the other nine, or to be referred to the absolute sovereignty of the Lord Jesus, it is not for us to say.

---

* Matthew says six days; but the reason of the difference between him and Luke is plain. He reckons both the day from, and the day to, which he is calculating. Luke gives the number of the intervening days.

† Mark v., 37. ‡ Matt. xxvi., 37.

The place to which he led them has usually been identified with Mount Tabor; but there seem to be insuperable objections to such an opinion. Our Lord was at the time of Peter's confession, and the conversation already alluded to, in the region of Cesarea Philippi; but Tabor is in the southeast of Galilee, and there is no record of any journey intervening between the incidents referred to and the Transfiguration; while the narrative of Mark* makes distinct mention of a departure thence, and a journey through Galilee immediately subsequent to the descent from the mount. Besides, as Ritter has said,† "The historical data which we possess show that the summit of Tabor was employed without any intermission between the times of Antiochus the Great, B.C. 218, and the destruction of Jerusalem under Vespasian, as a stronghold, and was by no means the scene of peace and solitude whither one would flee anxious to escape the turmoil of the world."

We are, therefore, constrained to lay aside the tradition which, taking the word "apart" in the narrative as qualifying the mountain, rather than the persons who went up to it, has designated Tabor as the scene of this wonderful manifestation of celestial glory; and we would connect it with some one of the many peaks of Hermon in the neighbourhood of Cesarea Philippi. Hanna has given us the following account of a personal inspection of the locality: "Standing upon the height which overlooks Cesarea Philippi, I looked around upon the towering ridges which Great Hermon, the Sheikh of the Mountains, as the Arabs call it, projects into the plain. Full of the thought that one of these summits on which I gazed had in all probability witnessed the Transfiguration, I had fixed upon one of them, which, from its peculiar position, form, and elevation, might aptly be spoken of as a 'high mountain apart,' when, casting my eye casually

---

* Mark ix., 30.

† "Comparative Geography of Palestine," vol. ii., p. 313. I am indebted for the quotation to Trench's "Studies on the Gospels," p. 192.

down along its sides as they sloped into the valley, the remains of three ancient villages appeared dotting the base. I remembered how instantly, on the descent from the mountain Jesus had found himself in the midst of his disciples and of the multitude, and was pleased at observing that the mountain-top I had fixed upon met all the requirements of the Gospel narrative."* The comparison of the whiteness of the Saviour's raiment to snow gives accidental corroboration to the view that the scene occurred at Hermon, where alone in Palestine the snow could be seen.

Up the sides of such a mountain Jesus led his three apostles as the day was declining, that the night might be spent by him in communion with his Father. He gave himself unto prayer, and they, heavy with slumber, had a hard battle to keep themselves awake;† but, having overcome their drowsiness, they were rewarded by such a vision as mortal eyes never before or since beheld. For the fashion of the Lord's countenance was altered, his raiment became white, flashing out like lightning, dazzling as the snow beneath the sunlight. We are reminded, as we read, of the case of Moses as he came down from the mountain, and of that of Stephen as he stood pleading his cause before the council; but both of these shone with a reflected lustre, giving back that which they had first received, whereas here the Saviour's radiance came from within. For the moment the glory of his Godhead broke through the veil of that humanity by which on earth it was so largely concealed; and he appeared "covering himself with light as with a garment." He was to meet a deputation from the realms of glory, and it became him to array himself in his celestial state. The night was filled with the splendour; the very darkness was light about them; and

---

* Hanna's "Life of Christ"—The Ministry in Galilee, p. 336.

† Alford translates διαγρηγορήσαντες (in Luke ix., 32) rightly by the words "having kept awake," and so vindicates the apostles from the accusation of indifference.

not all at once could the privileged spectators accommodate their vision to the brightness. But when they could see into the glory, they beheld with their Master two shining ones, whom they knew to be Moses and Elijah, and whom they heard conversing with him on that very death which had been so distasteful to them, and for deprecating which Peter had drawn upon himself such a startling reproof. It was such a spectacle that they were lifted up out of themselves; and Peter, in the ecstasy of the moment, and in his own hasty manner, from the best of motives, but without any consideration of what was involved in his request, exclaimed, "It is good for us to be here; if thou wilt, let us make here three tabernacles; one for thee, and one for Moses, and one for Elias."

He felt that this was a better atmosphere to breathe than that in which for the past days he had been moving. The visible glory made him forget for the time the cross through which alone it could be made permanent, and he said, "Let us stay here. Why should we descend again to conflict and humiliation?" But even as he spake, a bright cloud, the emblem of the presence of Jehovah, overshadowed them all; and as, recognizing the nearness of the great I AM, they bent in lowly reverence, they heard the words from the excellent glory, "This is my beloved Son, in whom I am well pleased; hear ye him." So deeply moved were they by this divine testimony and admonition, that they did not venture to lift themselves from the earth until Jesus came and touched them, and then, when they raised their eyes, the night had come again, and they saw "no man, save Jesus only."

As the morning broke they took their way down the mountain-side, and, because of their own imperfect apprehension of the meaning of what they had seen, no less than because of the unprepared condition of men's minds, to receive their report, they were commanded to "tell the vision to no man until the Son of man be risen again from the dead."

The purposes which this remarkable occurrence was designed to serve will appear only when we take into consideration the different individuals of whom the group on the mountain-top was composed. So far as Jesus himself was concerned, there can be little doubt that it was meant to sustain him through the dreadful ordeal of Gethsemane and Calvary. In the near future of his ministry, there lay before him those sufferings and that death of which he had so recently spoken to his followers; and in the hour of that awful agony when his sweat was as great drops of blood falling heavily upon the earth, as well as in the moment of that dreadful loneliness when he cried, "My God, my God, why hast thou forsaken me?" the memory of this voice upon the mount, and that other by the banks of the Jordan, must have come back upon his spirit with re-assurance and consolation.

Before the conflict with the prince of darkness in the wilderness, the vision at his Baptism was given to inspirit him for the fight; and now again, just before he set out on his last journey to Jerusalem, and when he had the near prospect of meeting the combined assaults of earth and hell, he is comforted and cheered by the words of Moses and Elijah, and by the voice from the Eternal Father. If there be a cross before us, God will grant us also a transfiguration, that we may not flinch in the time of trial. He "sendeth none a warfare on his own charges," and the glory of Hermon lightens the darkness of Gethsemane.

The presence of Moses and Elijah was designed to show that the old dispensation was but a preparation for the new. Moses represented the law, as did also Elijah, for, strictly speaking, the Tishbite was rather a reformer of the old than a prophet of the new. These two, therefore, were the men who might naturally have been supposed to be most zealous for the system which was inaugurated on Sinai; but even they are here to receive honour from Christ, and yield up the palm to Christ. Observe, their appearance did not precede the transfiguration of the Lord. The change on Christ came first, then his glory gave brightness and distinctness to them; and after they had been thus illuminated, they retired and left him alone, the master of the new dispensation. Thus, as I attempted to show in my discourse on this subject as connected with Elijah,* the special significance of the presence of these ancient worthies testifies to these three things, namely, that the glory of Christ is intimately connected with the decease which he accomplished at Jerusalem; that Christ, so glorified, gives new radiance to that old history and law of which Moses and Elijah were the noblest representatives; and that the ancient law, so glorified by Christ, is seen to have served its purpose, so that it ceases to be binding on men's consciences, while the new system of which Jesus is the head is inaugurated by the voice from the throne, of which this is the significance: "Moses and Elijah were my servants, and you did right to hear them; but now I bring to you my beloved Son in whom I am well pleased: hear ye him."

Thus viewed, the purport of the Transfiguration is parallel to the argument of the Epistle to the Hebrews, and especially to that of its first two chapters, wherein the superiority of Jesus as the Son is made a reason why we should give the more earnest heed to the things which he has spoken, "lest at any time we should let them slip."

One object secured by the presence of Peter, James, and John was that there were eye-witnesses of the Redeemer's majesty on this occasion, when for a brief season he resumed his regal state. But while that was a matter of undoubted importance, the effect produced on these three disciples themselves must not be overlooked; and to obtain a correct idea of that, we must take into account the conversations in immediate connection with which the Transfiguration occurred. The Lord had asked them first, "Whom do men say that I the Son of

---

* See "Elijah the Prophet," pp. 195-209.

man am?" and they had replied, "Some say that thou art John the Baptist; some, Elias; and others, Jeremias, or one of the prophets;" and now, Moses and Elijah themselves appear doing homage to Jesus, and setting that matter completely at rest.

He had asked again, "But whom say ye that I am?" whereupon Peter, speaking for the band, had said, "Thou art the Christ, the Son of the living God;" and, lo! as they gazed on his robe of light, they had ocular demonstration of the truth to which Peter confessed, while the voice out of the cloud left no room for any lingering doubt as the great God himself proclaimed, "This is my beloved Son."

Once more: he had now, for the first time, spoken plainly to them of his sufferings and death; and they were offended thereby; so that Peter, in their name, had protested against his enduring any such indignities at the hands of men; and all had marvelled at the force of the reproof which he had thereby drawn upon his head. But, behold! when Moses and Elijah come from heaven to hold fellowship with Christ, it is of this very death they speak. They say nothing of the glory of his miracles; they utter no word about any earthly monarchy, such as that which his followers supposed he was about to found; they have no conference concerning the conquest of Israel's Roman oppressors; they speak only of "the decease which he should accomplish at Jerusalem." In their estimation, that was the central point in his career; the most glorious and the most god-like thing he was to do was to give his life a ransom for many, for thereby he was to accomplish an Exodus* more far-reaching in its results and more illustrious in its renown, than that with which the name of Moses is imperishably associated.

The effect of all this upon the listening apostles must have been great. They would learn at once that in the dying of their Lord there was to be nothing really disgraceful to him, however much indignity men might endeavour to connect with it;

---

* The original word in Luke is τὴν ἔξοδον, the Exodus.

and though, for the time, they might not be able to comprehend how the death of the Lord could be a theme of such interest to celestial beings, and could be so intimately associated with their Master's honour, yet, in later days, after the Holy Ghost had been conferred upon them, they would, through their remembrance of this wonderful conversation, be enabled to understand more thoroughly the mystery as well as the majesty of the cross.

It is worthy of remark that these privileges came to the three apostles in the wake of the confession which Peter made in their name and his own. The whole evidence that exists for the claims of Christ upon us as our Redeemer and Lord is not to be expected to be known and appreciated by us before we confess him. If we see enough to convince us that he is the Son of God, then let us take means to publish that conviction, and when we have done that, he will take us to some mountain-top of experience, where he will unveil his glory to us, and give us an unwavering assurance regarding him that will resist the insinuations of the sceptic and the assaults of the gainsayer.

Men wait for this before they make their confession even though in their inmost hearts they feel that Christ has an indubitable claim upon them. But that is a mistake. Let them confess him *first*, and then there will come to them the Mount of Transfiguration, with its light in the midst of darkness, to confirm them in so much of their confession as was true, and to correct that which in it was false. "If any man be willing to do his will, he shall know of the doctrine whether it be of God." Act up to the light which you at present enjoy, and as you do that, new light will come to you. The way to the top of the transfiguration mountain is through the confession of the Lord Ah! if I could only persuade you of that, how many among you who are already "disciples, but secretly," would come forth and avow yourselves on the Lord's side! But I do not wish you to take it on my word. Ask any one of those who out of sincere affection to him, and humble confidence in him, have confessed Christ, if it be not even as I have said, and they will corroborate my assertion. The day of confession ushers in a new era in religious experience, and from that hour the disciple rises to a higher life in Christ. Try it, you who in your hearts are already yielding yourselves up to him, and after you have done it, and not long after it either, he will take you with him unto a high mountain apart, and give you a vision of his transfigured glory.

But it is time that I should glance a little at some of the more general lessons which we may learn from this striking scene.

And, in the first place, we are reminded by it that seclusion is needed for the highest sort of devotion. Luke tells us that the transfiguration of the Lord took place as he was praying, and so we are warranted in concluding that Jesus and his three disciples withdrew to the mountain-top for special communion with God. Nor was this a solitary instance of the kind; for the student of the Gospel narratives is struck by the frequency with which they record the facts that the Saviour went up into a mountain to pray, and that he spent whole nights in supplication. Now, if he who had no sins to confess and no forgiveness to ask, still felt it needful after his toilsome days with the multitude to refresh his soul by fellowship with Jehovah, how much more earnest ought we to be in securing seasons for devotional retirement! The very activity of the times in which our lot is cast ought to impel us to use means for keeping the closet undisturbed; yet it is to be feared that by many of us the privilege of private prayer is undervalued, and the blessing of communing with God in secret is unenjoyed.

We are living in a period of reaction in this matter. In former times, our fathers, Peter-like, sought to erect booths upon the mountain top, and were inclined to dwell there for ever, forgetting the duty which they owed to their fellow-men in the streets and lanes of their own cities, and in the far lands of heathenism. Hence, as we read their treatises and biographres we find many things concerning devotion, and comparatively few concerning work. They were great in meditation, but they did little for the elevation of the people around them. Now, however, a wonderful activity has sprung up among Christians. They are far enough yet, indeed, from what they ought to be in that respect; but still they are greatly in advance of some former generations; and in their consecration to these works of faith and labours of love they are apt to ignore the closet altogether.

It is told of Clarkson that when, on a Sabbath-day, Wilberforce called upon him and found him busily engaged in some work connected with the anti-slavery enterprise, the senator said to him—"Clarkson, do you ever think upon your own soul?" and the reply was, "Wilberforce, I can think of nothing about myself so long as this terrible evil is in existence." Now there was a certain nobleness in Clarkson's words; yet, even while we concede that, we must affirm that he was wrong, for the more we are called to do for God in the service of our generation, the more earnestly ought we to seek stated seasons of communion with him, for thereby only can we keep ourselves in the proper working spirit.

It was after the Saviour had been busiest with the people that we find him withdrawing from them for fellowship with his Father, and the more we have to do for the Lord, the oftener should we seek to be alone with him. I know that we may have genuine fellowship with him in our work, and that we may pray to him anywhere, in the brief, ejaculatory manner in which Nehemiah called upon him, even while the king's cup was in his hand. I gladly admit the truth of all that is advanced in that direction; but still that sort of fellowship must not be made a substitute for the other, else it also will soon drop altogether out of our lives. The fountain-head of devotion is in the closet. If we keep that full, it will irrigate the entire life, and at every favouring opportunity its waters of refreshment will bubble up to gladden us; but if we let that run dry, the whole experience of the soul will speedily become withered and barren.

Matthew Henry was right when he said that apostasy from God generally begins at the door of the closet; and in these days of holy convocations, when every day in the week, and many times in a day, we are asked to take part in some public gathering for the promotion of revival or the advancement of the Redeemer's kingdom, we need to be warned against the danger of putting such engagements in the place of the mountain top. Nothing will make up to thee, my brother, for the neglect of that; therefore, let nothing become to thee a substitute for it. He who is stimulated to pray long in public, but has no relish for private devotion, never prays to God at all, but is angling in his supplications for the applause of his human hearers. So I make the closet, rather than the prayer-meeting, the test of individual piety, and that alone is a profitable prayer meeting which gives to every one attending it a new relish for secret prayer.

In the second place, we are reminded here that a devotional spirit sees new glory in Christ and in his Word. When Peter and his brethren retired apart with Christ, he was transfigured before them, and Moses and Elijah shared his brightness. Now, when we give ourselves to the devotional study of the Scriptures, new radiance breaks forth from its pages for us. I think that one reason why we do not relish the closet as we ought is that we make it a place for mere asking, rather than for the study of Christ and his salvation as they are revealed in this book. It is worthy of remark that, in the Hebrew language, the word which signifies "to pray" means also "to meditate," proving that meditation ought to blossom up into prayer, and that prayer ought to have its root in meditation. Yet how little we give ourselves to meditation! We can talk to a friend at any time; we are always ready to take up an interesting book; we do not object, either, to give loose reins to our imaginations in day-dreaming: but meditation—the holding of our minds to a certain subject until we have discovered the principles which underlie it, and have traced its applications in different directions—that is not so much to our taste. But that ought to be the principal exercise of the closet, and in the prosecution of that every Biblical student will tell you that he has often seen Christ transfigured, and that frequently Moses and the prophets have stood out before him, arrayed in a glory given to them by the Messiah. Brethren, there are few joys greater than that which is awakened in us by the discovery of some new beauty in Christ, through the study of his Word, and if you will only give yourself to that work in your closet-hours, you will be rewarded with a happiness akin to that of Peter on the mount, when, in listening to the conversation of the glorified triumvirate on the death of Christ, he said, "Master, it is good for us to be here."

In the third place, we are reminded that devotion is not the whole of life. Peter wanted to remain on that summit altogether. But he knew not what he said. There was a world to be redeemed, and how could that be accomplished if Jesus were held back there from the cross? There was, even at that very moment, a poor demoniac in the valley, waiting their descent, in order that he might be cured. No! it could not be. Before Peter himself were the Pentecost, the prison, and the cross, for he was to be one of God's chosen vessels for the carrying of the Gospel to mankind. The present hour was a time of refreshment preparatory to a life of labour, and he must leave the scene of privilege for the field of toil. So it is still. Prayer is of highest value, and the ordinances of the Church can hardly be overestimated; but we cannot be always enjoying. No doubt there are some among us who may have sung at a communion season or elsewhere these lines—

> "My willing soul would stay
> In such a frame as this,
> And sit and sing itself away
> Into the realms of bliss."

Now that is all very well; but it is just as impossible as was Peter's proposal here to erect booths upon the mountain-top. The devotional is meant to be the handmaid of the practical. Prayer is not a mere sentimental thing. Wherever it is so, it is not true prayer. But, wherever it is genuine, it is the inspiration to work; and we who have been filled with ecstasy by the vision of the Christ ought to go down again among our fellows, and seek to lift them up with us to our former elevation. Thus the active and the contemplative balance each other in the Christian life. The former gives new zest to the closet, and the latter gives new vigour to the conduct; so that he is the noblest man in whom they are both equally developed.

Finally, we are reminded here that devotion furnishes support for the performance of the duties and the endurance of the trials of life. As I have already said, the Redeemer himself, even in the garden and on the cross, was upheld by the remembrance of this voice from the midst of the cloud; and we know that Peter long after, when contemplating his decease, looked back upon this whole scene as one of the strongest verifications of the Gospel saying, "We have not followed cunningly devised fables, but were eye-witnesses of his majesty, when there came to him such a voice from the excellent glory, this is my beloved son in whom I am well pleased; and this voice which came from heaven we heard when we were with him in the holy mount." Thus, through all his later experiences, the memory of Hermon's glory stayed up the heart of the apostle and sustained his faith. So it has been often with humbler disciples: their discoveries of Christ in their devotional study of his Word have sustained them under afflictions, and strengthened them in moments of temptation. "I could not have got through," said one to me, during the money panic two years ago, "if it had not been for prayer." My hearer, do you know anything of such an experience as that? Is it possible that you are one of those who ridicule prayer, despise the Gospel, and dishonour Jesus? Well, you have had some trials, for unbelief gives you no exemption from them; you have been in deep distress without Christ; you have just come, it may be, out of some dreadful agony, in which you could not recall one single promise of his grace, and dared not lay hold upon his hand? How was it with you then? Would you like to go through a similar ordeal again? Ah! you shudder at the very thought; you cannot contemplate such a thing without terror. Oh, what a privilege all the while you have been denying yourself in putting Jesus from you! Give him your hand, give him your heart to-night; and as the weeks revolve he will show you more and more of his grace, and take you too up with him to some Hermon-top of glory, the memory of which will be to you an anchor through life, and the influence of which will bear you up in death.

IX.

THE WASHING OF THE FEET.

JOHN xiii., 1-17.

PASSING over the finding by Peter in a fish's mouth of a piece of money, with which, by the command of the Lord, he paid the Temple tribute,* and merely alluding to the question † which he put to Jesus as to the frequency with which he should forgive an offending brother, we come now to the first of that series of interesting incidents which culminated in his denial of the Lord. From Gaulonitis the Saviour had gone to Galilee, and from Galilee he had set his face steadfastly to go up to Jerusalem, knowing full well the things that should befall him there. At first, as he entered the city in a certain kind of state, he had been received with popular enthusiasm; but under the influence of their selfish rulers the people had suddenly cooled in their attachment to him, and the week whose first day saw his triumphal entry, witnessed on its sixth day his crucifixion on Calvary. It was now the afternoon of the Thursday, and the Master and his disciples were reclining at table, in the upper room which Peter and John had prepared for their celebration of the paschal supper. It is true, indeed, that the Evangelist John, to whom we are indebted for the narrative which is now before us, gives no account of the institution of the Lord's Supper, but there is abundant evidence that the passover here spoken of was that at the close of which he in-

---

* Matt. xvii., 24-27. † Matt. xviii., 21.

stituted the memorial ordinance which is still so dear to all his followers.

But while all are agreed on that, there has been much learned discussion over the question whether the feast here observed by Jesus was the regular Passover, or whether he anticipated that by a day, so that his own crucifixion was simultaneous with the time of the offering of the typical lamb. And some have attempted to prove that the statements of the fourth Evangelist on this point are irreconcilably opposed to those of the other three. Thus, in the opening verse of this chapter, John speaks as if the feast of the Passover were still to come; and in a later passage (xviii., 28) he alleges that the Jews would not go "into the judgment-hall lest they should be defiled, but that they might eat the passover." Now Matthew (xxvi., 17) says that directions were given for preparing to eat the passover "on the first day of the feast of unleavened bread;" and Mark (xiv., 12) and Luke (xxii., 7) refer to "the first day of unleavened bread," when "the passover must be killed."

We have adopted the view of those who believe that Christ did eat the passover on its own proper and appointed day with his followers, and we find the principle of harmony between the sacred writers in the fact that by the term "passover" the first three Evangelists commonly mean the actual eating of the paschal lamb, while John uses it in a broader sense, to signify the festivities of the entire week of unleavened bread. It is proper to say, however, that this opinion is very far from being unanimously accepted, and when such authorities as Alford, Pressensé, and Farrar are on the other side, it would be presumption in me to dogmatize; but twenty years ago I had the privilege of reading an elaborate article * on this question by the late Dr. Robinson, of this city, and I have found his argument so convincing that nothing that I have read since then has disturbed the conclusion to which he conducted me.

---

* In the "Bibliotheca Sacra" for August, 1845.

While they were at table the Lord rose, and laid aside his upper garment; then, girding himself with a towel, and taking water in a basin, he proceeded to wash the feet of his followers. That was a work usually done by servants or slaves; yet, as not shoes but sandals were commonly worn in Palestine, and as the streets and highways were hot and dusty, the washing of the feet was a great comfort, we might even say a great luxury, to the traveller; so that, when he entered the house of a friend, the earliest courtesy extended to him was that of giving him water for his feet.*

To a Western reader it seems strange that Christ should have attempted to do this for his disciples while they were at table. But the customs of the Jews at that date were quite different from those which now prevail among us. The guests at a feast were arranged along three sides of a parallelogram, and they reclined on couches. Leaning on the left side, each one had his right hand free to help himself to the food prepared, and as their heads were toward the table their feet stretched out behind. Hence, one could go round behind them, and have free access to their feet without in any way disturbing their repast. It was in this manner that the woman stood at Christ's feet, behind him, when he was in the house of Simon the Pharisee,† and began to wash them with her tears, even while the entertainment was going on. So, in the present instance, while the apostles kept their places, the Lord went round outside and washed their feet. They were amazed at his procedure. They knew not what to make of it. But, as usual, it was Peter that broke the silence with which they were all stricken; for when the Master came to him, the impulsive and generous apostle could not think of allowing the Son of God to do for him the office of a slave, and said, "Lord, dost thou wash my feet?" To this the Saviour responded, "What I do thou knowest not now, but thou shalt know hereafter." As if he had said, "Submit

---

* Luke vii., 44. † Luke vii., 38.

to it now, and in a very short time you will see the significance of my act." Still the impulsive disciple would not consent. He replied, with even more emphasis than before, "Thou shalt never wash my feet." But the Master would not argue with him. He simply said, "If I wash thee not, thou hast no part with me." And when it was put thus to him, there was no longer any hesitation—nay, in the exuberance of his desire to manifest his determination to have part with Christ, he answered, "If it is urged by thee on that ground, I am ready for any thing. Wash not my feet only, but also my hands and my head." But that, again, was too much. True obedience is the doing of the very thing commanded—neither more nor less; and in this overplus of zeal there was as much to blame as there had been in his refusal to be washed at all. So the Lord checked that also with the words, "He that is washed needeth not save to wash his feet, but is clean every whit; and ye are clean," but with a suggestive arrow aimed at the conscience of Judas, he adds, "not all."

No one can read this narrative without observing the distinct and consistent individuality which is given to Peter by all the sacred writers. By whomsover of them he is described, whether by Matthew or Luke, by Mark or Paul, or by his beloved friend and coadjutor, John, you have the same characteristics delineated. He is always a man of impulse; and when he sees he has made a mistake, he is so eager to rectify it that he runs right into the opposite extreme. He is as explosive as nitro-glycerine, and while occasionally the force of the blast clears away some rock of offence, just as frequently it imperils the safety of those by whom he is surrounded. He is constantly uttering right things, but he very often utters them at the wrong time; so that the criticism once made on an eccentric Scottish minister might have been pronounced on him: "He is instant in season and out of season, but especially out of season." Yet, withal, he was so affectionate and so honest, that one is almost ready to forgive his mistakes for the

I

sake of the magnanimity with which he committed them, and the motive by which he was actuated. Here, for example, we can see that his blunder sprung out of the very reverence in which he held his Lord. In his wonted impetuosity, he did not stay to remember that obedience is better than sacrifice, and that the truest respect we can pay to the Lord Jesus is to have implicit confidence in him, and to give unquestioning allegiance to him. Still, in his own blind, blunt way he was trying to show his love to Christ, and to reveal the exalted conception which he had of his greatness. Hence, whenever he was told that washing was essential to having part in Christ, he yielded in a moment; nay, he would be all washed, and so he swung to an excess of submission which was as faulty as his refusal had been.

Now, this distinctness and consistency of individuality which we mark in Peter, wherever we meet him in the New Testament, is a striking proof, all the more striking because it is incidental, of the credibility of the sacred writers. The highest triumph of dramatic genius is secured when the poet is able to give through the actions of his characters a separate and easily recognized identity of disposition to each person whom he represents. Some have attempted to accomplish this by putting certain words into a man's lips, which he is made to speak on all occasions; others have tried to attain it by stamping the individual with some external mark, such as provincialism of dialect, or stammering in speech; but the unapproachable eminence of Shakespeare is apparent in the fact that he has succeeded in allowing his greatest characters to develop themselves before us in a natural yet consistent manner, so that we feel that we recognize them at each reappearance. Even he, however, has not always accomplished that. But here, in the Gospel narratives, and in the apostolic history, the sacred writers have done it successfully for the chief actors whom they introduce to our notice. You cannot mistake John for Peter, or Peter for Paul, or Paul for

Barnabas. Each has his own distinct individuality; and that is given to him without any attempt on the part of the writers to describe him to us. So far as I know, Barnabas is the only one of those whom I have named of whom we have any thing like a description, and even of him the historian only says, "He was a good man." They are allowed to define themselves to us by their words and actions, and yet each stands out before us in living distinctness, and is never found acting out of character. Here, for example, is Peter, who figures prominently in the works of Matthew, Mark, Luke, and John, and in one of the letters of Paul. Five writers, distinct from each other, producing their works at separate times, and entirely independently of each other, represent him in distinct situations. John has shown him in circumstances of which the other three are silent; Luke has things about him of which Mark and Matthew say nothing; and Paul has referred to his action at a time of which none of the others have any account; yet in them all Peter stands out before us the same man, easily recognizable by those features which I have tried to describe. Here, therefore, are five authors working separately and independently, yet they produce in their portrayal of Peter a dramatic unity of character which has been secured in poetry only by the loftiest genius, and not always even by that. How shall we account for this? We cannot explain it, if these records are forgeries, or have to do with things which did not occur. We can account for it only on the supposition that each of these five men was describing real occurrences in the history of a real man, and thus we have a valuable branch of corroborative evidence in behalf of the genuineness and credibility of the New Testament Scriptures.

But, while we give due attention to the important bearing of the consistency with which Peter's character is revealed to us by the sacred writers, on the question of the reliability of the record, we must not lose sight of the contrast here suggested by the Saviour's words, "but not all," between the disposition of Peter and that of Judas. The traitor was present all through this singular ministry of Jesus to his followers; and as we see from one of the early verses of the chapter (John xiii., 2), he had already formed the determination to betray the Lord, yet *he* made no objection to the washing of his feet. He accepted this token of his Master's affection as a thing of course. The mere onlooker might have preferred his demeanour to that of Peter, but in reality there was a tremendous difference between the two men; and though we cannot give Peter unqualified praise, yet it is better far to have his honest impulsiveness, even if it do blunder now and then, than the cunning duplicity of Judas; though, of course, it is still better to have the calm and trustful submission of John and the others, who let the Lord do to them as he pleased, and waited for his explanation in his own time.

But now let us ask what the meaning of the Saviour in this enigmatical action was. He has told us himself in these words, "Know ye what I have done unto you? Ye call me Master and Lord: and ye say well, for so I am. If I then, your Lord and Master, have washed your feet, ye also ought to wash one another's feet. For I have given you an example, that you should do as I have done to you. Verily, verily, the servant is not greater than his lord, neither he that is sent greater than he that sent him." He had condescended to do for them the office of a slave, and so they ought to perform similar offices for each other. Christian disciples are to help each other even if, in doing that, they should sometimes require to stoop to the lowly position of a servant. That seems to me to be the general lesson which our Lord meant to teach on this occasion, but we must beware of frittering away its force by restricting it to one stated sort of service.

We read that Thomas à Becket had "thirteen poor men daily introduced into his apartment, at the hour when they were least likely to be observed, and, having washed and kissed their feet, he regaled them with a plentiful meal, at which he himself waited on them, and sent them away with a present of four pieces of silver to each;"* and we are told that on a certain day of high ceremonial the Bishop of Rome washes the feet of twelve men. Now, it is to be presumed that Becket was sincere, and that the Pope is sincere, in the desire to follow in the footsteps of the Lord. But, in all such services as these, the repetition of the letter of the Lord's example is mistaken for the manifestation of the spirit which breathed through the Master's act. The outward thing which he did is done again once every day, or once every year, as the case may be, while that which he really enjoined was the constant exercise of that spirit of self-sacrifice which underlay and inspired his action. In the mere externalism of such ceremonials as these, the force of the Saviour's injunction is restricted to one special work, performed at some particular time, while he designed it to have free course through all the life. He meant that as his disciples we should always seek to serve each other, even if in doing so we should have to lay aside our dignity, or to deny ourselves our wonted comforts, or even to lay down our lives. Such an act as that of Becket's, no matter how sincerely it was performed, bears to the example of our Saviour here the same relation that a portrait does to a man: it is a likeness, but it wants the life; it catches one expression of the original and it fixes that, but it gives no conception of the manifold aspects of which it was capable. There is an immense difference between a copy and an imitation. The copyist works from without, and reproduces the external appearance; the imitator labours from within, and, catching the spirit, he lets that work itself out as it may. We are not to copy Christ, for every copy will turn out to be a caricature; but we are to let "this mind be in us which was also in him," and then the ever-varying circumstances of our lives will furnish new opportunities for the development of the principles on which the Master acted.

---

* "Becket, Archbishop of Canterbury; a Biography," by James Craigie Robertson, M.A., p. 58.

But while all this is true, I cannot help thinking that the words of our Lord to Peter, ere yet he began to expound the significance of his act to the apostles, suggest a certain special spiritual application of this general lesson of love and self-sacrifice. He said, in answer to that disciple's request to have his head and his hands washed as well as his feet, "He that is washed, needeth not save to wash his feet, but is clean every whit, and ye are clean, but not all." Now the one word "wash" in this text is used as the English equivalent for two distinct Greek terms. The first time it occurs "he that is washed," it is, literally ($\dot{o}$ $\lambda\epsilon\lambda ou\mu\epsilon\nu o\varsigma$), "he that has been bathed." The second time it appears, "needeth not save to wash his feet," it is ($\nu i\psi a\sigma\theta a\iota$) the exact equivalent of our word to "wash." The one verb denotes the washing of the body as a whole, the other the cleansing of any part of the body as distinguished from the whole. In its literal application it implies that he who has gone fresh from his own bath to the house of his host needs not to be bathed again, but requires only to have removed from his feet the dust which they have contracted in his walk.

But from the expression of the Lord, "Ye are clean, but not all," it is plain that he meant the whole sentence to be taken spiritually. And if this be so, then its significance may be thus expressed: He who has been once renewed by the washing of regeneration, does not require to be renewed again. A man is born but once spiritually, even as he is born but once naturally. Regeneration needs not to be repeated. All that one needs after that is to have his feet washed; that is, to have removed from him the impurities which adhere to him in consequence of his having to walk daily through this defiling world.

Now this we Christians, even at the cost of our dignity and comfort, must do for each other. Doubtless there is a sense in which Christ alone can take away sin; yet when one is overtaken in a fault,* Paul exhorts those who are spiritual to restore

---

* Gal. v., 1.

such a one in the spirit of meekness. Therefore that is the specific form in which, as interpreted by the narrative itself, we are to wash "one another's feet." We are to help to restore one another. We are to minister to the promotion of each other's holiness by being careful not "to suffer sin upon a brother." We are thus made each other's keepers in a very important sense. When we see one going astray, we may not content ourselves with sighing over "the pity of it," but we ought to endeavour to bring him back. And when a faithful brother, observing that we are in danger, comes to us with warning and expostulation, we are to welcome his offices as gratefully as the eastern visitor received the washing of his feet from the servant of the host into whose house he entered.

Every one will see that the delicacy of this duty makes it a very difficult one to perform; and if we are not very specially on our guard, even with the best possible intentions, we may do more harm than good. Hence, when in this sense we seek to wash a brother's feet, we must be very careful about three things, which I give in the quaint way in which I have somewhere seen them expressed:—

1. "The water must not be too hot." Above all things else, this office of love must be performed "in the spirit of meekness." We must not aggravate our brother's humiliation by an overbearing or patronising manner. It is a painful thing to be spoken to concerning our faults, be the manner of our censor what it may, and so we should see to it that we give no added cause of offence in the way in which we do it. Much may be learned from the Saviour's own dealings with his followers. "His gentleness made them great." His tenderness gave strength even to his reproofs; and it would be well if, like the woman with the Lord, we could wash our erring brother's feet with our tears.

2. "Our own hands should be clean." To no purpose will we seek to win a brother from sin if we be ourselves guilty of the very thing which is blamable in him. Among the peasantry of Scotland, on the night before a wedding, the bachelor

companions of the bridegroom contrive to catch him in an unguarded moment, and carrying him away to a convenient place, they pretend to wash his feet; but each one who dips his hand into the water has had it first blackened with soot, and it is not needful to describe what the issue is. Now, when I have heard one who is himself addicted to some sin seeking to expostulate with another for the same iniquity, I have been reminded of that national horse-play which so often made the Scottish homesteads ring with merriment. Only there is no merriment here; for it is not so easy to wash off sin as soot. He who, being guilty of an evil himself, seeks to deal with another for the same evil, will inevitably make that other worse than ever. Let him go first, and learn what that meaneth: " How wilt thou say to thy brother, Let me pull out the mote out of thine eye; and, behold, a beam is in thine own eye? Thou hypocrite, first cast out the beam out of thine own eye, and then shalt thou see clearly to cast out the mote out of thy brother's eye." *

3. "We must be ready to submit our own feet to the process." The washing is to go all round. See, it is written, "Ye also ought to wash *one another's* feet." That which when done by us is a kindness to a brother, is equally a kindness when done by him to us. We are not infallible; and, when we fall, we are ourselves often the persons who know or feel the least about the evil which has overtaken us.

In such minor matters as external habits we may be guilty of doing the most grotesque things, and yet be quite unconscious of the ridiculous figure we are constantly making of ourselves, so it is a blessing to have some one who loves us well enough to tell us about them. In the same way we may be falling into spiritual snares which are stealing away our strength, and yet we may not be aware of the fact until some kind brother opens our eyes to it. What a blessing it is to have some one who cares for us enough to do such an office! Seeing us with

---

* Matt. vii., 4, 5.

the impartiality of a stranger, yet loving us with the affection of a fellow-disciple, he enables us to observe and correct our faults, and thus renders us the best of all services. Let us gratefully receive it as such; and even if he should blunder in his manner, let us forgive that on the ground of the kindness of his intention.

Brethren, if the members of our churches were to act on these principles toward each other, church-membership would mean something, and we should furnish a noble commentary on the words of the apostle: "Consider one another to evoke one another to love and to good works."

But I cannot conclude without recalling, for the comfort of some and for the warning of others, these two sayings of the Lord to Peter, "What I do thou knowest not now, but thou shalt know hereafter;" and, "If I wash thee not, thou hast no part with me." What consolation and reassurance there is in the former of these expressions to those who are suffering under the afflictive dispensations of the providence of God! He sends upon us some sore bereavement, or brings upon us some dreadful calamity. We are cast upon a sick-bed, or our business is completely ruined, or, do as we will, we can find no means of earning our support, and are at our wit's end. We cannot see what he is designing. The valley is too dark, and, besides, the tears bedim our eyes. So we are dreadfully perplexed. But "we shall know hereafter;" and for that hereafter we have not always to wait until we have passed through death, for very frequently, even in our earthly lives, we see, before a great while, what the Lord meant; and, lo! he has been, as in the present case, "washing our feet." Ah, how often have we had occasion to say, "It has been good for me that I have been afflicted!" Our trials have been the means of purifying away our dross, even as the fire refines the gold. And since we have had such experiences in the past, we may surely trust him for the future. So, instead of repelling all his discipline and rebelling against it, let us calmly submit to his will, content to let him do with us as seemeth good in his sight. That is true faith which is submissive in the darkness, pillowing its head on this word, which, precious as it is, had not been spoken had it not been for Peter's waywardness: "What I do thou knowest not now; but thou shalt know hereafter."

But how terrible is this other saying, "If I wash thee not, thou hast no part with me!" That does not mean, as some modern ritualists would have us believe, "Except ye be baptised ye cannot be saved." Such an explanation is a pitiful perversion of the Lord's words, and reduces them to the merest externalism. He had a much deeper thought in his mind at the moment, and it was as if he had said, "If you will not accept washing at my hands, I can do nothing for you." The blessings of his salvation may be separately enumerated and considered by us; but they always go together. Just as one may make a separate study of heat and light in the sun's rays, though they invariably exist together, so we may speak of forgiveness and sanctification at different times; but in the experience of salvation they are inseparable. You cannot have the one without the other. You cannot have pardon and yet keep your sins. If you are to be saved at all, you must be saved from your sins, not in them.

Now, that is immensely important. Multitudes are willing enough to accept pardon if they can only retain the sin. They like well enough the forgiveness, but they dislike the holiness. Let these know, however, that if Christ wash them not, they "have no part in him." There is no salvation, nay, not even forgiveness, for those who are not willing to be purified. How is it with you, my hearer? Surely when the case is thus presented to you, you will make your prayer, in David's words, "Purge me with hyssop, and I shall be clean: wash me and I shall be whiter than snow."

X.

DENIAL.

MATT. xxvi., 69-75; MARK xiv., 54, 66-72; LUKE xxii., 31-32, 54-63; JOHN xviii., 15-18, 25-27.

FROM the supper table, shortly after the washing of his disciples' feet by our Lord, Judas went out to complete the arrangements for the betrayal, and then, after foretelling that he should be deserted by his followers and denied by Peter, the Saviour instituted that delightful ordinance which every true-hearted Christian loves to observe. This was followed by those tender addresses which John has preserved for us in his gospel; and then after singing a hymn together, and listening to that wonderful prayer of intercession which has more of heaven about it than of earth, the eleven went with their master out into the full moonlight, and took their way down into the valley, across the Kedron, and into the garden of Gethsemane.

There the favoured three were the near witnesses of that mysterious agony which pressed the blood through the pores like sweat; and the overhearers of those earnest prayers in answer to which a ministering angel came to him with strength. There, too, they saw the traitor come to point out their Lord to the band that were ordered to apprehend him; and thence two of them, namely, Peter and John, followed him to the palace of the high-priest, in or near the courtyard of which our usually courageous apostle weakly and wickedly denied his Master.

It is a sad and suggestive chapter in his history, the details of which, as gathered from the pages of the four evangelists, will come out as we proceed; but so much of general preface was needed, in order to connect the incidents which are to-night before us with those which we considered in our last discourse. Before proceeding, however, it will contribute to a better understanding of all the circumstances if we set before you as clearly as possible the place in which the several denials were made, and endeavour to harmonise the different accounts which the several evangelists have given of them.

As regards the place, all difficulty will disappear when we remember that an Oriental house is commonly built on the sides of a quadrangular interior court. Into this court there is a passage, sometimes arched, through the front part of the house, and closed at the end next the street by a heavy folding gate, having in it a small wicket for single passengers, and kept by a servant or porter. The interior court, often paved or flagged, and generally open to the sky, is the hall spoken of in the narrative where the attendants made a fire; and the passage beneath the front of the house from the street into the court is that which is called the porch. The chamber in which Jesus stood before the high-priest was probably an open room or place of audience on the ground-floor, in the rear, and open in front, such rooms being, in fact, quite common.

We have nothing exactly corresponding to this, so far as I know, in our own city; but I have been in a hotel in Paris which enabled me quite to realise all that is here described, and they who have visited the Langham Hotel, in London, may with a little imagination reproduce all the incidents recorded in this section of the sacred story. At least, by keeping in mind what has been said, we can easily understand how in the open room behind, the Lord could turn and look upon Peter standing with the servants in the court, when by the crowing of the cock he was, as it were, reminded of his servant's fall.

Then, as to the order of the incidents given by the evangelists, the following summary may serve to give a clear and harmonious account of what occurred: The first denial seems to have been connected with Peter's admission to the house through the wicket. By John we are told that the damsel that kept the door was his first assailant; by Matthew we are informed that she came to him as he sat without in the court; and by Mark and Luke it is said that this first denial was made while he was sitting with the servants by the charcoal fire. But we have only to suppose that the porteress followed him from the gate into the court, "chaffing" him all the way, and that when she came to the fire the other servants joined her in her taunts, and then we have a full and consistent harmony of all the four accounts.

The second denial, according to John, was made while Peter was standing by the fire, when it is represented that he was set upon by more than one at a time, for the words are, "They said unto him." By Matthew it is alleged that he went out into the porch, and another maid accosted him. By Mark he is represented as being attacked by the same maid as before; while by Luke it is simply said "another saw him." Now, here again, all difficulty vanishes when we suppose that the apostle was assailed by a number of persons at once, who followed him about from one part of the court to another, and to whom he made what was substantially the same reply, though it was repeated more than once in different forms, and was in one case accompanied with an oath.

The third denial is connected by John with the recognition of Peter by a kinsman of that Malchus whose ear Peter had cut off in the garden of Gethsemane. By Matthew it is said to have occurred "after a while," and more than one assailant is referred to, for the words are "they say unto him," while special allusion is made to his Galilean accent. Mark agrees with Matthew, and Luke says substantially the same thing, although he mentions only one assailant. But here, again, all is plain on the supposition that Peter was set upon simultaneously by a number of persons.

The narratives do not require us to believe that Peter utered words of denial only three times, each time to only one person.

Rather they suggest to anyone who is accustomed to sift evidence that he was, on three distinct occasions, assailed by a number of persons at once, who questioned him as to whether he had been with Jesus. He was made the object three times that night of general banter and assault by a company of the high priest's servants, who considered it a good joke to torment him by working on his fears.

This view of the case not only enables us to harmonise the narratives, but also helps us to understand more clearly the nature of the temptation before which Peter fell; for in the state of mind in which the apostle was, after all he had seen and experienced during the preceding hours, nothing could well have been more exasperating than to be baited, badgered, and bantered by a company of thoughtless and unfeeling lackeys, who to the malice of their masters added a coarseness that was all their own. But now, having obtained a clear conception of the circumstances in which the denials were made, let us attend a little first to the precursors of this fall.

Among these we give a prominent place to self-confidence. At different times during the Last Supper, and in the conversations after it, Peter expressed himself after this fashion: "Though I should die with thee, yet will I not deny thee." "Although all shall be offended, yet will not I." "I am ready to go with thee both into prison and to death." "I will lay down my life for thy sake."* And when he said these things he was sincere. He felt all he said. Hypocrisy was foreign to his nature; so foreign, indeed, that when he tried to practise it, he made such poor work of it as to lay himself open to the banter of his assailants. It will not do, therefore, to speak of him as insincere in his protestations of attachment to the Lord. We must not forget either that he was the only one of the eleven, save John, who followed Jesus into the palace of the high-

---

* Matt. xxvi., 35 ; Mark xiv., 29 ; Luke xxii., 33 ; John xiii., 37.

priest. The others had forsaken the Master altogether for the time, and so, in a sense, Peter's greater guilt than theirs was owing to his greater love. But the root of the evil in him was that "he trusted in his own heart." Just as when he set out upon the water to go to Jesus, he thought he could do more than the others, and in trying to do that he began to sink; so now again, in attempting to manifest more courage than they, he fell into a deeper humiliation than theirs. His self-confidence threw him off his guard, and made him think that he had no need to pray for strength, and so he fell an easy victim to the tempter's stratagems.

But the same effect will follow boastfulness and self-confidence in us. "A proud look goeth before a fall," and it is the man who thinketh he standeth who has the greatest need to take heed lest he fall. The most confident swimmers are they who are most in danger of drowning, just from the rash venturesomeness which their over-assurance inspires. The most conceited drivers are they who most frequently upset the coach. And the greatest braggadocio in the camp is sometimes also the greatest coward in the field. Let us, therefore, not be highminded, but fear. We cannot depend too much on God; for when we sincerely trust him, we shall also implicitly obey him. But we cannot depend too little on ourselves; for "he that trusteth in his own heart is a fool."

Another precursor of this denial was rashness. When Jesus was in the garden, and about to be apprehended, Peter drew the sword which he carried, and cut off the ear of Malchus, one of the servants of the high priest. The Lord himself immediately interfered, and miraculously cured the wound. But Peter's act was rash, and it has always seemed to me that it had much to do with his denials. John was known to be a disciple of Jesus; but he was in no danger, and was not assailed. Peter, however, had undeniably committed an assault which made him amenable to the law, and might subject him to punishment; and it is not improbable that he was tempted to deny that he knew the Lord in order to save himself from being apprehended for that crime. This view seems to be corroborated by the fact that it was when the kinsman of Malchus spoke to him that he began "to curse and swear."* Perhaps, therefore, if he had not been so rash with his weapon, the fear of man might not have been so strong within him as to induce him to declare that he was not a disciple. But whether this were true in his case or not, it is indisputable that many men by their injudicious recklessness have put themselves into circumstances where they were sorely tempted to utter a false word. And it might have been said regarding them that if it had not been for their foolhardiness in the first instance, they would not have felt any force in the temptation in the second. Misplaced bravery is very often, as in this instance, the forerunner of cowardice. If by our folly we put ourselves in jeopardy, we are on the highway to falsehood in order to get ourselves out again. The safe course, therefore, is to be upon our guard, and to follow the advice of that official in ancient Ephesus whom I have generally found to be my wisest counsellor, and who said to his fellow-citizens that they should "do nothing rashly."†

Another precursor of these denials was distance from the Lord. One of the evangelists tells us that "Peter followed —afar off."‡ It was well that he followed at all; but there was peril in the distance at which he kept from Jesus. It would seem that Peter and John came to the porch of the high-priest's palace some time after Jesus had been conducted through it, and that John, being known to the servants, entered first alone, and then came back for Peter. John, as we may conjecture, went immediately forward to the place where Jesus was, but Peter lingered among the servants, and so

---

* John xvii., 26, 27, with Mark xiv., 70, 71.
† Acts xix., 36. ‡ Matt. xxvi., 58.

exposed himself to their attacks. Had he gone straight up, and placed himself at the side of his Master, the sight of the meek majesty of the patient sufferer would at once have given him strength; and neither man nor devil would have moved him to do him dishonour. But he was in the midst of evil surroundings, and he fell. As a good Scotch woman used to say about him, "He had nae business among the flunkeys." This witness is true: he ought to have been close by his Lord. If we are going to follow Jesus at all, the easiest as well as the safest way to do so is to follow him fully. Decision wards off attack. If Peter's assailants had not seen that they were annoying him, they would have stopped at once. But when they observed him wincing under every blow, they only struck the harder. Often a weak army has held a stronger one at bay by simply making a judicious show of force; so we may keep our adversaries from assailing us by the very decision of our course. And who should be decided, if not we? Is not Christ on our side, if we be on his? And while we keep true to him, what real harm can come to us? Trimming is a courting of attack; decision carries all before it, because it carries God with it. If, therefore, you propose to follow Christ at all, see that you keep close to him and follow him fully.

But now let us look a little at the aggravations of these denials. These were many. For one thing, Peter had been well warned of his danger. Away back, months before, under the parable of his walking on the waters, the Lord had let him see into his own heart, and had shown him the peril of a disposition such as his. One would have thought, too, that the discipline to which he had been subjected for his rebuke of his Master, for his foolish request upon the mountain-top, and for his conduct in connexion with the washing of his feet, might have taught him to be less boastful and self-confident. But to all these had been added plain and direct statements of the precise sort of weakness before which he was to fall; and still he took no heed. We have a proverb to this effect, "Forewarned, forearmed." Yet even though the Lord spake to him in the solemnest manner,* and told him of the searching nature of the ordeal to which he was to be subjected, his words produced little effect, and Satan found in him an easy victim. But similar warnings have been given to us. We, too, have been put upon our guard, in such passages as these, "In the world ye shall have tribulation;" "Watch ye, stand fast in faith, quit you like men, be strong;" and if, after these commands have been addressed to us, we allow ourselves from lack of vigilance to be taken prisoners by the enemy, our guilt will be greater far than that of those to whom no such messages have been sent.

Another aggravation of Peter's denials was connected with the time at which they were uttered. It was with Jesus himself "the hour and the power of darkness." He had just risen, all breathless and bleeding, from the endurance of that inscrutable agony which came upon him in Gethsemane. His cheek was yet almost moist with the impress of the traitor's lips upon it; and his heart was sore at the thought that, of the other eleven, only two cared to be near him in the climax of his necessity. Was this the time then for Peter to wound him yet more deeply by his denial? It is never right to turn the back on Jesus; but surely it is most disgraceful to do so when he is suffering indignity at the hands of others. If for no other reason than because so many others had forsaken him, the apostle whom he had so loved and honoured ought to have been firm. And in days like these in which we live, when men in many circles are mocking Christ, as truly as the Roman soldiers did when they arrayed him in the garments of a make-believe royalty; when Judases in the Church are betraying him with the kiss of falsehood; and when Sadducean philosophers in the world are robbing him of his deity, it will be a sad shame in us, who owe to him all our happiness now, and all the

---

* Luke xxii., 31, 32.

hopes we are cherishing for hereafter, if we let ourselves be influenced by such examples, and deny the Lord that bought us.

Further, these denials were aggravated in Peter's case by the fact that the Lord had given him many special tokens of his regard. He had been peculiarly privileged. One of the first three of the chosen band, he had witnessed the raising of Jairus's daughter; he had been on the Mount of Transfiguration; and had been taken as far into Gethsemane as it was possible for human sympathy to accompany a divine sufferer. Nay, he had received certain individual marks of favour at the time of his memorable confession. Yet he denied the Lord. Truly "the best of men are but men at the best." Privilege does not guarantee perfection; and even a holy apostle is seen here as a blaspheming sinner. But what had Peter's privileges been thus far to ours? There is scarcely a scholar in our Sunday-schools to-day who does not know more about Christ, and has not received more from Christ, than Peter at this stage of his history. We often speak as if it were otherwise. But the more you think it out, the stronger will be your conviction of the truth of our assertion that we know far more of Christ, and owe far more to Christ to-day, than the first apostles did. If, therefore, we should betray him into his enemies' hands, or deny him through fear of men, our guilt will be immensely greater than that of Judas or of Peter. Do not think, therefore, that you cannot sin after this fashion. Realize your danger, and let your prayer ascend, "Hold thou up my goings in thy paths, that my footsteps slip not."

Finally, here these denials were aggravated by the manner in which they were made. Peter was not content with one denial. It was repeated. It was repeated with an oath. It was repeated with "cursing and swearing." In his early years the son of Jonas had been a fisherman on the Galilean lake. He belonged to a class of men engaged in perilous labour, and living a wild and reckless life. Among them, therefore, it is probable that he had contracted the habit of profane swearing; and though he had broken it off for years, it came back upon him now in his moment of weakness, and added its element of guilt to the general enormity of his conduct. When one has recovered from a dangerous disease, such a local weakness is left in the organ which had been affected that whenever a severe strain comes upon the constitution it is sure to feel it first and worst. So even after one has conquered an evil habit, there is left in his character a proneness to fall back into it again at every time of crisis, and thus God makes us frequently to possess "the sins of our youth." How important it is, therefore, never to acquire evil habits, lest in some hour of weakness they come back upon us with seven other sins, more and worse than themselves! Behold, too, how iniquities seldom come singly! The lie links itself on to the oath, and the oath, being already blasphemy, prepares the way for the curse.

> "Ah! what a tangled web we weave
> When first we practise to deceive."

Peter did not think of all this when he rose from the supper-table a few hours before. But he went on step by step; and the first error was in his self-confidence. That was the germ from which all these evils sprung; and had he kept himself from that "secret fault," he had never been guilty of this "great transgression."* Let not the lesson be lost on us.

But let us look now at the sequel of these denials. When Peter said for the third time "I am not," the cock crew. Mark tells us that the same thing followed the first denial; but these circumstantial variations strengthen, rather than weaken, the force of the testimony given by the evangelists, establishing as they do their perfect independence of each other. Luke informs us also that, just at the moment when the cock crew, "The Lord turned and looked upon Peter."

---

* Psa. xix., 12, 13.

What a look that was! It was a mingling of reproof, of tenderness, and of entreaty. It reminded Peter of the warnings he had received, of the kindness he had so ungratefully met, and especially of the words of love which had been so recently addressed to him: "Simon! behold, Satan hath desired to have you, that he may sift you as wheat; but I have prayed for thee, that thy faith fail not; and when thou art converted, strengthen thy brethren."* He saw then what he had done, and in a moment the fountains of the great deep within him were broken up, for, overcome with shame and sorrow, "he went out and wept bitterly." Yet all through the bitterness there remained with him the memory of that loving look and of these assuring words, "I have prayed for thee, that thy faith fail not." He lived on that look till the Master met him after the resurrection; and the thought of that prayer kept him from falling into despair. Had it not been for these things, he, too, might have gone, like Judas, and hanged himself; but, as it was in the cases of these two disciples, we have clearly unfolded to us the difference between repentance and remorse. Repentance springs from the contemplation of our sin, in the light of Christ's love; remorse from the consideration of our sin in the mere light of conscience and of law. Repentance keeps us in hope; remorse drives us to despair. Repentance brings us back to Jesus; remorse drives us farther from him. Repentance leads to newness of life; remorse sends us yet more deeply into sin.

Whoso, therefore, seeks to repent, must have Christ as the centre of that exercise, for we can obtain a true view of our sins only at the foot of his cross. It is an anticipation of the history, but we must add that the Lord recognised the genuineness of Peter's penitence in that private interview which he had with him on the day of his resurrection, and in that public restoration of him to his apostolic office by the sea of Galilee,

---

* Luke xxii., 31, 32.

the account of which forms the appendix to John's gospel; while, as we shall see when we come to analyse his epistles, some of the sweetest passages in them were the result of this painful chapter in his personal history.

I have endeavoured throughout this discourse to give a practical turn to the subject, and anything like formal application is almost unnecessary. I content myself with one or two inferences which are too important to be overlooked. In the first place, great prominence in Christ's service does not keep us from peril. Peter was one of the first three of the apostles, yet he fell. The truth is, the only safeguard for any man is in keeping close to Christ, and trusting implicitly to him. So far from eminence in Christian service insuring one against attack, it very often makes him only the more prominent as a mark for the fiery darts of the wicked one. When Satan thinks it worth while to bestir himself about a man, it is because that man is doing yeoman's service for his Master. He does not waste his skill upon nobodies. He looks for "foemen worthy of his steel." He tries to pick off the officers in "the sacramental host of God's elect;" and just when one is most useful and eminent in the service of the Lord, he is in the greatest possible danger. His fiercest onslaught was on the Lord himself, and those who are nearest him in character and devotion are still the objects of the adversary's most insidious assaults. Whenever Christ is honouring you by making you instrumental in bringing many into his kingdom, look out for being sifted as wheat by Satan! and if you would save yourselves from falling before him, be humble, be vigilant, be prayerful. Above all, follow Christ fully, and keep the servants of the world's highpriests at a safe distance from you.

Remember, in the second place, that our greatest danger does not always lie where we are weakest, but is sometimes where we are usually strongest. Peter's characteristic was honesty; yet he fell into deceit. Peter's nature was courageous, yet here he manifests cowardice. So eminent as Abraham was in faith, it was in faith that he most signally failed; remarkable as Job was for patience, it was in that very thing that he gave way; and though Moses was "meek above all the men that dwelt upon the earth," his meekness gave place to irritability at Meribah, and that, too, before a provocation which seems to us to have been the smallest of his life. Let us learn, therefore, not to relax our watchfulness in any one particular. If we begin to think ourselves strong in any characteristic, then is the moment of our danger. By many sore experiences Paul was led to say, "When I am weak, then I am strong;" for his weakness sent him to the Lord, who said, "My grace is sufficient for thee; my strength is made perfect in weakness." But the converse of his words is also sadly true; for when we are strong, then are we weak, and when we begin to think that some one principle is powerful in us, we are in danger of failing in that very thing. What need, therefore, of unslumbering vigilance in our daily lives!

Finally, if Peter's fall is a warning against overconfidence, his restoration ought to be an antidote to all despair. We have seen how aggravated his guilt was, yet Jesus took him back; and no matter how heinous our iniquity may have been, he will heal our backsliding also, if we go to him in penitence and prayer. The greatest sin we can commit against him is to despair of his grace. Oh, if there be anyone here to-night who has been denying Christ, let me beseech him now to return! As you think of your father's house, where you were taught to know and love the Lord, as you remember the privileges you enjoyed in the Sunday-school, and at your mother's knee, where first you learned to lisp the words of prayer; as you recall the ecstasy of the hour when, before the Church and the world, you confessed Christ as your Saviour and Lord; and then, as you reflect on all that you have done since—on your falseness, your impurity, your profanity, aye, it may be your dishonesty—you may be apt to sink into despair. But no! no! no! Do not despair. Do not judge the Lord Jesus by the standard of your own heart; do not judge him even by the character and conduct of those who call themselves his followers. Judge him only by his own words and actions! Is it not written, "If from thence thou shalt seek the Lord thy God, thou shalt find him, if thou seek him with all thy heart and with all thy soul." Even from thence! What do these words mean! They mean anywhere this side of hell. Think of Peter, then, and go back to Jesus. He will heal your backsliding; he will love you freely. Go, and weep your tears of penitence at his feet, for he saith unto thee, "Thy sins are forgiven thee."

XI.

BY THE LAKE OF GALILEE.

JOHN xxi.

THE twenty-first chapter of the Gospel by John, to which we are indebted for the incidents which are now to come under our review, may be regarded as an appendix to the treatise in which it is incorporated. But, though bearing upon it the mark of having been written at a later date than the main narrative, it has also unmistakable indications of the same author's hand. The simplicity of the style, the incidental allusions in the story, the recurrence of certain forms of expression which are frequently found in his other writings, and the personal references in the closing verses, are all characteristic of "the disciple whom Jesus loved;" and, as we pass from the body of the Gospel into this epilogue, we are conscious of no such transition as that which we must have felt had we been going from the writings of one author to those of another. Like the side-chapel in some beautiful cathedral, while it has certain features of distinctive excellence, it so harmonizes in manner and appearance with the principal edifice as to convey the impression that it is the creation of the same great architect who designed the structure of which it is an adjunct.

Nor is it difficult to divine the motives by which its author was actuated in making this addition to his former work. Principally and especially, he desired to commend to his readers the gentleness of Christ, as that comes out in his treatment of the apostle who had thrice denied him; but incidentally he gives us also an account of the renewal of Peter's commission, and so accredits him to all his readers. I call particular attention to this incidental effect produced upon the student by this chapter, because Renan has affirmed that "in his old age the Apostle John commenced to dictate a few things which he knew better than the rest, with the intention of showing that in many instances in which only Peter was spoken of, he had figured with him, and even before him."*

But who that has read the Gospel even in the most cursory manner can accept such a statement? Is it possible that the divinest book in the world could have had its origin in the personal pique and petty pride of its author? Is it conceivable that the man who throughout his treatise has never mentioned his own name, and has kept himself studiously in the background, was yet at the very same time filled with jealousy of Peter? But, in addition to these weighty considerations, we point to this supplementary chapter, and ask if it be not patent to every one who cares to see it, that John has written this narrative with a kind of brotherly pride in his fellow-disciple, and with the view of exalting him in the estimation of his readers? No doubt there is an implied reproof of Peter's curiosity in the twenty-second verse; but why should John, in recording that, be accused of being jealous of Peter, any more than Matthew should be blamed for the same thing, because he tells that on one occasion the Master said to the same disciple, "Get thee behind me, Satan."

The truth is, that John here has supplied us with information without which it would hardly have been possible for us to understand how the Peter of the denials became in the short space of fifty days the Peter of the Pentecost. The other evangelists, indeed, have given us hints of his repentance; but if it had not been for the account which John has furnished of his running to the sepulchre, and of his interview with the risen Lord by the Lake of Galilee, we might have been disposed to accuse him of forwardness and pre-

---

* Renan's "Life of Jesus," English people's edition, pp. 15, 16.

sumption in taking such a prominent part in the organization of the Church. As it is, however, this commission given to him by the Lord is the warrant for his activity on the day of Pentecost.

But to give an intelligent presentation of the subject, we must go back to the point at which we closed our last discourse. After Peter's denials our Lord was taken from the palace of the high-priest to the hall of Pilate, and thence to the house of Herod, who sent him back to the Roman governor, by whom he was given over to crucifixion. At the ninth hour of the sixth day of the week the Lord yielded up the ghost; and as the reality of his death was ascertained by the spear-thrust of the Roman soldier shortly afterward, there was still time before the Sabbath began for a hasty funeral. So Joseph of Arimathea and Nicodemus, having obtained from Pilate the necessary permission, took the body, and, with the assistance of Mary Magdalene and Mary the mother of Joses, "wrapped it in linen and laid it in a sepulchre which was hewn out of a rock," and which had been only recently finished in a garden hard by Calvary. In this tomb the body of the Lord Jesus lay all through that silent Sabbath. But on the morning of the first day of the week, in spite of the sealed stone which had been put at the door of the sepulchre, and to the dismay of the soldiers who had been set as a watch beside it, he came forth, "having burst the bands of death because it was impossible that he should be holden of them." At what precise moment he arose from the dead we are nowhere informed. We know, however, that he did not hurry from the tomb, like as a criminal runs to make his escape from prison; but that he was calm as one rising refreshed from his couch, for the napkin that had been bound around his head was found folded with care in a place by itself, and the other grave clothes were laid decently by themselves.

It belongs not to my present purpose to speak of all the appearances which the Lord made to his followers after his resurrection. We have to do now especially with Peter; so we restrict ourselves to those incidents with which he was connected.

It would seem, then, that when the women who went first to the sepulchre on that eventful morning saw that the stone was rolled away, Mary Magdalene immediately conjectured that something was wrong; and, without waiting a moment to see what had occurred, she ran into the city, and told Peter and John. While she was absent on this mission, the other women had a vision of angels, and as they were returning to the city met Jesus himself, who said unto them, "All hail!" and gave them a message to his followers. They had left the garden before Peter and John had time to reach it, and so there was no one there when John came in eager haste, followed by the panting Peter. The beloved disciple only looked into the sepulchre, but the bold and impulsive apostle went into it at once; then John followed, and while they were there, they saw in a moment what had occurred. The faith of the women was so faint that angels were needed to confirm it; but already these two apostles were so strong in this grace that, even without the assurance of the angelic attendants, they believed.

It has been usual with expositors to remark on the fact that John outran Peter on the way to the sepulchre, as if it indicated that love is swifter than zeal; but, in truth, there was nothing very remarkable in the case, for Peter was considerably the older man, and it was natural, therefore, that he should fall behind. But in his prompt entrance into the tomb on the very moment of his arrival at it, there was character, and we recognise at once the rapid and decisive movement of the impulsive man. After their departure from the garden, Mary Magdalene returned to it, and had that deeply touching interview with the Lord which John has described. Then, some time in the course of the day, Jesus met Peter alone, and we may suppose that, in that interview, the penitent disciple was re-assured by the reception of forgiveness from his Lord.

In the afternoon Jesus appeared to the two disciples who were going to Emmaus, and in the evening to the company of his followers, who, with the exception of Thomas, had assembled in an upper room. Then, eight days afterward, he came again into the midst of them, and convinced Thomas that he was indeed risen from the dead. On both of these occasions Peter must have been present, but nothing was said in either interview which had any special reference to him. The Lord waited until he met him again on the margin of that lake where first he had called him to the apostleship, and there, amidst the scenes and memories of the past, he gave him, in the presence of his brethren, a fresh commission to the pastoral work.

The apostles had gone to Galilee in obedience to the command which Jesus had given them, and there Peter, and Thomas, and Nathanael, and James, and John, with two others whose names are not mentioned, were together, when Peter proposed to go on a fishing expedition, and the rest volunteered to accompany him. They went forth at once; but, though they toiled all night, they caught nothing. At length, when the morning broke, they saw One standing on the shore, and as they drew near he called to them, "Children, have ye any meat?" They answered him, "No;" and he called again to them, "Cast the net on the right side of the ship, and ye shall find." The command could not fail to remind them of the former occasion when their Master had, after a night of failure, brought to them, by a similar injunction, a signal success; and there is little doubt that the alacrity of their obedience now was due to their remembrance of their experience then. They cast at once, and "they were not able to draw the net for the multitude of fishes." In a moment the keen intuition of John detected the presence of their beloved Lord; and so soon as he indicated his belief to Peter, that disciple, with his wonted impetuosity, girded his upper coat about him, and threw himself into the lake, swimming a hundred yards or so in his eager haste to be the first to do homage to the Master.

With greater deliberation, that they might save all the fish, the others came in the boat, and after they had counted their take, they found—how provided they knew not, and we are not informed—a fire of coals, and fish thereon, and bread. Then, at the invitation of the Lord, they partook with him of a simple meal, well assured that it was he, yet feeling too much reverence in his presence to ask any definite question upon the subject.

One cannot read this narrative without comparing the circumstances with those to which I have already alluded, and in connection with which the fishermen of Bethsaida were first called to be apostles. On both occasions the miraculous success was given after a night of disappointment. In the former case, there was no record of the fish; in this they were carefully counted. Then the fish were taken into the boats on the lake; now they are drawn at once to the shore. There the net was in danger of breaking; here there was no sign of any such weakness manifested. After the first miracle, they were called to be fishers of men; after the second, they are invited to eat with Christ.

Now, if it be true, as it undoubtedly is, that the miracles of Jesus were symbols as well as wonders, we cannot help seeing in these two, so similar and yet so distinct, something like that which Trench and Wordsworth have indicated. We give the condensed summary which the commentary of the latter furnishes: " The former miraculous draught represents the fishers tossed in the ship of the Church, on the sea of this world, and drawing the fish into the net of the Church visible..... This second miraculous draught—that after the resurrection—represents her labour done, the fish drawn to the land of everlasting life, and the fishers.... sitting down to a spiritual banquet with their Lord, on the peaceful shore of Life Everlasting, after their own resurrection through the resurrection of Christ."*

---

* Wordsworth's "Commentary on the Greek Testament" on the passage.

After the repast was ended, the Lord addressed to Peter, three times over, the searching inquiry, "Lovest thou me?" and three times over received, substantially, the same reply, "Thou knowest that I love thee," which on each occasion was followed by a command having special reference to his future life-work. Now, here so many things call for remark that for the sake both of clearness and of brevity, we shall take them in formal order.

First, you will observe that the Lord in his first inquiry gives prominence to Peter's former comparison of himself with his brethren. You remember that the over-confident disciple said, "Though all men should deny thee, yet will I never deny thee;" and now, after his terrible discovery of his own weakness the Saviour says to him, "Lovest thou me more than these?" The humbled Peter, feeling all that the words imply, is careful in his reply to say nothing about his brethren, and is as far as possible from putting himself above them, so that the Lord is satisfied on that point, for he does not repeat the painful expression in his later questions.

Second, I ask you to bear in mind that there is a variation between the third question addressed by our Lord to Peter and the former two. In our English version, indeed, they are apparently identical; but in the Greek language there are two verbs which signify "to love." The one denotes the love of reverence such as is borne toward God by the pious man; the other means more especially the love of personal warm human affection, a less exalted thing than the former, more intense for the moment, but more liable also to grow cold. Now, in his first and second questions to Peter, the Saviour employs the word which has the former of these two significations; but Peter, unwilling to assume the assurance of employing such a term, answers by using the verb that speaks of personal endearment. Then, on the third occasion, as if to probe the apostle to the very quick, the Lord adopts Peter's own word, saying to him virtually, "Well, taking even thine own term, art thou indeed so sure that thou art thus attached to me by personal affection?" In his humility and grief the apostle would not dare to say that he loved the Lord with that reverence with which as God he ought to be regarded, but he was sure he loved him with an ardour similar to, but more intense than, that which his heart cherished for his dearest ones on earth; and then, descending to his own level, the Master asked if he were indeed convinced that he loved him even in that lower sense.

I ask you to remember, in the third place, that there are similar variations in the words which convey the Saviour's charge to Peter. In our version, indeed, we have the one word "feed." But in reality there are two different Greek words so translated.* The one first used signifies "to provide food for;" that employed on the second occasion denotes "the doing of the office of a shepherd for;" and the third is identical with that first employed. So, again, the words denoting "the flock"† are, first, "lambkins;" second, "sheep;" and, third, "sheeplings;" and we may translate the three injunctions thus, "Feed my lambkins," "Shepherd my sheep," "Feed my sheeplings." Probably Alford gives the best explanation of these distinctions when he says: "Perhaps the feeding of the lambkins was the furnishing of the apostolic testimony of the resurrection and facts of the Lord's life on earth to the first converts; the shepherding, or ruling of the sheep, the subsequent government of the Church as shown in the early part of the Acts; the feeding of the sheeplings, the choicest part of the flock, the furnishing of the now maturer Church of Christ with the wholesome food of the doctrines contained in his epistles."‡ It is difficult to give the precise shades of difference between the expressions, yet we must believe that some such distinction as Alford has thus

---
* The first and third are βόσκε; the second, ποίμαινε.
† They are ἀρνία, πρόβατά, and πρόβατιά.
‡ Alford's "Greek Testament" on the passage.

drawn out was intended to be marked by the employment of these several terms.

In connection with these repeated injunctions, the Lord goes on to speak of the manner of Peter's death. Drawing a contrast between the vigour of youth and the weakness of age, the liberty of freedom and the constraint of imprisonment, he said, with a tone of pathos trembling through his words, that a day should come when his servant would stretch forth his hand, and another should gird him and carry him whither he would not.

Now let us mark the intimate connection between the giving of this prediction at this particular time by Jesus, and the spirit of humility which Peter had first manifested. On the occasion of the disciple's overconfidence when he had said, "Though all men should deny thee, yet will I never deny thee; I will lay down my life for thy sake," the Saviour replied, "The cock shall not crow until thou hast denied me thrice." But here, when in deep humility he will not put himself above the others, and will not even bring himself to say that he loves the Lord with that exalted and reverential affection which Christ's own word implied, while yet he affirms that he did love him in a very true and real sense, the Master virtually says to him, "Now thou hast attained to the martyr spirit: keep that humble disposition always, and the day will come when, as thou wantedst so much to do, thou wilt follow me even to the cross. Thou couldst not understand why I said to thee, 'Whither I go thou canst not follow me now, but thou shalt follow me afterward,' and thou saidst somewhat impatiently, 'Why cannot I follow thee now?' I could not explain it to thee at the time, but thou seest the reason now. Thy present temper is that of the martyr, and with that self-distrustful spirit and that love to me which thou hast just confessed, thou shalt follow me even to the cross, and glorify me in death."

That Peter did thus die for his Lord has been the uniform tradition. The story is that he was crucified, and that he requested that he should be fastened to the cross with his head downward, because he considered that it would be too great an honour for him to suffer precisely as the Saviour did. But whatever weight may be given to the testimony of tradition as to the manner of his death, the point of the allusion to it here lies in the fact that while his former self-confidence made him a coward in the hour of trial, his present humility and love would give him such steadfastness that, even though his death should be of the most torturing description, he should glorify God in dying.

As he heard this prediction regarding himself, Peter chanced to see John, the well-beloved, coming up behind him, and either from his deep interest in one who had been his partner, first in secular business, and afterward in spiritual labours, or from simple curiosity, or on the mere impulse of the moment, he said to Jesus, "Lord, and what shall this man do?" But that was a matter with which he had really nothing whatever to do. So the Master answered, "If I will that he tarry till I come, what is that to thee? follow thou me." Different interpretations have been given of this reply. Some take it as an intimation that John should live until the coming of the Lord, understanding by that coming the destruction of Jerusalem. Others, however, believe that the words give no indication whatever of the duration of the life of the beloved disciple, and regard the whole sentence as hypothetical, understanding the coming of Christ alluded to as his final coming to judgment. With these last we agree, inasmuch as the Evangelist's own comment on the words seems to us to be designed to draw special attention to the hypothetical character of the saying. It was a reproof to Peter, put in the strongest form, as if he had replied, "Thou hast nothing to do with that: even if it should be my will concerning him that he should remain upon the earth till I come again to judgment, that would be no affair of thine. Thy duty, present and perpetual, is to follow me."

"If you drive nature out with a fork, yet it will come back again." That was an old Roman saying, and one cannot but be reminded of it here. Even at this solemn moment, just after his searching examination by the Lord, and when his mind had been directed to the time and manner of his own death, Peter's temperamental disposition asserts its power, and he goes off at a tangent after a matter that did not concern him at all. We do not think the less of him for it, yet we can hardly help smiling at it. And as we read the record we say to ourselves, "That was Peter all over"—ever blundering without intending it, and almost without knowing it! Wherever we find him, he is the same big-hearted, impulsive, generous, yet awkward and indiscreet man. Reliable in the main, he was very uncertain in minute matters, and exceedingly apt to be switched off into some ridiculous siding, when he should have kept on the right line of duty and devotion to his Lord. Yet with all his blunders we love him still; and we can almost condone his awkwardness when we think of the valuable principles which, in the way of expostulation and reproof, they elicited from his Lord.

I have gone so fully into this delightful chapter that I have left myself but little time for any practical improvement of the subject; yet I cannot conclude without giving prominence to three things suggested by the subject as a whole.

Observe, then, in the first place, the wide range of the pastoral office. When Jesus called his apostles, he said to them, "Follow me, and I will make you fishers of men," and his words on that occasion seem to point most especially to the bringing of men to him; but on the occasion before me he takes his illustration from the office of a shepherd, and thereby reminds us that the true and faithful minister must exercise himself as much in the feeding and shepherding of those who are already Christians as in labouring for the conversion of sinners. This is a point which is apt to be lost sight of among us; for our church arrangements have, I fear, been made too exclusively for the bringing of souls to Christ, and not enough for the feeding and training of Christians. Thus the pastor preaches, the Sabbath-school teacher labours, the brethren exhort, and the devout generally pray, that souls may be brought into the kingdom. Church membership is the goal they set before them; and when those in whom they are interested come so far as to make a public confession of their faith, that is enough; they are forthwith left to take care of themselves, and the zealous labourers go after others.

Now, no doubt, this ought to be done, but just as surely the other ought not to be left undone; and whenever the minister is exclusively a fisherman, and neglects the labour of the shepherd, he is only doing half his work. He is like a man in a boat who seeks to propel it with one oar, and who succeeds only in making it spin round in a ceaseless circle. He will make no progress and his people will lack intelligence. They will be Christians, indeed, but they will belong to the invertebrate species, having no backbone, and they will be of small account in the conflicts and controversies of the times.

The evangelist who passes from place to place may restrict himself to the duties of handing sinners through the wicket-gate, and starting them out on their pilgrimage; but the stated pastor must make up to the wayfarers at the separate stages of their journey, and give to each the direction he requires. He must not neglect to preach to sinners. So far from that, he must embrace every opportunity of proclaiming to his perishing fellow-men the good news of salvation through Christ; but neither must he neglect to feed the lambkins already in the fold, or to shepherd those who have already found the Lord. He must rightly divide the word of truth, and give to every one his portion of meat in due season. Hence, it is unjust in the highest degree to compare the work of the devoted pastor who is seeking to lead out his flock with that of the evangelist.

I rejoice with my whole heart in the success of those earnest men who go from city to city holding aloft the cross of the

Lord Jesus Christ; but let them settle down as pastors for years over the same flocks, and they, too, will have to look for the results of their labours in the growth of character among their people as much as in the number of conversions. The pastor is to be a teacher as well as an evangelist. He has to combine in himself the work of the baptist as a preacher of repentance, with that of the Christian apostle as a writer of doctrinal epistles; and his labour is as needful as a supplement to that of the evangelist as that of the evangelist is an introduction to his own.

You cannot, therefore, measure the success of a church by the number of conversions. No doubt it is highly desirable that there should be many of these; but there should be also the development of Christians in meekness, purity, benevolence, liberality, and steadfastness. We must not be so occupied in getting the sheep into the fold as to forget to feed those who are already in it.

Observe, in the second place, the true motive for Christian work. The Lord did not say to Peter, "Lovest thou the work?" or "Lovest thou my lambs?" but "Lovest thou ME?" for the most potent principle in the Christian heart is love to Christ. Yet we are too prone to forget that this is the case, and so we dwarf even our best efforts by engaging in them from motives which, though good enough in themselves, are lower than the highest.

Some of us work mainly from a sense of duty. Now, I will not say a word against that principle. There is much in it which is truly laudable; and many noble men have been nerved by it to do good work and true in the Church and in the world. But, after all, duty is a cold and stern thing when compared with love, and though it may carry you through labour without difficulty, yet the work itself will not be so noble as it would have been if it had been inspired by love. Let anyone try it in his own experience, and he will understand the difference at once. You see a friend in spiritual jeopardy, and you feel you ought to say to him a word of warning. Your conscience is alive; and you go to him because you feel you must. But what is the result? Either you do the work in a perfunctory manner, so as to satisfy conscience with a plausible attention to its requirements, or, wishing to be very thorough, you overdo it, and you wound the heart of your friend by your unfeeling sternness. Now suppose you had gone to him from a regard to Christ, and with a vivid remembrance of the Lord's own gentleness to you, how different it would have been! The very effectiveness of your expostulation would have been in tenderness, and your friend would have embraced you even in the moment of your faithfulness.

Others work from love to their fellow-men, and that also is a good principle enough. There is much to be said in its favour, and in some cases it may lead to better results than those which are produced when one is animated only by a sense of duty. But that also is defective. For our fellow-men may meet us with ingratitude, and it is hard to continue to work for those who do not care to receive our good offices. Hence, if we have no higher motive than the love of our neighbour, we shall very soon become weary in well-doing, and give up the whole enterprise in disgust. But we shall never do that while we are working from love to Christ. How he bore with our defiance of him, with our ingratitude to him, and with our rejection of his proffered salvation! How he continued to work for us until he led us at length to peace and joy in himself! When we think of these things we can never despair of another, and we can never be reconciled to give up our exertions on his behalf. There is no zeal so patient, persevering, persistent, and undying as that which is rooted in love to Christ. Hence if we would do the noblest possible work among men, we ought to be animated by this lofty principle. Is not the secret of our failures in the past to be found in the fact that we have not been working from this motive?

If you would have pressure in the water-pipe, you must bring your water from a lofty reservoir. I remember that on one Lord's day in Liverpool, a fire broke out in the topmost story of one of those lofty cotton warehouses that line the docks, and when the firemen fastened the hose to the hydrants there was not force enough to send the water up to the place where the conflagration was; so the whole was burned. Now something like this is constantly occurring in spiritual things. We try to extinguish the flames of sin and misery in the world, and we mean right well; but we cannot reach by our efforts the seat of the evil, for we are not drawing our water from the loftiest reservoir; there is not pressure enough to send it up, and therefore it falls short of that at which we aim,

"Lovest thou ME? Feed my lambs." There is the principle. "Inasmuch as ye have done it unto one of the least of these my brethren, ye have done it unto me." There is the reward. Oh, who may tell what like that banquet shall be on the shores of immortality, when Jesus shall say unto his servants, "Blessed are ye who are called to the marriage supper of the Lamb?"

Finally, observe that difficulties about those things with which we have nothing to do ought not to keep us from performing the plain duty of following Christ. Beneath these words of our Lord to Peter, "What is that to thee? Follow thou me," there is a principle that is applicable in many circumstances still. There is a clear obligation resting upon each of us to strive to enter in at the strait gate, and to follow Christ. These things have to be done by us if we would be saved ourselves, and it is folly for us to incapacitate ourselves for that which ought to be the great business of our lives, by allowing our minds to be pre-occupied with difficulties which we never can solve, and for the existence of which we are not responsible. The practical, which lies before us, which we can accomplish, and for the accomplishment of which we shall be held responsible—that is for us the important thing. The speculative, the unrevealed, the insoluble—these belong to God; and if we would have the greatest enjoyment in our lives, and make the best out of them for ourselves and others, we shall leave these to God, and be content, each one for himself, to work in his little portion of the great pattern of history, ignorant of its bearing upon the rest, but believing that, if we follow Christ, all will be right at last. When, therefore, I hear friends distressing themselves about the entrance of sin into the world, or about the mysteries continually recurring in the administration of Providence, or about the doctrine of the divine purposes, or even about the meaning of unfulfilled prophecy, I am disposed to say unto them, What are these things to you? Follow Christ. These matters belong to God. He has chosen to put them in his own power. You are not responsible for them. He will take care of them. Depend upon it, the judge of all the earth will do right. Leave these matters, therefore, to him. Walk in the light. Do the work which the Lord has plainly set before you. Cultivate the Christian character, and give yourselves to the advancement of the Gospel of Christ. That is yours—all else is God's. These intricate matters will become hopelessly tangled in your hands. Let God unwind them in his own time, and he will keep them clear. Ah, how much happier we should be if we troubled ourselves less about the government of the world, and concerned ourselves more about our own personal duty!

XII.

PENTECOST

ACTS ii.

FROM Galilee the apostles and many of the brethren returned to Jerusalem, in the neighbourhood of which, forty days after his resurrection, they saw the Lord ascend from Olivet into heaven. Immediately before he was parted from them by the cloud which received him out of their sight, "he commanded them that they should not depart from Jerusalem, but wait for the promise of the Father," and assured them that they should be "baptized with the Holy Ghost not many days" after. So soon, therefore, as they returned to the city, they gave themselves to devotiona preparation for the great blessing which they were thus early to receive; and took measures, at the suggestion of Peter, to secure the appointment of one who should be numbered with the apostles in the place of Judas. Then on the day of Pentecost the expected Spirit came, and the work of the Church was inaugurated by a success as signal as that which attended the efforts of the fishermen when the Master said, "Launch out into the deep, and let down your nets for a draught."

The name Pentecost, which is simply the Greek word signifying fiftieth, was given to this Jewish feast from the mode in which its date was fixed. It was to be held forty-nine days after the presentation of the first ripe sheaf; and as that service was performed on the second day of the Passover, Pentecost was just fifty days after the first day of the Passover. It was also called the "feast of the harvest" and the "feast of the first-fruits," because a part of its ceremonies consisted in the offering to God of the first-fruits of the crop as actually realized and ready for use. This was done by the "waving" of two baked loaves; but in addition to that service, which was performed by the priest for the whole nation, each individual worshipper was enjoined to give his personal offering of first-fruits,* "a tribute of the free-will offering of his hand, which he was to give according as the Lord his God had blessed him." Jewish writers say that the particular form of confession and thanksgiving prescribed in Deuteronomy xxvi., 5-10, and beginning with the words, "A Syrian ready to perish was my father," was used on this occasion. The feast at first only lasted one day, but in the later years of Jewish history it was prolonged into several days. It was primarily designed to teach the people to acknowledge the goodness of God in giving the blessing of the harvest, and was, in brief, the Thanksgiving-day of ancient Israel.

Two reasons may be assigned for its selection as the date for the first great manifestation of the power of the Holy Spirit in the Christian Church. One is connected with the typical character of the feast itself. In its reference to the Christian life, the services of Pentecost suggest to us the duty of presenting ourselves as redeemed and regenerated to God. They say to us, "Ye are not your own," and they exhort us to make our bodies "living sacrifices, holy and acceptable to God, which is our reasonable service." On the day of the Passover, Christ, by the sacrifice of himself, ushered in the harvest of the world. On the day of Pentecost the Spirit descended, turning the fruits of grace into the bread of life, received and fed upon by the souls of men, and leading them to offer themselves unto God according as James has said, "Of his own will begat he us with the word of truth, that we should be a kind of first-fruits of his creatures."

---

* Deut. xvi., 10.

The second reason for the selection of Pentecost for the descent of the Spirit is to be found in the number of Jews from all quarters of the world who attended that feast. The city was filled with strangers who had come to take part in the popular festival of the Mosaic year; and so, through the conversion of many of them to Christ, the seed of the Gospel was introduced at once to many lands, in which it grew up and brought forth abundant fruit.

In the early morning, the whole number of the disciples, amounting, as we learn from the preceding chapter, to one hundred and twenty, had assembled in all likelihood, as on the previous days, for prayer in one place. Some have supposed that they met in one of the chambers connected with the Temple; but besides the fact that is not even hinted at in the narrative, it is in itself very improbable; for the chief priests and scribes must have had still within them that enmity to the Gospel which showed itself in the crucifixion of the Lord, and we cannot believe that they would permit his followers thus statedly to come together within the sacred precinct. It is, therefore, in my judgment, much more likely that they met in the upper room, already dear to them from its association with the Last Supper, and with their first meetings with the risen Lord. But, however that question may be settled, we are informed by the historian that, while they were together, there came a sudden sound as of a tempest, which filled the house where they were sitting; and along with that sign to the ear there was another to the eye, in the appearance of fire parted into separate tongue-like flames, each of which sat upon the head of one of the disciples. Amidst these external manifestations, there was communicated to each the gift of the Holy Spirit, so that he was lifted up into a loftier spiritual condition, in which his perception was clearer, his emotional nature more active, and his whole experience so exalted, that it found utterance for itself in a tongue which up till that moment had been strange to him.

The loud sound as of a tempest was heard through all the city, and created such a ferment as would be produced to-night on this island by some immense explosion. As a consequence, a multitude soon assembled round the house to which the peculiar phenomenon had been traced. But as the crowd stood round, a still greater marvel was perceived; for as the disciples within continued to praise God for his wonderful works, each one of the foreign spectators heard some one of the speakers use his own vernacular. "And they were all amazed and marvelled, saying one to another, Behold, are not all these which speak Galileans, and how hear we every man in our own tongue, wherein we were born?"

Much has been written regarding this miracle, and many different opinions have been entertained concerning it, but we cannot give anything like an exhaustive treatment to the subject here. The following things, however, seem to be clear:

1. It was a special gift to the disciples, enabling them to do something which up till that time had been to them impossible. So much is apparent on the very surface of the record; and we wonder how any interpreters could imagine that the effect wrought by the Spirit was produced by miracle on the ears of the hearers rather than on the tongues of the speakers. If this had really been the case, then the proper name for the Divine blessing would have been "the gift of ears" rather than "the gift of tongues," and the symbolical fire would have rested on the multitude rather than on the disciples.

2. The effect of the miracle was that the disciples spoke intelligibly in certain known and recognizable languages. We cannot tell whether they were endowed with a knowledge, for the time, of so much of these languages as they required for the employment of them in the praise of God, or whether the Holy Spirit used their vocal organs simply as the vehicles for the utterances which he himself was making. It is more in harmony with his general procedure in the inspiration of his servants, however, to suppose that he employed their intellects

as well as their tongues, using them thus dynamically rather than mechanically. But, however that may have been, the result was that they spoke, not in unintelligible sounds or in an unknown tongue, but in dialects used at home by the different foreign Jews who were at the moment hearing them. This is clear from the confession made by the multitude, "We do hear them speak in our tongues the wonderful works of God." And I scarcely think that any other idea would have been derived from the words of Luke, had it not been for the fact that many expositors have allowed their minds to be confused by the opinion that the phenomena of Pentecost were identical with those described by Paul in the fourteenth chapter of Corinthians, and which there he calls a "speaking with tongues."

Now, it is beyond all doubt that there were certain points of similarity between the two, suggesting the common origin of both; but it is equally plain that some things at Pentecost were quite different from those described by Paul among the Corinthians; and it may contribute to clearness in our understanding of the subject if we pause a moment to indicate the things in which they were similar, and those in which they were distinct. I cannot do this better than it has been done by Lechler, in his commentary on this book.*
"(1) It was in both cases an extraordinary influence and gift of the Holy Spirit. (2) On both occasions the Spirit of God took possession of the soul of the speaker with great power, insomuch that the free action of the will, and the self-consciousness of the (individual) at last receded; a mental state ensued so strange and mysterious in its character as to produce on the minds of some spectators the impression, corresponding to their general views, that they beheld a state of drunkenness, while others regarded it as a case of madness. (3) In both instances this speaking with tongues (γλώσσαις λαλεῖν) did not

---

* In Lange's "Critical, Doctrinal, and Homiletical Commentary."

result in a didactic discourse, but was the language of devotion, in which the praise and honour of God were proclaimed. On the other hand each case exhibits distinctive features of its own: (1) The speaking of the disciples (Acts iv.) was intelligible, and was consequently understood by the hearers without the assistance of others; whereas the Corinthian speaking with tongues could not possibly be understood without the aid of an interpreter. (2) The speaking described in Acts was clearly a speaking in foreign languages, whereas not a single distinct and unequivocal expression in 1 Corinthians xiv. intimates that such was the case." We conclude, then, that while the two things were generically the same in their origin, they were specifically different in their manifestations, and that here the presence of the spirit was indicated by the speaking, on the part of the disciples, of certain foreign tongues, so that, without the aid of an interpreter, their language was intelligible to those to whom these tongues were vernacular.

Thus one of the earliest effects of the work of Christ was to counteract the evil of the confusion of tongues, which came as the punishment of human pride; and it may be, too, that in the company who in that upper room were praising God for his wonderful works in many different tongues, we have an anticipation and prophecy of the white-robed throng, "a great multitude whom no man could number, of all nations, and kindred, and people, and tongues," whom John saw standing before the throne, and whom he heard crying with a loud voice, and saying, "Salvation to our God, which sitteth upon the throne and unto the Lamb."

3. The narrative here does not furnish us with sufficient data on which to form an opinion whether this speaking in foreign tongues was a permanent endowment, or a mere temporary thing. The common idea is that the first apostles were miraculously gifted with a knowledge of languages, so that, when they went to foreign lands, they did not require to

spend a long while in acquiring the vernacular. But there is nothing here, or in the rest of Luke's history, that makes it certain that such was the case. We know that Greek was so widely understood at that time throughout the world that one familiar with that language could easily make himself intelligible anywhere; and it is nowhere said in the account, for example, of Paul's missionary journeys that he spake to his hearers in their native tongue. On one occasion, indeed, it would seem that his ignorance of the local dialect prevented him from taking as prompt measures as he otherwise would have done to keep the men of Lystra from offering sacrifice to him and Barnabas;* and, on the other hand, it does appear that in his intercourse with the inhabitants of Malta he evinced a familiarity with their speech,† which suggests that he had a special and peculiar endowment in that department. On the whole, therefore, we have not here, or indeed anywhere else in Scripture, sufficient grounds for dogmatically asserting either that the gift of tongues was or was not a permanent endowment of the primitive Church.

As the multitude listened to the strange sounds, and gazed upon the singular spectacle, different opinions were expressed regarding them. Some, recognizing their own language, cried, "What meaneth this?" Others, not hearing, perhaps, their own mother-tongues, and deafened by what must have seemed to them an unmeaning babblement, cried, "These men are full of new wine."

. And now, the miracle having served its purpose in arousing attention, or, as John Foster has very admirably put it, "the miracle having rung the great bell of the universe," and thus gathered together an eagerly inquisitive multitude, Peter stood forth to vindicate his brethren, and to proclaim the truth as it is in Jesus. He began by affirming that it was impossible that intemperance could account for the things which they

---

* Acts xiv., 13-18.   † Ibid. xxiii., 1-10.

had seen and heard, since, as they knew, it was only nine o'clock in the forenoon, and it was the custom of their countrymen neither to eat nor drink before the hour of morning sacrifice. And, having thus disposed of the sneer of the mockers, he went on to answer the inquiries of the serious and well-disposed.

He alleged that all that they had witnessed was the beginning of the fulfilment of a prediction made by Joel, which they had often heard in their synagogues, and with which, therefore, they were perfectly familiar. He did not say, indeed, that Joel's words were so completely fulfilled by the events of Pentecost that we may not look for any further verification of them. All he affirmed was, that this was an instalment of that promise which God, by the mouth of Joel, had made, and that it was the result of the pouring-out by Jehovah of his Holy Spirit upon them. Then he proceeded to connect the bestowment of that gift at that particular time with the resurrection and ascension of the Lord Jesus Christ. Sketching the character and career of his Master with a bold and manly eloquence, he reminded his hearers that they had crucified and slain him, and then he startled them with the assertion that he had risen from the dead.

Seeing the amazement which that statement produced, he fortified it by a reference to a prophecy which they all admitted to be Messianic, because, though it came from the pen of David, it could have no reference to David's own history. The passage which he quoted is taken from the sixteenth Psalm, and the pith of it is in these words: "Because thou wilt not leave my soul in Hades, neither wilt thou suffer thine Holy One to see corruption;" and it is interesting to mark how Peter expounded it, and raised a doctrinal inference from an historical fact. He said, David died and saw corruption, for his sepulchre is with us unto this day; therefore he could not here be speaking of himself: but, being a prophet, and foreseeing that Messiah should sit upon his throne, he spake in this wise of his death and resurrection. This prediction, therefore, was verified in Jesus of Nazareth, for we are witnesses of his rising from the dead; and because he has now ascended into heaven, he hath shed forth this which ye do see and hear.

Nor, he continued, let it seem strange to you that I speak of his ascension; for that, too, is the fulfilment of a prediction in another Psalm,* in which David said, "The Lord said unto my Lord, Sit thou on my right hand." The Psalmist could not mean himself in this prophecy any more than in the former, for he is not ascended into the heavens. It remains, therefore, that he was referring to the Messiah; and so, as Jesus of Nazareth has been raised from the grave, and has been exalted by the right hand of God, it follows that he whom ye crucified is both Lord and Christ.

The effect of all this was overwhelming. They discovered he whom they had so cruelly put to death was alive again, and that he was, in very deed, the deliverer toward whom their eyes by all the prophets had been turned. Therefore they were cut to the heart, and cried, saying, "Men and brethren, what shall we do?" and in response, Peter preached to them the Gospel, bidding them repent and be converted, and exhorting them to make themselves publicly the disciples of Christ by receiving baptism in his name. He had wounded only that he might heal; for he proclaimed that the promise was unto them and to their children, and to all that were afar off, even as many as the Lord their God should call; and the result was that three thousand were added that day to the Church. Nor was it a mere ephemeral epidemic. The converts continued steadfast, and proved, by their love, their liberality, their fervour, their fortitude, and their fidelity, that they had indeed been born again.

In reviewing this discourse, one cannot but be struck with the marvellous progress made by Peter in Christian knowledge

---

* Psa. cx., 1.

in the brief space of fifty days. What a difference between his utterances now and those which he made before the Master's death! How is all this to be explained? Much of it is to be traced, of course, to the influence of those instructions in the things pertaining to his kingdom which were given by our Lord to his apostles at intervals during the forty days which elapsed between his resurrection and ascension into heaven. But more of it was due to the enlightening agency of the Holy Spirit, by whom he had just been filled. The Lord promised that the Comforter would bring all things to their remembrance, whatsoever he had said unto them; that he should teach them all things; that he should guide them into all truth, adding to all the rest these precious words, "He shall glorify me: for he shall receive of mine, and shall show it unto you."* And in the discourse of Peter upon this occasion we have a beautiful instance of the manner in which that blessed agent commonly proceeds in the enlightenment of men. You observe that, under his inspiration, Peter is led to the Old Testament Scriptures, and that he sees in the sections to which he refers more than he ever saw before. These passages, so far as Peter was concerned, had been always there, but now he understands them in a new light; and in the same way the Spirit leads him to a correct interpretation of the facts in the Saviour's history which had occurred before his own eyes.

Now, so it always is. The Spirit guides into the truth, not by putting new things into the Word, but by bringing out more fully those which are already there; and in proportion as we grow in the intelligent apprehension of the revelations thus made to us, we shall increase in Christian courage and steadfastness. Thus, while the effusion of the Holy Spirit sufficiently explains the transformation which we see in Peter here, that transformation itself requires some such supernatural cause to account for it; and so the history is perfectly consistent and

---

* John xiv., 26; xv., 26; xv., 13, 14.

entirely credible when we take it as a whole; while, if we follow the example of some rationalistic interpreters, and endeavour to abstract from it everything that is miraculous, it will entirely vanish under our hands, and leave the early existence of the Church an unsolved and insoluble enigma.

But leaving the mere interpretation of the chapter, let us see what light it throws on that subject which is occupying so much the thoughts and prayers of God's people among us at this hour. We have here the history of the first Christian revival. Let us trace it through, and mark at once its origin and its characteristics.

In the first place, it was ushered in by prayer. There is nothing said, indeed, in the opening verses of this chapter of united supplication. But in the preceding context we read, that after the ascension, the disciples, to the number of one hundred and twenty, met in the upper room, and continued in prayer and supplication; and it is reasonable to suppose that when they came together on the day of Pentecost, they had the same exercise in view. Now, what did they pray for? We are not told in so many words, but, as the latest injunction given them by Jesus had reference to the promise of the Holy Spirit, we conclude that they prayed for him. It might seem, indeed, that just because he had been promised, they did not need to pray for him. But they did not reason after that fashion. When a father promises a gift to his child, he gets many a reminder, and night after night as he returns from business he is met with the eager enquiry, "Papa, have you brought it yet?" So, like true children of God, these first disciples waited and prayed, asking evermore, that they might receive the Holy Ghost according to his word. And herein they rebuke us severely, for in our petitions do we not far too largely neglect the Holy Ghost? We do not deny his personality or repudiate his agency, but we ignore him, and we pray that men may be converted, and that Christians may be edified, forgetting to go behind these effects to him through whom alone they can be produced. Let us honour the Holy Spirit more, and then we may expect a fresh baptism from above.

But we see here, again, that the revival began in the Church in the quickening and enlightening of those who were already disciples. The one hundred and twenty were first blessed, and through them the thousands were converted. Now, this is to be the course yet. When we cry for revival, we think too largely of other people. We dwell in imagination upon the unconverted, and supplicate that they may be brought in crowds to Jesus; but we forget that they are to be brought through our being first filled with the Holy Ghost ourselves. The purging of the Church with searching fire is to be the precursor of any great revival in the world. In the case before us, the attention of outsiders was attracted by the fact that the disciples spake with foreign tongues, and so made themselves intelligible in many languages; but to-day there is one way of testifying to Christ which is independent of all languages, and is the same in all lands: that is, by character and life; and when the eyes of men everywhere are turned with admiration upon Christians for the holiness of their conduct, the love of their fellowship, and the liberality of their benevolence, then will be a glorious opportunity for some new Peter to stand forth, and, tracing all these effects to Christ as their cause, preach the truth in him with such power that multitudes shall be born in a day. To have the world converted, we must have the Church purified and ennobled, through the enjoyment of a rich effusion of the Holy Ghost.

Further, the revival here was characterised by the preaching of the truth. Peter stood forth and testified for Christ. In all probability he said a great deal more than has been preserved here; but even in this outline we have much to arrest our attention. His discourse was Biblical. He brought the Bible to the front, and by its simple exposition he proved that Jesus of Nazareth was indeed the Messiah. Nowadays we have a great deal said in the pulpit that might be just as appropriate in the hall of the lyceum, or in the class-room of the professor of philosophy. But Peter began and ended with the Word of God; and when our ministers will give over apologising for the Bible, or criticising it, and will let it simply speak for itself, then we, too, may look for a new day of Pentecost. What mean the crowds that everywhere throng to hear those evangelists whom God has so signally honoured? They are the proof, if men only care to be convinced, that no book is so interesting to the common people as the Word of God, and that no magnet is so potent in its attraction as the cross. Let us put God's word foremost, and revival will not be long in coming.

Again, Peter's sermon was experimental. It was a testimony. He could and did say "whereof we are witnesses," and so his words had in them that attribute of eloquence which the French preacher has called so happily "the accent of conviction." Men saw and felt that he himself believed what he was saying, and therefore they were inclined to believe it themselves. In proportion as the minister of the Gospel merges himself into a witness, he will succeed in turning men to Christ. True, that will not afford much room for the display of self, but it will give ample opportunity for displaying Christ; and he has said, "I, if I be lifted up from the earth, will draw all men unto me."

But still more, this sermon of Peter's was pointed and courageous. He did not flinch from giving his view of the career of Jesus of Nazareth; neither did he go about to find soft words for the sin which he charged home to the consciences of his hearers, but he said right out, " Him ye have taken, and by wicked hands have crucified and slain;" "that same Jesus whom ye crucified is both Lord and Christ." Can this be, indeed, the voice of Peter? Did he not quail before the maid-servant, and say, "I never knew the man;" and now does he speak after such an uncompromising fashion? What has come over him? The explanation is easy. On the former occasion he was full of self; now he is filled with the Holy Ghost. So he calls things by their right names, and strikes both home and hard. Let our preachers speak thus to men's consciences, and they, too, shall have many inquirers crying, "What shall we do?"

For, to mention only one thing more, this revival was characterized by many conversions. First, there came conviction of sin; then, inquiry; then, after Peter had given them direction, there came faith, repentance, and confession of Christ before men, and all these so rapidly that three thousand were converted ere the evening closed around them. Nor was this a mere temporary thing. They who thus gave themselves to Christ continued steadfast, and adorned their profession by a walk and conversation becoming the Gospel. "Will it last? Will it last?" That is the inquiry made by antagonists when they hear of a great revival and many conversions. Let them read the closing verses of this chapter, and they will see that wherever the Spirit is really operating, his work is permanent. The suddenness of a conversion is no discredit to it, else we should have to suspect such cases as that of the Apostle Paul, and Colonel Gardiner, and ten thousand others. But the way to send back those who profess to have been thus suddenly translated from darkness into light, is for other Christians to treat them to cold shoulder, and put them into quarantine, until it is seen whether or not they shall endure. Was that the manner in which Christ met us? It were better for us far to make a few mistakes in receiving such as are not quite genuine, than to injure some timid, seeking soul, and mar his usefulness for life. Therefore let us not look coldly and indifferently on when God is working in the midst of us; but let us rejoice that Christ is preached, and let us open our hearts to all who profess to be his disciples.

XIII.

THE LAME MAN HEALED.

Acts iii.

WHEN the bud begins to burst, and to expand into the flower, it does not all at once slough off the external casing by which it had been bound. Gradually, as the leaves and petals unfold themselves, they bend back their former covering until at length it seems a mere excrescence, and of itself drops off like a withered thing.

Now, as the Christian Church was a development out of the Jewish, we find a similar process in its early history. It did not assume all at once a separate and independent existence. Its first members had their own meetings, indeed, in each other's houses and in upper rooms; but with these they combined a regular attendance upon the Temple services. They differed from other Jews in the fact that they believed in the Messiahship of Jesus of Nazareth, and were knit to each other in the bonds of a brotherhood which had its origin in a common experience of the great salvation; but they kept up also a strict observance of the Mosaic law. Very probably they had at this time no clear idea of the shape which their movement was finally to take; and perhaps the thought of separation from the Jewish Church had never entered into their minds. God was leading them by a way which they knew not; and, as we follow the steps of the apostle of the circumcision, we shall find that even he was prepared, little by little, for the acceptance of the truth that Christ by his work had abrogated the entire ritual of their nation, and introduced a system of worship which, because it was spiritual, was to be universal.

Luther was at work as a spiritual reformer long before he felt himself impelled to come out of the Church of Rome; and though the organization which Wesley formed tended inevitably to separation from the Church of England, that venerable evangelist, to the very end of his days, repudiated the very idea of leaving that communion. With such examples before us, therefore, we cannot be surprised that the first Christians continued to frequent the Temple of Jerusalem at the hour of prayer.

Prominent among them on all such occasions were Peter and John. Since the day on which Jesus had sent them to engage the upper room for the celebration of his last passover with his disciples, these two apostles seem to have been almost inseparable companions. They had been together in the high-priest's house; they had vied with each other who should be the first to reach the sepulchre; they had been close beside each other in the boat on the lake when the Lord beckoned to them from the shore; and it was Peter's eager interest in the welfare of his friend that drew upon him the reproof, "What is that to thee? follow thou me."

Brought up at first in the same town, and following there for years the same occupation as partners, they were already fast and familiar friends before Jesus called them; but now their relation to each other had been elevated, refined and strengthened by their constant intercourse with each other as fellow-disciples; and in the white-heat of the fiery trials of the crucifixion time their hearts had been fused together, so that they were of one mind and soul.

Theirs was emphatically a holy friendship, and it would be well if in our choice of companions we could secure such reciprocity and counterbalance as Peter had in John, and John in Peter. They were in many things most unlike each other, but that made them only the more valuable to each other; since the defects of the one were supplemented by the excellences of the other. The impulsiveness of Peter was checked by the caution of John; while occasionally, as at the sepulchre, the hesitation of John was put to flight before the bold decisiveness of Peter. They were to each other very much what Luther and Melanchthon were in a later age. John had the eagle eye; Peter had the ardent soul. John could thunder, too, on occasion, for the Lord called him and James, Boanerges; but his general demeanour was calm and still. Peter was active, impetuous, and frequently abrupt. John's character was the deeper and the more intense; Peter's the more energetic and demonstrative. John resembled a clear deep river, giving you the idea of peace, as it mirrors on its bosom the calm repose of the unclouded sky. Peter resembled a river churning on in full flood, broken now and then by a rocky fall, but giving you withal the idea of tremendous power as it sweeps every obstacle before it. John was intuitional and meditative; Peter was observational and practical. John was the Mary among the apostles; Peter was the Martha. They were both noble men. Their union would have made an almost faultless character; and next to that, for influence on the world around them, was their intimate and endearing friendship.

As these two companions were entering the Temple one afternoon by the gate called Beautiful, they were accosted by a beggar who was privileged to have a seat there because he had been lame from his birth. Indeed, it would almost seem, from the force of the original word, that his friends were in the act of carrying him to his accustomed place at the very moment when the apostles were passing, and that he had only time to make application to them for help before they should enter the sacred precinct. In response to his entreaty, Peter said, "Look on us;" and he immediately raised to them an expectant eye, supposing that he was about to receive, as indeed he was, some very unusual and precious gift. But how must his hopes for a moment have sunk within him when he heard the words, "Silver and gold have I none!" I could almost fancy how at first he might be tempted to say, "That's a poor joke. You might surely find something better to do than to make fun of an impotent man like me " But when he heard the rest of the sentence, "In the name of Jesus, of Nazareth, rise up and walk," and when he saw the apostle advance to take him by the hand, his heart thrilled with a peculiar anticipation. He said within himself, This cannot be a mockery, and, grasping the hand of Peter, he swung himself to his feet, and felt a strange, tingling life run prickling along his nerves as his limbs grew firm beneath him. Then, half walking and half leaping, like one yet unaccustomed to the exercise of locomotion, he went into the Temple to praise the Lord for his goodness.

Now, as it is said by objectors, with truth, that no miracles can be so easily counterfeited as cures, it may be well to set clearly before you the circumstances of this case, that you may be able to answer every gainsayer regarding it. The man on whom it was wrought was well known. He was over forty years of age, and for a long time, as seems to be implied in the words of the historian, he was regularly to be seen at the Temple gate. His disease was not a slight ailment of recent origin, but was brought with him into the world. His cure was performed not in secret, and before a chosen conclave of spectators, but in open day, and in a place as much frequented at the hour of evening prayer as Cheapside is in the height of business. The case was inquired into at the time by those who were openly opposed to the cause with which the apostles were identified; yet even they were compelled to admit the genuineness of the work of healing, and had no argument wherewith to oppose the disciples, but that of the prison. Now, if an event so authenticated is to be accounted false, how shall we be certain of anything which history has recorded?

But this was a miracle; and men are suspicious of that word. Some, in the ranks of philosophy, maintain that such a work is impossible, because it is inconsistent with the uniformity of nature, which the achievements of science have so amply demonstrated; and others, in the ranks of theology, have cast off the miracles as evidences of the Gospel altogether, believing them to be only hindrances to faith, and imagining that the Gospel can stand without their support. Let me, therefore, pause here for a few moments, and see whether I may not wipe away this double reproach from the miracles of the New Testament.

By a miracle, then, I understand a work out of the usual sequence of secondary causes and effects, and produced by the direct agency of God. It is of its very essence that it shall be a particular departure from that uniformity which is the general characteristic of what we call nature. But it is not, except in a very limited sense, a suspension of a law of nature; and it is unfortunate that such an expression should ever have been employed in its definition. When I lift any thing, say, for example, this book, I do for the time being, and in the case of the book, suspend the law of gravitation; but I do so only by the introduction of a higher cause, namely, my will, acting through my muscular nature, and even while I do so the law of gravitation remains the principle on which the material universe is conducted.

A suspension of any law, throughout the universe, even for the briefest time, would issue in the most disastrous results; but a miracle is not such a suspension. It is the production of a new and sufficient cause, which is the agency of God; and which brings about not the suspension of any law, but only a deviation, in a single instance, from the ordinary course of things. There need, therefore, be no jealousy on the part of scientific men against a miracle, for it would be impossible to recognize a miracle at all, if there were not in nature that very uniformity for which they contend. There could be no exceptional deviations, if there were no uniformity; and so, it is as essential to the advocates of the supernatural as it is to the disciples of science to contend for the regularity and constancy of the operations of nature.

Then, as to the possibility of a miracle: if we accept the personal existence of God, there can be no difficulty felt upon that point; for if we admit that the operations of nature are carried on by a person in a certain uniform way, we cannot hesitate to admit, also, that he may, if he so choose, deviate from that uniformity in a certain instance, for any purpose which he accounts sufficient. Thus the real matter at issue is not the possibility of miracle, or the truth of Christianity—it is the existence and personality of God. The question raised is that between atheism and faith in God, and that must be settled on other grounds than those of revelation; for the one grand postulate of the Bible is God. If one accepts that, he will not stumble at miracles. If one does not admit that, we must begin to reason with him a long way farther back than miracles.

But some theologians, following the leadership of Coleridge, say, "The Gospel can stand without the miracles; therefore let them go; we have evidences enough without them."

Now, to this I reply, that the Gospel cannot stand without the miracles; for, be they true or false, the narratives of these supernatural works are so inwrought into the whole fabric of the record that you cannot cut them out without destroying it. Nay, more, the moral character of the Saviour must be sullied if we repudiate his miracles, for he laid claim to the possession of supernatural power. Nor is this all. Every reader of the fifteenth chapter of Paul's first letter to the Corinthians must see how much depends on the fact that Jesus Christ rose again from the dead; but that resurrection was a miracle. So, too, every student of John's Gospel must observe the importance with which that evangelist has invested the fact that the Word, who was God, became flesh, and dwelt among us; but the incarnation was a miracle. Now, if you give up the fact of the incarnation, and allege that Christ never rose from the grave, how much of the Gospel will remain? You see, therefore, how absurd it is to say that the Gospel can stand without the miracles. They who speak after that fashion are talking either thoughtlessly or treasonably, for we cannot surrender the miracles without giving up everything which we have heretofore associated with Christ, and repudiating the Bible itself as a revelation from God.

"But," some one says, "allowing all that to be true, you need not insist so strongly on the miracles as evidences: surely the internal are better than the external. Let the Gospel be its own witness. If its doctrines be true, they will attest themselves. Nothing can be truer than truth."

Now, to this I reply that though it be the case that one truth cannot make another true, yet some things may be more apparent than others, and one fact may help to make another clearer. What is the use of evidence else? Take, for example the case of a prisoner in a court of law. Either he is innocent or guilty from the first. Yet evidence is had, but that evidence does not make him either the one or the other; it only makes manifest which he is. So, again, in mathematics; every proposition in Euclid is true, altogether independently of its demonstration. The demonstration only makes the truth apparent. Similarly the Gospel is true and of Divine authority altogether independently of the miracles wrought by Christ and his apostles; yet these miracles being performed in the plane of ordinary life, and in a department with which men are familiar, make evident the truth of those statements which the Gospel contains regarding things which belong to a region beyond the sphere of our observation or the possibility of our investigation. When Jesus said to the paralytic,* "Son, thy sins be forgiven thee," he made an assertion the verification of which was impossible by his hearers, for it referred to a region beyond their reach. So they said, "Why does this man thus speak blasphemies? Who can forgive sins but God only." As if they had replied, "It is a safe thing to make a claim like that, because you know we cannot investigate its truth." But the Lord, knowing how they felt, makes a reply which, as

---

* Mark ii., 5-11.

Trench has paraphrased it, amounts to this: "You accuse me that I am claiming a safe power, since in the very nature of the benefit bestowed no sign follows, nothing to testify whether I have challenged it rightfully or not. I will therefore put myself now to a more decisive proof. I will speak a word. I will claim a power which, if I claim falsely, I shall be convinced upon the instant to be an impostor and deceiver. I will say to this sick man, 'Rise up and walk.' By the effects as they follow, or do not follow, you may judge whether I have a right to say to him, 'Thy sins be forgiven thee.' By doing that which is submitted to the eyes of men, I will attest my right and power to do that which in its very nature lies out of the region of proof."*

Now, what that one miracle of the healing of the paralytic was to the one claim of Christ, in connection with which it was wrought, that the miracles of the New Testament, as a whole, are to the Gospel as a whole. The doctrines of the Gospel refer to supernatural things in that spiritual department which is beyond the limit of our observation; the miracles are supernatural facts in the province of nature and of daily life, which is open to our investigation, and so the performance of them by him who utters the doctrines is a confirmation or attestation of their truth. Both are true. The doctrines are true altogether independently of the miracles; and the miracles are true altogether independently of the doctrines; but the truth of the miracles makes that of the doctrines more evident; and for that reason miracles were employed at the inauguration of the Gospel.

In the Palazzo Rospigliosi, at Rome, Guido's famous painting of Aurora is on the ceiling, and the visitor cannot therefore examine it without much discomfort and great disadvantage; so a mirror has been placed in the room at such an angle as to catch the reflection of the picture and present it to the spectator at a point where he can conveniently in-

---

* "Notes on the Miracles," pp. 205, 206.

spect it. So the spiritual declarations of the Gospel are far above us, and we cannot verify them; but in the miracles they are reflected in material facts as in a mirror, and these we can investigate. Thus the supernatural in the one attests the supernatural in the other.

I have dwelt thus at length on this subject because the miracle of Peter has afforded me a convenient opportunity for meeting the plausible objections of modern philosophers, and for exposing the hollowness and absurdity of the reasonings of many theologians on a question which seems to me to be of vital importance. But we must pass on now to consider briefly the address delivered by the apostle in connection with this miracle.

The report of the cure of the lame man spread with marvellous rapidity among the worshippers in the Temple, and when they saw the grateful beggar, clinging in his gladness to Peter and John, they crowded round them and followed them to Solomon's Porch. This was one of a series of piazzas which were built on the inside of the outer walls of the Temple. On the eastern, northern, and western sides, there were two rows of these porches, and on the southern, three. They were about twenty feet in width, and paved with marble of different colours; they had flat roofs of costly cedar wood, supported by marble pillars; and they afforded a grateful shade to the people. The porch on the eastern side was distinguished for its beauty, and, standing as it did on the vast wall which Solomon had raised from the valley beneath, and which was the only thing of his work that remained in the second Temple, it was called after his name.

When Peter saw the throng, and marked the expression of amazement mingled with inquiry which was upon the countenances of the people, he spoke to them as he had done to the multitudes on Pentecost. His address on this occasion was characterized by the same qualities as his former discourse, and whether we consider its honesty, boldness, and simplicity, or its full presentation of the way of life, and its comprehensive brevity, we must place it on a level with the utterances of Paul, and second only to the loftier and more suggestive sayings of the Lord himself.

He begins by alleging that there was in reality no ground for the astonishment which they felt. It would have been, indeed, a wonderful thing if John and himself had cured the lame man by their own skill, or as a reward for their own piety. But as it was, there was nothing to marvel at, for the miracle had been wrought by Jesus Christ, whom God had raised up and glorified after he had been denied and delivered up to Pilate, and killed by them. He was indeed the Holy One and the Just, the Prince of Life, the Servant of Jehovah, and yet the Son of God; and so it was only natural, and what in the circumstances was to be expected, that the faith which was by him should give this perfect soundness to the lame man. No doubt that made their position very serious indeed; for this miracle demonstrated that he whom they had put to death was now alive, and at the right hand of God, as the Prince of Life; yet, though they and their rulers had rejected him, they need not despair, as though there were no possibility of salvation for them. God had been, through these things, only fulfilling his own gracious purposes; and if they changed their minds regarding the Messiah, and turned from their opposition to him, so as to become his servants, their sins would be blotted out, and they would enjoy times of refreshing from the presence of the Lord. The grandest era of the Jewish nation was not in the past, but in the future, and it was contingent on their repentance and conversion; for when they had all turned unto the Lord he would send Jesus Christ a second time to them. But meanwhile, until the fulfilment of all the prophecies which God had spoken by his servants since the beginning, he must remain in heaven. Still, they must not despise him on account of his absence, for he was the prophet of whom Moses spake, and whom he described as like unto himself, saying also, "It shall come to pass that every soul which will not hear that prophet shall be destroyed from among the people." On the one hand, therefore, they had to fear the most dreadful punishment if they rejected Jesus; and, on the other, if they received him as their prophet, they might expect the fulfilment of the promise which God made to Abraham when he said, "In thy seed shall all the kindreds of the earth be blessed," for unto them first, God, having raised up his Son Jesus, had sent him to bless them in turning away every one of them from his iniquities.

Every separate verse of this address might furnish matter for a sermon; but I content myself with having set before you thus the relation of its several parts to each other, and the design which the apostle had in view. But he was not permitted to dwell at any greater length upon the subjects on which he touched, for the Jewish authorities, unwilling that the people should be taught by any but themselves, laid hold of him and John, and, as the easiest way of getting rid of them for the moment, put them in prison until the next day. There, therefore, we must meantime leave them, while we gather up a few of the more valuable lessons which this chapter of early Church history suggests.

We are reminded, in the first place, that there are some things more valuable than money. The end is always of more importance than the means by which it is gained; and if it can be attained without the use of these means at all, then they become, comparatively speaking, of little moment. Now, the value of money is not intrinsic. It arises simply from the fact that it furnishes a ready medium of exchange. Silver and gold thus are worth only what they can purchase; but there are certain things which they cannot buy, and to which, therefore, they are, and always must be, inferior. Health is a boon which no pecuniary price can purchase. Happiness is a commodity which cannot be bought even with the wealth of a millionaire. Acceptance with God is a blessing which untold gold cannot secure. And, as we see from the record here, Peter with his gift of healing was of infinitely greater service to this lame man than if he had possessed the riches of Crœsus. Let the wealthy among us, therefore, see that they keep their treasures in the proper place. The moment wealth becomes an end to be sought simply for its own sake, it ceases to be a blessing. Its employment in that wise beneficence which helps the poor to help themselves will promote the happiness of all who are assisted by it, and their enjoyment will come back to the giver of it with a richer interest than the usury of earth, causing him to say, "It is more blessed to give than to receive."

But, on the other hand, let not those of us who are poor in this world's goods imagine that we are thereby quite prevented from doing good to others. Behold what a blessing Peter, though he had neither silver nor gold, bestowed on this beggar! There are other ways of helping our fellowmen than by giving them money; and, God be praised for it, there are continually occurring, even in our lanes and alleys, our cellars and attics, cases of kindness done by the poor to the poor that show like redeeming features in our fallen nature, and sound like variations in that "still, sad music of humanity" which rings so ceaselessly in the ear of the thoughtful observer. Ye that have money, therefore, use it for God's glory in the world's good; and ye who have to make the confession of Peter, and say, "Silver and gold have I none," give of what you have; so shall you catch the spirit of these first apostles, and, like their Master, "go about doing good."

We are reminded, secondly, that fidelity is the true kindness in the end. Mark how pointedly Peter here addresses the multitude. He charges home upon them, in unmistakable terms, the crucifixion of the Lord Jesus Christ. He says, "Ye delivered him up;" "Ye denied him in the presence of Pilate;" "Ye desired a murderer to be granted unto you;" "Ye killed the Prince of Life." Yet he was not indiscriminate in his censure, for he says, "I know that through ignorance ye did it."

Now, in all this he was a model for us. Faithfulness is to be tempered with justice in all things, but especially when we are dealing with the unconverted. We must speak plainly, yet we must speak kindly, and let those with whom we are conversing feel that, while we cannot but condemn their course, we thoroughly understand their procedure, and have the tenderest compassion for themselves.

It is delightful to see how, after the strong things which he had uttered about their guilt, Peter comes round at last to tell them of the mercy and the love of God, and to invite even the murderers of the Messiah to receive a blessing from the hands of him whom they had crucified; and it would be well if all who feel prompted to speak to men about their sins would study well the method which the apostle pursued. Impertinence is not faithfulness. There is a right as well as a wrong way of approaching every man; and if we wish to succeed with him, we must study him until we have discovered how he is to be treated. Many earnest disciples, with the best possible intentions, have disgusted those to whom they have spoken, and sent them farther away from Christ and his salvation than they ever were before. Behold how it was here. The good deed done to the impotent man drew the people's attention; then, when they were impressed by that manifestation of the divine beneficence, the apostle spoke to them of their guilt; and after he had impressed that deeply upon their hearts, he addressed to them his appeal to repentance, and declared that God was waiting to be gracious unto them.

Now, let us follow a similar plan. We can not work a miracle, indeed, but we can do a kindness that shall make as wholesome an impression as this work of healing did; and then, when we have thus secured the confidence of those whom we have benefited, the way is open for our speaking to them of their guilt. By pursuing that plan, we shall, by the help of God, succeed in bringing many to Jesus. But let us not make up to one who is a perfect stranger to us on the street, and say to him, "Do you know, sir, that you are going to hell?" That is an insult; and it will be well if when we are guilty of such folly, we meet with a man who will say to us, as a Christian did to a youth who had so addressed him, "My young friend, you mean well, and if I did not know that, I should be very angry at you. For many years I have been trying to serve the Master whom you love, and you had no right to speak to me in that fashion. You will do more harm than good if you prosecute your missionary work after the fashion of a highwayman, and call upon every man you meet to stand and deliver up his soul, under your threatening of hell. He that winneth souls is wise." Be faithful, then, but be tenderly faithful. Do not perform the work of the shepherd in the spirit of the wolf.

Finally, let us remember that the enjoyment of times of refreshing from God's presence is inseparably connected with our return to God. The literal rendering of the nineteenth verse is this: " Repent and be converted, that your sins may be blotted out, in order that times of refreshing may come from the presence of the Lord." And I cannot but think that Peter here, addressing Jews, was guided to the use of words which, while they are true in the experience of individual converts, shall have their highest fulfilment in that day when "all Israel shall be saved." The grandest era of the Jewish nation is not in the past, but in the future, and the coming of that era is dependent upon their repentance and conversion.

But while that may be the primary reference of his words, the principle underneath them is susceptible of the widest application. If a soul wants refreshment, let it turn to the Lord, changing its mind in regard to Jesus and its conduct before men; let it become one with God in Christ, and then,

> "Sweet as home to pilgrim weary,
> Light to newly opened eyes,
> Flowing streams in desert dreary,
> Is the rest the cross supplies."

Does a church want revival, then let its members put away from them everything that is offensive to God ; let them return to walk in his ways, and to wait on his ordinances, and times of refreshing will surely come. Do we wish revival in our city and in our land; then we must begin by preaching repentance. John the Baptist yet must be the precursor of the Christ. So let us raise the cry "Repent! repent!" for the greatest blessing God can confer upon us, a blessing carrying every other boon of a spiritual sort within it, is "when he turns us away from our iniquities." There is the whole difficulty. You cannot have both the refreshing and the iniquities. Now, which will you give up for the other? There is much prayer for revival now— God grant that it be sincere !—but if you pray for revival with iniquity still enshrined in your hearts, your supplication is a mockery, and will be answered with judgment rather than with blessing. Let us have a revival of repentance, and the times of refreshing will be at the door.

XIV.

BEFORE THE COUNCIL.

ACTS iv.

THE first antagonists of the apostles were of two classes. The one was composed of the priests, who were then engaged in the Temple, headed by the Levitical official whose special function it was to prevent disturbances in the sacred precincts. Their motive in seeking to silence the new preachers was personal; for, belonging, as they did, to a separate body, whose members had peculiar privileges, they were naturally jealous of the rise of others to influence and importance. They wanted to keep the instruction of the people in their own hands, and so they availed themselves of the slight confusion which was created by the coming together of so great a crowd as a pretext for laying hold of Peter and John, and putting them into prison.

Nor has this spirit been peculiar to these earliest antagonists of the Gospel. Wherever the ministers of religion account themselves priests, there similar intolerance is cherished and, if possible, enforced. In those countries where Popery is the religion of the State, no spiritual instruction is allowed to be communicated to the people, save under the oversight of the priests; and even in lands where religious equality is the law, you will find that the notion is industriously circulated among the people, that in consequence of their office, the words of the priests have a certain power and virtue to which those of others can lay no claim. Priesthood, wherever you find it, means spiritual monopoly; and by whomsoever it is claimed, whether by papal priest or Anglican clergyman, or Presbyterian minister or Congregational pastor, it is alike unscriptural and intolerant.

It is right and proper, of course, that there should be office-bearers in the Church; but their appointment to office does not give them the warrant to forbid anyone from using without the Church the gifts which God has given him; nor does it give to things done by them, or words uttered by them, a character which they would not possess equally if done or said by an unofficial member. Let us testify against this arrogant and offensive spirit when it is manifested by others, and let us strive against it in ourselves. Let us cultivate the disposition of Moses, who, when Joshua ran to request that he would forbid Eldad and Medad to prophesy in the camp, said, " Would God that all the Lord's people were prophets!" Let us imitate the example of Paul, who, though some preached Christ of contention, supposing to add affliction to his bonds, rejoiced therein. Above all, let us drink in the spirit of our Divine Master, who, when his disciples told him that they had forbidden one to work miracles in his name, because he followed not with them, replied, " Forbid him not; for there is no man which shall do a miracle in my name that can lightly speak evil of me."*

The other class of antagonists to the first preachers of the Gospel was formed of Sadducees, who were moved not so much by personal as by doctrinal considerations. They were the radical party in the Jewish nation, as opposed to the Pharisees, who were the conservative. The Pharisees were jealous for all the restrictions of the law of Moses, in order that they might the better keep the nation isolated from surrounding countries. The Sadducees, on the other hand, wished to enter into fuller fellowship with their neighbours, and therefore they desired to break down as much as possible those barriers of religious ceremony and belief which stood in the way of the attainment of their desires. Thus their political position influenced their religious creed, and they pared down and explained away the distinctive tenets of the Jewish faith

---

* Numb. xi., 29; Phil. i., 15-18; Mark ix., 39.

until they had reached the level of utter naturalism. They were the Broad school of the Jewish Church. Their creed consisted in negations rather than in affirmations. It would be easier to tell what they did not believe than to say what they really received. As we learn from another passage of the New Testament, they denied the existence of angel or spirit. They repudiated, also, as it would seem by necessary inference from the fact just mentioned, the doctrine of immortality; and that of the resurrection of the body was their special aversion. Now, as Peter put in the very forefront of his defence the assertion that Jesus Christ was risen from the dead, they were stirred into antagonism, and joined in the attempt to coerce the apostles into silence.

It has often been alleged by the advocates of infidelity that they are the most tolerant of men. It has been affirmed, also, that while every religious sect in turn has been guilty of persecution, infidelity has never through its adherents attempted to interfere with anyone for the maintenance or diffusion of his religious faith. But in the conduct of those Sadducees who endeavoured to gag Peter, we see that even they who boast of the widest liberalism may be guilty of the greatest intolerance. The origin of persecution is in the human heart; and only when that is changed by the power of the Holy Spirit through the word of the truth as it is in Jesus, may we hope to see intolerance disappear, and true charity take its place.

In the prison the apostles remained for the night; and on the morrow they were formally arraigned before the Council. This was a body composed of twenty-four priests, twenty-four elders of the people, and an equal number of scribes and lawyers. It met in a hall called Gazith, supposed by some to have been situated in the south-east corner of one of the courts near the Temple building. It sat every day from the termination of morning sacrifice till the evening sacrifice, save on the Sabbath and the festival days. The president occupied an elevated seat: on his right hand was the vice-president, and on his left the referee; while the members, seated on low cushions, with their knees bent and crossed in the Oriental fashion, were arranged according to their learning and age in a semicircle, so that they could all see each other, and all of them be seen by the president and vice-president.

Before this august assembly, then, Peter and John were placed, and the question was put to them, "By what power, or by what name, have ye done this?" a question, be it observed, which admitted that a miracle had been performed, and inquired only what its significance was.

In answer, Peter begins courteously, yet with a quiet irony almost akin to humour, saying, "Since it is so, that we stand at your bar, not as malefactors, but for the good deed done to the impotent man, and you desire to know how he was made whole, be it known unto you all, and to all the house of Israel, that by the name of Jesus of Nazareth, whom ye crucified, whom God raised from the dead, even by him doth this man stand here before you whole." Then, according to his custom, and guided by that Spirit by whom he was filled, he fortifies his statement by a reference to the Jewish Scriptures, quoting a passage which had been similarly employed by the Lord himself, and implying that it had been verified in his case, "This is the stone which was set at naught of you builders, which is become the head of the corner;" and, rising from the particular instance before him, and with his heart all aglow with the fervour of a lofty enthusiasm, he gave utterance to one of those sentences which every great crisis in the world's history strikes out of some one of God's apostles, and which, becoming the watch-words of the army of progress, are in themselves "half-battles." He said, "Neither is there salvation in any other; for there is none other name under heaven given among men whereby we must be saved."

These pointed words produced a deep impression on the minds of the members of the Council, and so turned the tables upon them, that, though they occupied the position of judges, they felt that they were themselves put upon their defence. They could not deny that a real miracle had been wrought; neither could they gainsay the accusations which Peter brought against them; and so, reminded, by the words and bearing of the prisoners, of Jesus and his trial, with its terrible termination, they thought the prudent course would be to hush the matter up in the quietest possible way. Hence, after a little private consultation they put on a stern front, and commanded them never to teach again in the name of Jesus. But their admonition was to no purpose; for the more they threatened, the bolder and more resolute did their antagonists become. Nay, more, they expressed their determination to disobey the injunction which they had received, and that in such language that their very judges were put to silence, for they said, "Whether it be right in the sight of God to hearken unto you more than unto God, judge ye; for we cannot but speak the things which we have seen and heard."

Thus the two plain unlettered men set them at defiance; and the members of the Council, finding that they could do nothing with them, dismissed them from the assembly.

Immediately on their release, Peter and John betook themselves to their brethren, and together with them poured out their earnest prayer that God would sustain them in the arduous work on which they had entered, and, delivering them from the fear of men, would enable them boldly to proclaim the truth as it is in Jesus. Nor did they need to tarry long for an answer; for while they were yet speaking, Jehovah heard them, and, amidst visible tokens of the divine majesty, they received a fresh baptism of the Holy Ghost, and came out of this, their first tribulation, more devoted than ever to the Lord Jesus, and more determined than ever to preach his Gospel.

Such, in brief, is the substance of this section of apostolic history. Let us see what practical inferences we may draw from it appropriate to ourselves.

In the first place, we may learn that if we are really Christ's disciples we may expect to encounter antagonism. Jesus had said to his followers, "In the world ye shall have tribulation," and Peter and John were now beginning to experience what he meant. In our day, and in our land, it is happily all but impossible for one to be put into prison or condemned to death on account of his religious belief; but it would be a mistake to suppose that the Christian has no opposition of any sort to fear. The world being as it is, one cannot be earnest in carrying out religious principle in any department of society without provoking some sort of animosity. It may take the form of a sneer or a taunt; or that of dismissal from some situation; or that of the perpetration of a series of practical annoyances, each in itself too paltry to be important, but all of them when combined sufficient to constitute a heavy burden. But in some form or other it will come; for Christ's words are as true to-day as they were when he first uttered them, and we have reason to stand in doubt of our earnestness in the spiritual life, if we know nothing whatever of the world's antagonism. We have no need, indeed, to go out of our way for opposition, or to do anything on purpose to provoke animosity. That would be both foolish and unchristian. But when, in our ordinary course of serving Christ, we are opposed by those who hate him, let us be thankful for an opportunity of standing up for principle, and let us accept it as an evidence that our discipleship is genuine.

But we may infer, in the second place, that if we are really Christ's disciples, there will be something about us that will remind the world of him. The priests and rulers as they listened to Peter's words, and looked upon his dauntless demeanour, "took knowledge of him that he had been with Jesus." The inner springs of character may be hidden, but the life will make evident of what sort they are. "As a man thinketh in his heart, so is he."

No doubt there is such a thing as hypocrisy, which consists in a discrepancy between so much of the conduct as is seen and the real disposition. But the possibility of that arises from the fact that no man can see the entire conduct of another. If we could observe all the actions of a man in all circumstances, it would not be possible for him to impose upon us by making himself pass for what he is not. There are no hypocrites before God. Hence, the occurrence of cases in which we have been deceived by outward appearances does not invalidate the position that from a man's conduct, generally speaking, you may tell his character. Whatever is in him will come out sooner or later; and if Christ be in him, he too will appear in well-defined characteristics. Not, of course, that the Christian will study to attract men's attention by his peculiarities, for the beauty of Christ-likeness is its unconsciousness of itself. Peter and John here were as far as possible from seeking to thrust themselves on the notice of the Council. They were trying simply to serve their Lord; yet in seeking to do that they so acted as to bring prominently before the minds of their judges the fact that they had been with Jesus.

And it is interesting to observe what those qualities were that specially produced such an effect. They were their "boldness," and "want of learning." Mark, not their boldness alone, but that taken in connection with the fact that they belonged to the common order of the people, and were destitute of all rabbinical learning. It may at first seem strange that boldness should have reminded these councillors of Jesus, for that is not a quality which we usually associate with Christ. Had it been written, "When they saw their humility, or benevolence, or calmness, or meekness, they took knowledge of them, that they had been with Jesus," we should have thought it more natural. But when we take their boldness along with the fact that they were unlearned men, all difficulty disappears, for that combination presented to the rulers the same puzzle which they had seen in Jesus.

Here were two plain men, of no education, and only a short while before labouring as fishermen; yet disregarding all worldly considerations, and standing undauntedly in their presence testifying to Christ. They could neither bribe them, nor threaten them into silence. There was no principle in their natures to which they could make such appeals. There was no handle by which they could take hold of them. They knew not what to do with them. They presented to them the same insoluble enigma as Jesus had done, when, in heroic silence, and with unruffled calmness, he had stood at the bar of Caiaphas and Pilate, and had endured at length the agonies of crucifixion. This, then—the incomprehensibility of the men—it was that reminded them of Christ. They could not understand the motives by which they were actuated. They were perplexed by the self-possession and the utter unworldliness which they manifested. They had seen many men act from love of money, or of fame, or of pleasure, but here was a new and unintelligible thing to them. They had seen nothing like it, save in Jesus Christ, and so they "took knowledge of them that they had been with him."

But it is always so. The Christian is a mystery to other men. In their view, his conscientiousness is crotchetiness; his disregard of worldly gains, when they are inconsistent with rectitude, is foolish squeamishness; his earnestness is fanaticism; his piety is weakness. They marvel at him. This has been the case in all Christian centuries; it is the case to-day. Find me a man whose whole life-work is a devoted service of the Lord Jesus, and I will show you in him a man who is a puzzle to all the unconverted around him.

Now, is there anything of this about us? Have we always acted so as to render it impossible for worldly men to explain our conduct on any other supposition than that we are Christians? Are our aims too high for them to see—our motives too exalted for them to comprehend—our standard too elevated for them to reach? Then may we take comfort in all that as an evidence that we are like the Lord. But if they see only too plainly that our principles are identical with theirs;

if they behold in us the same regard for worldly considerations, the same fawning on the wealthy in the expectation of receiving something at their hands; the same fear to be true to conviction, lest profit should be lost; the same paltry littlenesses of every kind that they are conscious of in themselves, then it is to be feared that we have never been with Jesus, and never learned of him that "man shall not live by bread alone, but by every word that proceedeth out of the mouth of God."

We may infer, in the third place, that if we are really Christ's disciples, the one rule of our lives will be to hearken unto God. What noble words are these, "Whether it be right in the sight of God to hearken unto you more than unto God, judge ye!" "Right in the sight of God"—that is ever what the Christian seeks to do. As in the natural world the one great principle of gravitation pervades the universe, so that amidst multiform variety there is still unity of operation, so in the Christian life the all-regulating principle is obedience to God springing out of love to the Lord Jesus Christ. In little things as in great; in secular things as in those which are called sacred; in private matters as in public; in politics as in religion, his rule is to do that which is "right in the sight of God." His conscience takes the law from God, and, no matter what will come, he will act upon its dictates.

See how this was exemplified in the life of the Christian soldier, Henry Havelock, who, though he was at length the saviour of the British empire in India, was for a weary while only a lieutenant. He writes thus to a friend in regard to his prospects: "Let me ask what it is you mean by prejudices against me? Tell me plainly. I am not aware of any. Old —— and others used to tell me that it was believed at the Horse-guards and in other quarters that I professed to fear God as well as to honour the Queen; and that Lord Hill and others had made up their minds that a man could not be at once a saint and a soldier. Now, I dare say such great authorities must be right, notwithstanding the example of Colonel Gardiner, and Cromwell, and Gustavus Adolphus; but if so, all I can say is, that their bit of red ribbon was very ill bestowed on me; for I humbly trust that in that great matter I should not change my opinions and practices though it rained Garters and coronets as the reward of apostasy." The man who wrote these words had been with Jesus, and was already a hero—long before the victory of Lucknow.

Do not, however, misunderstand me here, so far as to suppose that a Christian should never be found working in any matter with a man of the world. On the contrary, there are many occasions when the line of duty for him will lie along that which worldly men are taking; but then he follows it, not because they are on it, but because he believes that it is "right in God's sight" for him to take it. And when the two roads part, it is clearly seen who his Master is. If you were to observe him only when he is going along-side of some godless men, you might, perhaps, for a moment, stand in doubt concerning him; but when you mark his course from first to last, you discover that when he joins the unconverted it is not to conform to them, and when he leaves them it is not from love of singularity, but that in both cases he is doing what he believes to be right. Here, then, ought to be our rule—to do the right. The right, not the profitable; the right, not the pleasant; the right, not the fashionable; the right, not that which leads to earthly honour. And to know what is right we must betake ourselves, not to any human statute-book, but to the divine law —for the Christian rule is, to do that which is right in the sight of God.

Brethren, are we prepared to act according to this law? Merchant, art thou willing to do what is right in the sight of God, even though heaps of gain may be set before thee to seduce thee from thine integrity? Statesman, wilt thou take this noble stand, though place and power may beckon thee to leave the high ground of patriotism and duty? Workman, wilt thou be true to this holy law, though the tyranny of thy fellows should seek to overwhelm thee with destruction? Employer, wilt thou seek always to keep by this standard, though capital and cabal may strive to push thee to the wall? Minister of Christ, wilt thou obey this divine maxim, though popularity and fame wait not upon thy faithfulness? Are not these the questions which the events of every day are putting in ever-new forms to every one of us? Oh, brethren! how are we answering them? God send to us the holy boldness and determined thoroughness of Peter, that we say to every adversary, "Whether it be right in the sight of God to hearken unto you more than unto God, judge ye."

We may infer, in the fourth place, that if we are really Christ's disciples, our chosen fellowship will be with those who are already his. We read that, "Being let go, they went unto their own company." There had been an external pressure put upon them which had kept them from following the bent of their inclination, but the moment they were free to act upon their own impulse they went to their brethren with whom they were associated. Now, it is similar with men yet. There are times when, though we may not be actual prisoners, we are kept by the force of politeness, or the demands of business, from those with whom we would otherwise be found; but so soon as that pressure is withdrawn, we betake ourselves to the friends in whose fellowship our greatest happiness is enjoyed. There is thus a kind of elasticity in our nature, such that it stretches to a certain extent under the influences to which at the moment we are exposed; but when these are removed it goes back to its original condition.

Hence we are furnished with two tests, by the use of which we may discover our true character. When is it, let us ask, that we feel ourselves under constraint? Is it when through necessary business we find ourselves associated with men who have no regard for Christ? I can conceive that, in the prosecution of his proper calling, a Christian may find himself in most uncongenial society; and that, though he will leave it as soon as possible, he may not find it possible to leave it as soon as he wishes. But all the while he is uncomfortable. He is not in his element. He longs to be away, and, like the bird in the cage, which, so soon as the door is open, leaps out to seek its own familiar grove, he hastens to the company of his believing friends the moment that he can break away. Now, if we know anything of such an experience as that, we may take it as an evidence that we are Christ's.

On the other hand, if the constraint be felt by us when we are in Christian society; if we feel obliged to go to God's house, it may be even to God's table, simply to keep up appearances, but feeling all the time that we would rather be elsewhere; if, because we have become involved in a Christian family, we are entangled into going with its members to the prayer-meeting, or into joining with them in evening worship; if all through the religious services we appear to be devout, while inwardly we are voting them a bore; and if as we leave the house we feel that we are indeed "let go," and have within us some such emotion as the prisoner has when he hears the heavy jail-doors shut behind him, and finds himself again a free man, then we may be thoroughly sure that we are none of Christ's.

It is only another side of this same thought when I add that we have here a valuable test in the questions, "What is our own company? With what sort of people do we find our highest enjoyment?" The proverb says that "a man is known by the company he keeps;" and if you, a Christian professor, have for your peculiar and innermost friends men who are utterly regardless of all spiritual things, then you have reason, not only to suspect that you are wrong, but also to believe that you are still in the gall of bitterness and the bond of iniquity. "What communion hath light with darkness? What fellowship hath Christ with Belial?" Remember that you are only what you are in your deepest and innermost nature; and if your religion be merely a surface thing, while the entire under-current of your being is going in the opposite direction, you are simply

O

an irreligious man. You cannot be really a follower of Jesus, and find your highest satisfaction in the fellowship of those who depise him.

On the other hand, if your highest pleasure is in the companionship of Christian brethren; if, when you are worn and weary with contending with sin within you and with sin around you, there is still for you a solace in the fellowship of believers; if your deepest happiness has been in Christian ordinances, Christian friendship, and Christian work; if the company to whom you belong be men of God, "full of the Holy Ghost and of faith;" if your experience of their communion be that given in the poet's words:

> "As birds of social feather helping each
> His fellow's flight, we soared into the skies,
> And cast the clouds beneath our feet, and earth
> With all her tardy, leaden-footed cares,
> And talked the speech, and eat the food of heaven—"*

then you have a striking evidence that you belong to Jesus himself, and a strong assurance that your home at last will be with him and his redeemed.

Finally, we may infer that if we are really Christ's, we shall betake ourselves in every time of trial to the throne of grace. When the apostles had reported to their brethren the troubles into which they had been brought, and the threatening which had been pronounced against them, they lifted up their hearts with one accord in supplication to God. The prayer which they offered is remarkable for its Scriptural allusiveness, its homely directness, its recognition of God's hand in everything, and its comprehensive brevity. Scarcely was it finished, when the place was shaken as on Pentecost, and they were all anew baptized with the Holy Ghost, so "that they spake the word of God with boldness."

Now, here again we are furnished with a test whereby we may discover our real character. To whom do we go in

---

* Pollok.

time of perplexity? Some repair to fellow-men; but they can give no effectual help in our deepest extremities, for they are simply on a level with ourselves. Others have recourse to poisonous drugs, such as opium, alcohol, and the like, that they may steep themselves in insensibility, and so forget their affliction. But that only aggravates the evil by bringing a terrible reaction at the last. All such expedients are really beneath us. But the Christian looks up. When he is in perplexity, he prays to be led to "the rock that is higher than he." He believes that precious word of promise, "When the poor and needy seek water, and there is none, and their tongue faileth for thirst, I the Lord will hear them, I the God of Israel will not forsake them. I will open rivers in high places, and fountains in the midst of the valleys; I will make the wilderness a pool of water, and the dry land springs of water,"* and he looks for its fulfilment in his time of need. Nor does he look in vain; for answers to prayer are not confined to this book. The life of every saint is full of them; and he is daily encouraged to tell the Lord "all that is in his heart." But if we never call upon God in supplication, if our troubles only drive us farther from him, if in our secret souls we cherish the desire to be independent of him, then it is clear that we are none of his. God has no dumb children in his spiritual family; and if no voice of praise proceeds from our lips, and no word of prayer is sent up from our hearts, then are we "bastards, and not sons."

A prayerless heart, a prayerless home, a prayerless life! Brethren, there are no darker things on this earth than these; and they who have these things are depriving themselves of the richest solace which humanity can enjoy. If there be such a one here to-night, let him become a little child again, that he may enter the kingdom of God; let him recall the days when he knelt beside his mother's knee, and, with her

---

* Isa. xli., 17, 18.

soft, white hand upon his head, repeated after her his evening prayer:

> "Now I lay me down to sleep,
> I give my soul to Christ to keep."

And as the holy memory of that happy time comes back upon him, haloed by the glory of the heaven in which his mother now is, let him repeat the dedication, this time with intelligence and decision, "I give my soul to Christ to keep." It is the best thing he can do. This is the best time to do it; and if he do it not now, it may never be done at all. Therefore, in the prayer of his childhood let him make to-night the consecration of his manhood to the Lord.

XV.

ANANIAS AND SAPPHIRA.
Acts v., 1—11.

THE description given by the inspired historian of the Church in the early days of its triumph and trial is exceedingly suggestive. "The multitude of them that believed were of one heart and of one soul: neither said any of them that aught of the things which he possessed was his own; but they had all things common. And with great power gave the apostles witness of the resurrection of the Lord Jesus: and great grace was upon them all."* The union and liberality of the members gave weight to the discourses of the preachers. The light in the hands of the apostles shone with an intenser brilliancy, because it was reflected by purity of character and disinterestedness of conduct in those who stood behind them. One feels, in reading the record, as if he were perusing the description of a new Paradise; but, alas! he has not gone far before he comes upon the trail of the serpent, and sees the evidences of the presence of him who is the enemy of God and men.

"The corruption of the best thing becomes the worst of all things," so says the proverb; and in the history which lies before us this evening we have abundant corroboration of its truth. Perhaps no feature in the life of the primitive believers is more attractive than their holding of all things at the service of the brotherhood; and in all ages since their days there have been those who have looked longingly back on the picture

---

* Acts iv., 32, 33.

which the Evangelist has here painted, and sought to reproduce it in the societies with which they were connected. But as the brighter the light the darker ever is the shadow that is cast by that which stands in it, so, in connection with this most delightful characteristic of early Church life, and, indeed, springing out of it, was the first manifestation of hypocrisy.

To understand how it came about we must go back a little to the practice which was followed by the disciples when they were going hither and thither in Palestine with the Lord Jesus. They had a common fund, which was kept by a treasurer, and out of which he paid the expenses of the company. This arrangement, however, was not inconsistent with the possession of personal property by each as an individual. It was a matter of convenience; and was doubtless in existence among them when the events of Pentecost occurred, which in one day widened the circle of the disciples from one hundred and twenty to three thousand. Naturally, there would be amongst such a number some poor and needy to be provided for. Perhaps some of the strangers then in Jerusalem would desire to remain for a time in the city, and would be in want of hospitality. Perhaps, also, some of the converts would be alienated, because of their conversion, from their friends and employers, and so cast for the moment on charity, while there would be the usual proportion of the destitute and the sick to be cared for. Now, it would be quite likely that, in seeking to relieve such cases, the apostles would begin by using their own fund. But that would be soon exhausted; and we find that it was replenished at once by the generous enthusiasm of those who were in better circumstances among them. Indeed, it came to be the case that each one held his property, not for himself alone, but for the brotherhood, and so they had the fellowship of giving and receiving.

It has been supposed by some that there was a real and absolute community of goods among the first Christians; and it must be confessed that some of the expressions which Luke has employed read very much as if it had been the purpose of the believers "to abolish the external distinction between rich and poor."* But in regard to that matter the following facts need to be borne in mind: The state of things here described was not inconsistent with the possession of private and personal property, for we shall by-and-by find that Mary, the mother of John, surnamed Mark, had a house of her own in Jerusalem.† There was no command issued by the apostles to the effect that each convert should lay his property at their feet. It was not a term of membership in the new society that each individual as he entered it should denude himself of all his possessions and surrender them to the brotherhood. They might sell their land or not, as they pleased; they might give the proceeds of their property to the Church or not, as they pleased. There was no compulsion in the case. They might be members, and yet retain their wealth at their own disposal, subject only to the approval of Christ. The movement described in the thirty-fourth verse of the fourth chapter was entirely a spontaneous thing; and if we knew all the circumstances of the Church at the time, it might appear to be simply "a special service for a special need." It would seem, indeed, that in the Church at Jerusalem there were some peculiar difficulties in the way of securing the temporal support of its members, for repeated appeals had to be made even to the Gentile churches, in subsequent years, on their behalf. So, when we take into consideration the points which have been advanced, we may see reason to agree with Neander that "a common chest was established, from which the wants of the poorer members of the Church were supplied, and perhaps, also, certain expenses incurred by the whole Church were defrayed; and in order to increase their contributions many persons parted with their estates."‡

---

* Schaff, "Apostolic Church History," § 114. † Acts xii., 12.
‡ Neander, "Planting and Training," Bohn's edition, vol. i., p. 26.

If, however, any one should insist that this explanation is unsatisfactory, and that the words of the history can mean nothing but an absolute community of goods, then, though I cannot agree with him in that opinion, I would ask him to remember these three things :—

1. Even supposing that communism of the Christian sort is here portrayed, it does not follow that we are bound to adopt such an arrangement now. The matter here was a development. It connected itself with a certain set of circumstances; and it was natural as an outgrowth from them. But in our case it would be different. Nothing but mischief can result from attempting to produce by external management that which was here a spontaneous expression of benevolence. What is binding upon us is the cultivation of the spirit which dictated this arrangement, not the particular form of the arrangement itself. That we should "do good unto all men, especially to those which are of the household of faith," is a constant law of the Christian life; but the particular channels in which our benevolence shall flow for the help of the brethren must be dug for us by the exigencies of present need. And our wisdom is not to adopt any stereotyped form, but to seek in the most appropriate and serviceable manner to help the poorer ones among us to help themselves.

2. Christianity does not seek to destroy society, but only to regenerate it. Now, the existence of social distinctions is inseparable from any society in which free play is given to the abilities and idiosyncrasies of individuals. As naturally as the hand divides itself into fingers, or the tree into branches, does society divide itself into classes. Judging therefore from the analogy of its operation in other cases, the influence of the Gospel will be exerted in regulating the relations of these classes to each other, not in obliterating the distinction between them. The community must not swallow up the individual; neither must the individual develop himself at the expense of the community; and it is the office of Christianity

to regulate the relation between them. It seeks by infusing love into the individual to keep him in harmony with the community. But communism, on the other hand, sacrifices him to the community, and the result is that neither attains to the highest prosperity.

3. If this which is described by Luke were communism, then with all reverence be it said, the attempt to establish it was not so successful as to attract us to imitate it; for not only did the hypocrisy of Ananias and his wife spring out of it, but it gave rise not long after to murmurings and disputings concerning the daily ministrations, and altogether so distressed the apostles that they handed its management over to the deacons. Moreover, we find no trace of anything like community of goods in the churches founded among the Gentiles, and so it is evident that the apostles did not consider it an essential part of the Christian life. Besides, in almost all the cases in which it has been attempted, this system has led to evil results. Monasticism began by companies of poor brothers seeking to have all things in common, and it has culminated in the existence of rich fraternities holding in a dead and unproductive hand some of the finest territories on the surface of the earth. Political Saint-Simonianism, on the other hand, would loosen the bands of society, break up the home circle, reduce statesmanship to a copartnery in selfishness, and put a drag on the wheels of all true and noble ambition.

These facts are enough to show that even if an actual community of goods existed among the first Christians, we are under no obligation to follow such an example now. But, as I have already said, all the statements which are here made are perfectly consistent with the idea that Luke is referring to a fund for the support of the poor, while the words of Peter to Ananias, "While it remained, was it not thine own? and after it was sold, was it not in thine own power?" are to my mind utterly irreconcilable with any such communism as is advocated in modern times.

We suppose, therefore, that there was among the Christians of Jerusalem, now several thousands in number, a common benevolent fund to which the wealthier members of the Church were encouraged to contribute, and for which many among them willingly gave up their all. One most illustrious example of this sort was Joses, surnamed Barnabas—a man well known and much beloved in after-days as the companion of Paul; and perhaps the great estimation in which he was held for his noble deed may have been the special occasion of which Satan took advantage, for the purpose of filling the hearts of Ananias and his wife with the temptation, before which they so ignominiously fell. At any rate, it would appear that this couple were possessed of property which they sold, and the price of which they professed to lay at the apostles' feet. But, as the land was, most probably, at a distance from Jerusalem, and they had effected the sale of it in such a way as to keep secret the true amount which they had received, they retained a portion, while they professed to give the whole. Thus they wished to obtain credit for a liberality equal to that of Barnabas, while yet they withheld a part of their property for themselves. They attempted to obtain a crown from God, and at the same time to keep as much mammon as they thought they might require—with what result we are now to see.

Outwardly the act of Ananias was no way different from that of Barnabas; but when he came in with his offering, Peter received a special revelation of his wickedness, and said unto him, "Ananias, why hath Satan filled thine heart to lie to the Holy Ghost, and to keep back part of the price of the land? While it remained, was it not thine own? and after it was sold, was it not in thine own power? Why hast thou conceived this thing in thine heart? thou hast not lied unto men, but unto God." Scarcely had the apostle ceased, when, smitten by the hand of God, Ananias fell down dead, and was carried out for burial.

Some hours after, his wife Sapphira, apparently in ignorance of what had occurred, made her appearance in the place of assembly and Peter asked her if they had sold their land for a sum which he specified. One would have thought that such a question would have probed her conscience to the quick, and made her feel that the secret of herself and her husband had been discovered, but, defiant to the last degree, she answered " Yea," whereupon the apostle, having pointed out her wickedness, told her of the death of Ananias, and declared that she too must die. "Then fell she down straightway at his feet, and yielded up the ghost. And the young men came in, and found her dead, and carrying her forth, buried her by her husband." Such, in brief, are the incidents recorded in this section of apostolic history; but they will bear, and they will reward, a more thorough scrutiny.

Let us look, then, first, at the sin here charged upon Ananias. It is "lying to the Holy Ghost;" "lying not unto men, but unto God." I pass, with a simple mention of it, the remarkable proof here incidentally furnished of the Deity of the Holy Ghost, and fix your thoughts for a little on the sin which these words describe. What was it? Some make it virtually identical with sacrilege, which consists in the using for a common purpose of that which had been exclusively consecrated to God. But Ananias had never really consecrated his entire property to God; he only pretended to do so, and therefore his guilt was not that of sacrilege. Others would understand the words thus: "Why hast thou belied the Holy Ghost?" and would explain them in this way, "Thou hast received the Holy Ghost, and thou professest now to be moved by him, in laying this money down at our feet, whereas thou hast been animated throughout by pride and selfishness; and thus thou art belying him." But there is no need for all this circumlocution. The meaning is very plain: he told a lie to the Holy Ghost. Doubtless, it was to Peter and his brother apostles that the allegation was made; but then these men were not only endowed with the Holy Ghost, but also the divinely appointed rulers of the Church in which the Holy

Spirit dwelt. Hence the lie told to Peter, as an office-bearer of the Church, was told to the Church. And the lie told to the Church was told to the Holy Ghost, whose habitation that Church is. He made a false representation to that Church which is the body of Christ and the temple of the Holy Ghost.

Then mark the aggravations by which the guilt of this sin was increased. "Aggravations!" I think I hear someone say, "Should you not rather speak of mitigations, for is it not all traced here to Satan in the words, 'Why hath Satan filled thine heart?'" But there is nothing in that objection. I admit that the suggestion came from Satan, and for the making of that he will be held responsible. But it was the duty of Ananias to repel the incitement; and because, so far from doing that, he fostered the evil germ until it sprung up into actual sin, he was guilty. Temptation does not excuse iniquity. It is to be resisted, not yielded to; and only when it is yielded to is there guilt. No man sins until he wills to sin; and for that act of volition no one but himself is responsible. It will not do, therefore, to throw the entire blame on Satan.

And here we plainly perceive some serious aggravations. In the first place, it was a deliberate lie. It was not the result of some sudden impulse; neither was it told under the influence of some temporary excitement, or extorted from them by the rack of some persecutor's cruelty. They agreed together to tell it; and to this agreement some mutual deliberation was necessary, so that it was fully planned between them.

Then it was a defiant sin. They agreed to tempt the Lord. Now reflect a moment on what that implies. It means that they had determined to put the Lord to the proof. They had arranged to test whether or not he could find out their wickedness. You remember that it is written of ancient Israel, "They tempted the Lord, saying, Is the Lord among us or not?"* And, again, it is affirmed in the historic psalm that "they

---

* Exod. xvii., 7.

tempted God in their heart by asking meat for their lust. Yea, they spake against God; they said, Can God furnish a table in the wilderness?"* So here the conduct of Ananias and his wife was a direct defiance of the Holy Spirit, as if they had said, "Let us see if God be in the Church or not; if he be, let him find out our deception."

In this view of the matter their guilt assumes a very crimson hue. "It is written, thou shalt not tempt the Lord thy God."† So said our blessed Lord to the arch-fiend, when he suggested that he should cast himself from the pinnacle of the Temple, and put his Father's promises to a presumptuous test; but fearful as was the sin which Satan thus attempted to get the Saviour to commit, this wickedness of Ananias was more dreadful still. For it has in it a questioning of the deity and omniscience of the Holy Ghost, and a determination to put that to the test of one instance. It was the same in kind with that committed some years ago by an infidel woman who was lecturing in a town in Lancashire, England, and who said, "If there be a God, I give him ten minutes to take away my life." Oh, the long-suffering of that Jehovah who did not take her at her word!

But once more, this was a gratuitous sin. They went out of their way to commit it. There was no obligation other than that which their own consciences imposed, which bound them to sell their land, or give all the proceeds for the general good. They might have continued Christians in good and regular standing even if they had not done so; for it was not a term of communion in the primitive Church that every one should sell all that he had and give to the poor. But under a desire to have a reputation for benevolence, while yet they kept a sum sufficient to sustain them, they committed this sin. If it had been in some matter of essential importance, perhaps we might have found something more to say in their behalf; but as it was,

---

* Psa. lxxviii, 18, 19.   † Matt. iv., 7.

they stepped aside from the path for the very purpose of committing this iniquity. Their ambition for the good opinion of men, and their unwillingness to part with mammon, were the two roots from which their sin did spring. Covetousness and love of approbation led them to their ruin. Of how many more than they might the same thing be said!

But now look at their punishment. It was immediate death, and that, too, to use a modern legal phrase, "by the visitation of God." I am aware, indeed, that some of those commentators, who are unwilling to admit the supernatural in the very slightest degree, have alleged that Ananias died of apoplexy; and that others have not scrupled to say that he was put to death by Peter's orders, if not, indeed, by his own hands; but there is nothing in the narrative which affords the slightest warrant for any such beliefs. The simplest explanation of both deaths is to attribute them to the hand of God, and this is also the vindication of their doom; for shall not the Judge of all the earth do right? Indeed, I do not see why we should be called upon to defend a case like this just because it is recorded in this book, when other similar instances have occurred in God's ordinary providence. It is true that we are not always warranted to infer that special things of this nature are the indications of special sin; but still there are cases in which such a conclusion seems to be utterly irresistible. It has been well said here by Dr. Dick that "as it discovers rashness and presumption to construe common calamities as proofs of the peculiar guilt and demerit of the sufferers, so not to observe the clear tokens of the divine displeasure against individuals which appear in the nature and circumstances of their punishment indicates a high degree of stupidity, a temper approaching to atheism, under whatever pretences of caution and charity it may be disguised."* Nay, the common sense of mankind may be safely trusted in regard to such things. In

---

* "Lectures on the Acts of the Apostles," p. 81.

the market-place of the town of Devizes, in England, there is a tablet, which records that near to the spot on which it is fixed a woman dropped down dead, having just uttered the words, "If I have got the half-crown, may God strike me dead!" and the coin was found firmly fixed in the hand of her corpse. Now, there was nothing in the cases of Ananias and Sapphira which requires vindication more than there was in that. God's hand was in both alike, and that to the sincerely pious heart is enough.

But notwithstanding that, we can see a special reason why, at this particular time, this warning came in the history of the Christian Church. In the beginning of the Mosaic economy Nadab and Abihu were stricken down for burning strange fire upon the holy altar; in the beginning of the conquest of Canaan, Achan was put to death for secreting a portion of the devoted spoil of Jericho in his tent; and so now in the commencement of the Church's history, when its members were laying their offerings, that is, themselves, upon the altar of consecration, and when they were girding themselves for the holy war which is yet to issue in the conquest of the world for Christ, it was meet that they should be put on their guard against hypocrisy, and warned of the danger which ever haunts a divided heart. "I will be sanctified," says Jehovah, "in them that come nigh me, and before all the people I will be glorified."*

The record is silent as to the eternal condition of these hapless ones, and we undertake not to push aside the veil which it has hung over their after-state. They went, like another, to their own place. Let us follow them no farther, but seek to learn from their history the lessons with which it is so fully fraught.

We may see, in the first place, the two-fold effect of a faithful ministry. On the one hand, we read that great grace was upon them all, and that Joses made a complete sacrifice of his

---

* Lev. x., 3.

property to the Lord. And on the other, we have this dreadful history of Ananias—both under the immediate presidency of the apostles. From the very first, therefore, it has been vain to seek after a perfectly pure Church. But what I am most concerned with now is, that we may account for both of these results by the faithfulness of the ministry. The good are made better, and if the bad are not converted, they are made worse under the instruction of a devoted pastor. If some develop into Barnabases, to cheer his heart, others, alas! become like Ananias, to sadden his spirit. Paul, in writing to the Philippians, where his success had been very signal, had to speak of some even among them as "the enemies of the cross of Christ."* And in one of his letters to the Corinthians, he says, with great solemnity, "We are unto God a sweet savour of Christ, in them that are saved, and in them that perish. To one we are the savour of death unto death and to the other the savour of life unto life. And who is sufficient for these things?"† Every earnest minister understands this well. As the years revolve, he is encouraged not only by the conversion of many to the Lord, but also by the perception in many of those who are already Christians of a deepening of character, and enlargement of heart, and increasing consecration of life. He sees the blade shooting up into the stalk, and the stalk developing into the ear, and the ear filling and mellowing into ripeness; and his heart is made glad thereby. But, alas! alongside of these very cases he observes others who are becoming more gross and sensual and selfish under his ministrations. His appeals seem only to harden them into more stolid insensibility, or to stimulate them to a hypocrisy like this of Ananias, which is sure, in the end, to terminate in the death of reputation and respectability, even as here it resulted in the death of the individual. I have known two men sit for ten years side by side, every Lord's day, under a

---

* Phil. iii., 18. † 2 Cor. ii., 15, 16.

ministry in which both at first took great delight; but while the one became a Christian, and passed through the Church to the highest offices which it was in the power of his fellow-citizens to bestow upon him, the other went through hypocrisy into intemperance, and through intemperance into a drunkard's grave. The same process is going on among us here. What then? Shall the minister be less faithful? Nay, verily, for necessity is laid upon him, and woe is unto him if he "preach not the Gospel."* But let the hearers beware; for if, under the proclamation of the truth, they do not gradually approach nearer to the unselfishness of Barnabas, they must be on the way to the hypocrisy of Ananias.

We may learn, in the second place, that it is impossible to combine the services of God and Mammon. The one is sin, the other is holiness; the one is selfishness, the other is benevolence; the one has its terminus in heaven, the other has its destiny in hell. How, then, is it possible to amalgamate the two? Yet the attempt has been often made, and always with the same result. Remember "Balaam, the son of Bosor, who loved the wages of unrighteousness." With a conscience so scrupulous that he would not allow himself to speak in Jehovah's name otherwise than as the Lord had bidden him, he yet did not hesitate to take the reward which Balak offered him; and after he had predicted the glory and perpetuity of Israel, he lent himself to a diabolical plan to corrupt the tribes to their destruction, and died upon the field of battle, fighting against the army of the Lord. There was the earthly issue of his attempt! Remember also Judas, who, pretending friendship for the Lord Jesus, kissed him only that he might betray him, and then, having received the thirty pieces of silver for which he had covenanted, he went and hanged himself. That was the end of his attempt. And you see what it was in this case of Ananias. The determination to combine these two

---

* 1 Cor. ix., 16.

services ends always in hopeless and eternal failure. Nay, the man who makes it becomes at length more devoted in his allegiance to Mammon than ever, and draws down upon his head a more dreadful doom.

Will you think of all these cases, and be wise in time? It were easier to bring the East and West together than it is to combine these incompatible characters; yet, alas! in all our churches there are too many who may be described in the words of the German Horn as "having all the desire in the world to build God Almighty a magnificent church, at the same time, however, not giving the devil any offence; to whom, accordingly, they set up a neat little chapel close by, where you can offer him some touch of sacrifice at a time, and practise a quiet devotion for him without disturbance."* But God will have a whole heart or none. He will not be contented with the profession that you give him your undivided homage, while yet you retain some secret sin, or some darling lust, or some cherished ambition in some hidden recess of your heart. Either you must pluck that out, or that will shut you out for ever from his presence. Surely, then, we shall sing with new fervour these searching lines:—

> "The dearest idol I have known,
> Whate'er that idol be,
> Help me to tear it from Thy throne,
> And worship only Thee."

We may learn, thirdly, that it is extremely dangerous to allow any one evil principle to gain the mastery over us. You can see that clearly in the case of a habit that is partly physical and external, like intemperance. Every one understands the drunkard's slavery; but we do not all see that there is really a similar bondage in every habitual sin. "Whosoever committeth sin is the slave of sin." Take such a principle, for example, as covetousness; and though it may begin in small things, it holds

---

* See Carlyle's "Essay on the State of German Literature."

its victim in as tight a grasp as his appetite holds the drunkard. It keeps him from being just, even to himself, and it prevents him from being generous to others. It stands between the man and his God, and is, in a word, his chosen good; but at length, as the name "miser" indicates, when the passion has thoroughly developed itself, it makes its victim utterly wretched.

So, again, the love of approbation, when it is suffered to gain the ascendancy, absolutely enchains the soul. The question, "Is it right?" has to give place to this other, "How will it look?" and the temporary applause of men is made to count for more than the eternal approbation of God. So with all other evil principles. Whatever we prefer to God does in the end enslave us in some way. Of his service alone can it be said that it is "perfect freedom."

And, remember, it does not take many such things to hold us fast to our destruction. One will do it. A man went, one day, when the tide was out, to gather sea-plants on the rocks; and, in stepping from ledge to ledge, his leg slipped down, and became jammed in a crevice. He tried to pull it out. He shrieked, he shouted, he prayed; but all in vain. By-and-by the tide came remorselessly in, and rose up, and up, and up, until it flowed over him, and stifled his last gurgling cry. Yet he was held only in one place! So one secret bosom sin cherished, one evil habit practised out of sight of men, will, by-and-by, gain such strength that it will hold us fast while the deluge of eternal judgment comes sweeping over us. "If thy hand offend thee, cut it off: it is better for thee to enter into life maimed, than having two hands to go into hell, into the fire that never shall be quenched."*

Finally, we may learn here that it is vain to think of deceiving God. Ananias and his wife had formed their plan with care, and used every precaution to escape discovery. But they had not taken God into account; and so, at length, they were covered with confusion, and overwhelmed with swift des-

---

* Mark ix., 43.

truction. Let us be warned by their exposure and doom, lest we, too, share at last their fate. We may deceive ourselves; we may deceive those who are living in the home beside us; we may deceive the office-bearers and members of the Church of Christ; but we have not deceived God. His eye has been on us from the beginning, and has searched us through and through. If, therefore, we have been living a lie, he will somehow confront us with the truth, and put us to "shame and everlasting contempt."

I have somewhere read that, when one king had been vanquished in war by another, the conqueror offered terms which were satisfactory to the conquered in every respect save this: that they required him to do public homage to his victor. That, however, was at length so far modified, that he was to be permitted to render his obeisance in the tent of his rival. But when the hour came, and he was in the very act of doing homage, his enemy, by some machinery which he had prepared, stripped off the canvas covering, and revealed him to the gaze of both the armies on his knees before his conqueror. So, if we allow a sinful ambition or an evil appetite to overmaster us, and think we can save ourselves from humiliation by doing our homage to it under the secrecy of some curtained tent, we may be sure that when we are in the very act of owning our allegiance to it, the Lord will throw down the covering, and unveil our degradation before the eyes of men and angels. Is it not written that he "shall bring every work into judgment, with every secret thing, whether it be good, or whether it be evil?" * Hath he not set "our secret sins in the light of his countenance?" † Ah, who of us can stand before such a scrutiny? Do we not feel, in the light of these truths, more than we ever felt before, our need of "the redemption that is in Christ Jesus?" Come, then, and apply to him for his cleansing blood and his renewing spirit, that we may obtain emancipation from the slavery of sin, and have "boldness in the day of judgment."

---

* Eccles. xii., 14.   † Psa. xc., 8.

XVI.

BEFORE THE COUNCIL AGAIN.

Acts v., 12-42.

AFTER the healing of the lame man at the Beautiful Gate of the Temple, it would seem that Solomon's porch * became a stated place of meeting among the primitive disciples. I do not suppose that all their assemblies convened there; but as the Christians at this date, and for some considerable time later, maintained their observance of the Mosaic law, it would be convenient for them, as they went up to the Temple at the regular hours of prayer, to arrange for conferences with each other at the same times. Nor were they at first molested; for, although the rulers threatened the apostles with violence if they should continue to preach in the name of Jesus, yet the reality of the miracles which they performed, and the boldness which they manifested, as well as the attractiveness of the Gospel which they preached, attached to them a great number of followers from among the common people. The deaths of Ananias and Sapphira, indeed, had produced a very deep and solemn impression, and kept those who were actuated by mere worldly motives from connecting themselves with the new society. Still, the numbers of the faithful steadily increased, and quite a new impetus was given to the movement by the development among the apostles of the miraculous gift of healing with which the Holy Ghost had endowed them.

They cured all manner of diseases; and such was the eagerness and faith of the people, that "they brought out their

---

*Acts v., 12.

sick into the streets, and laid them on beds and couches, that at the least the shadow of Peter passing by might overshadow some of them." Nay, more: this great opportunity for the diseased was so talked of throughout the district that a multitude came "out of the cities round about unto Jerusalem, bringing sick folks, and them which were vexed with unclean spirits; and they were healed every one."

After the argument which I presented to you in a former lecture on the possibility of miracles, and the nature of the testimony which they bear to the Gospel, I need not now say anything on these subjects.* But as the advocates of the supremacy of the pope found something on what is said here concerning Peter, and as some have supposed that this reference to Peter's shadow has in it an element of superstition, I may make a passing allusion to these matters.

In regard to the primacy of the pope, let me frankly admit, what indeed is too patent to be denied, that Peter did occupy the foremost place in the Church at this time, and that this was in fulfilment of the promise which the Lord had made to him. But what that has to do with the supremacy of the pope, or on what grounds the Bishop of Rome can be regarded as the successor of Peter and the inheritor of his priority, I am unable to discover. The argument of the Papacy here may be reduced to a syllogism, thus: the apostle Peter was the first of the apostles in the primitive Church; the Bishop of Rome succeeded to the place and power of Peter; therefore the Bishop of Rome is the primate of the Church. Now, the *major premise* of that argument must be admitted to be in some sense true, and Protestants only weaken their cause when they cavil at or deny its truth; for, as we have seen, ever since the day of Pentecost Peter was the leader of the disciples. But the *minor premise* is a flagrant assumption. It takes for granted that the apostles could have succes-

---

* See *ante*, p. 185.

sors; it assumes that the Bishop of Rome was the successor of Peter, and that the prerogatives which were bestowed upon that apostle as a reward for his noble confession of his Lord must descend to the holders of a certain office altogether independently of their character and conduct. Of these things no sort of proof worthy of the name is offered, and, what is more, no proof whatever can be given. Therefore, the argument, as a whole, is a failure. But while we admit the primacy of Peter at this time, it would appear that it was not intended that he should continue to retain pre-eminence; for at a later date we shall find James in the presidential chair at the Council of Jerusalem, while Peter speaks as an ordinary member; nay, more, we shall discover that Peter's advice was declined, while the suggestion of James was accepted.

Farther, if it be supposed that the reference to Peter's shadow here sets him on a pedestal above the others, then the reply is easy; for, in the first place, the healing power resided neither in Peter nor in his shadow, but in the Lord Jesus Christ; and, in the second place, similar miracles were afterward performed through the media of handkerchiefs and aprons that had been in contact with Paul.*

But some ask, in astonishment, "Was not all this superstition?" To which I reply that it would have been so, if the minds of the applicants had rested simply, and only, on the shadow. But they came to be cured, not by the shadow in itself, nor by Peter himself, but by the Lord. Hence they were exercising faith, sincere and strong as hers who stole behind the Lord himself, and said within herself, "If I may but touch his garment, I shall be whole."† The great thing was, that they who sought a cure were looking to Christ for it; and when they were doing that, and recognized that the power of healing lay in him alone, it was a matter of indifference through what means they sought it. If the Lord were pleased to act, he

---

* Acts xix., 11, 12. † Matt. ix., 21.

could do so through any sort of instrumentality. All methods adopted by him were only signs. A word, a touch, a shadow—each alike—was but a symbol designed to help the faith of the applicant, and to meet his individual necessity. There was no virtue in it; that came out of Christ. Thus regarded, therefore, the act of those who sought that only the shadow of Peter might fall upon their sick rises almost to the height of the faith of him who said to Jesus, "I am not worthy that thou shouldest come under my roof: but speak the word only, and my servant shall be healed;" and of which the Lord said, "I have not found so great faith, no, not in Israel."*

These miracles attracted still greater attention to the apostles and their message. They had larger audiences to address, and much success accompanied their preaching, so that multitudes, "both of men and women, were added to the Lord."

It is a little remarkable that this is the first express notice we have of female membership in the Christian Church. We know that during the days of his public ministry many Galilean women distinguished themselves by their kindness to the Lord, and we can never forget that those who were the last to leave his remains in the sepulchre, and the first to greet him on the morning of his resurrection, were women. So, too, there were women in the upper room, and there must have been many among the converts on Pentecost and afterward; for Sapphira was not the solitary representative of her sex: but here first it is plainly asserted that females were received into the Church.

Perhaps the very mention of Sapphira's name in connection with her sin may have suggested to the historian the importance of specially recording this noteworthy fact; and we may not pass it by in silence, for the Gospel alone has been just to woman. All other religions have more or less debased her, and made her the slave of man. The savages of the East and the West have been alike in this, that they have driven the weakest

---

* Matt. viii., 8, 10

to the wall ; and she who was intended to be the helpmeet of her husband, sharing all his cares, doubling all his joys, and throwing a halo of glory round his home, has been trampled under the hoof of cruelty, or branded with the mark of violence, or treated as an inferior being. But the Gospel has recognised her true position, and has educated her to fill it; for in the highest of all earthly fellowship—that of the Christian Church—she stands by the side of man. "In Christ Jesus there is neither male nor female." Thus the Gospel has given dignity to womanhood, and thereby it has raised the whole tone and character of social life ; for, restored to her rightful place, woman has elevated the home with her, and all within it, husband and children alike, are the happier for her exaltation. The treatment of woman is everywhere the gauge of true religion and civilization; and she is then only in her proper place when she is neither the drudge of oppression, the idol of chivalry, nor the plaything of fashion, but the fellow-Christian and companion of her husband.

The increased stir made by the apostolic miracles and successes roused anew the antagonism of the Jewish rulers, who determined, if possible, to put an end to the whole enterprise, apprehended the apostles, and put them "in the common prison." But he who could work miracles by his servants could also, when it was needful, work miracles for them ; and during the night, by the ministrations of an angel, he opened for them the doors of their dungeon, and sent them forth, saying, " Go, stand, and speak in the temple to the people all the words of this life." Every word in this commission is emphatic. They were to tell of life, spiritual, immortal—resurrection-life. They were to tell of *this* life as connected with the Lord Jesus Christ. They were to tell all the words of it, keeping back nothing from regard either to the frown or the favour of the multitude. They were to tell of it in the temple, the place of daily concourse; and they were to tell of it to the people as a whole, without respect to class or caste. "To the people." This is the divine charter of Gospel rights and privileges, and it gives them, not to any conclave of priests or any order of men, but to the people. Wherever, therefore, any measures are adopted to keep them from hearing or reading its "words of life," the great design of the Lord Jesus is counteracted.

The Gospel rings the death-knell of all monopolies, and is the pioneer everywhere of popular liberty, popular education, and popular progress. Hence its dissemination among the masses which crowd the streets and lanes of our large cities is one great indispensable thing for the securing of the prosperity and permanence of the nation. There is but one panacea that will heal our social and political maladies. If the habits of the working-people, as a class, are intemperate and improvident; if the relations between employers and employed are hostile and disagreeable, breaking out ever and anon into lock-outs, on the one hand, and strikes on the other; if the lobbies of our halls of legislation are scenes of corruption, and enactments are bought and sold for a bribe; if scarcely a day elapses without the revelation of some new dishonesty at which the world stands aghast; then there is but one remedy for all these evils. It is to be found in the Gospel of Christ; and the incidents of our days are saying to us, as clearly as the angel said to the liberated apostles, "Go, stand and speak to the people all the words of this life." Multiply your agencies for the reaching of those who never enter a place of worship; send forth a thousand-fold more labourers into the dens and purlieus of vice among us; organize new efforts for the neglected rich in the midst of us; send missionaries into our avenues and among our legislators, as well as into the low places of the city and among our sailors; and, with these efforts for their good, do not forget your own spiritual interests. Thus, speaking of this life to the people as a whole, you will begin at the fountain-head of all evil, and at length a virtuous nation will be the fruit of your endeavours.

One cries up education; another speaks of temperance; a third calls for better houses for the working-classes; a fourth insists upon the necessity of mutual understanding between capital and labour; and all these things are good enough in themselves. But they are all dealing with matters which are themselves effects. The Gospel alone touches the one prolific cause by which they have all been produced. It alone, by the grace of God, can change the selfish nature of men into self-sacrificing benevolence, and teach them to live in purity, in peace, in brotherhood, in love. Here is a centennial text for us. It lies at the very root of our national life; and only in so far as we obey its commands shall we secure that "government of the people, by the people, and for the people," shall not disappear from the earth. Ring it out, then, clear and loud; obey it yourselves, and see that others give it good heed: "Go, stand and speak to the people all the words of this life."

Obedient to the angelic injunction, they went forth to do their Master's work; and early in the morning "they entered into the Temple and taught." Much about the same time as they went to Solomon's porch, a special meeting of the Council was convened; and the first thing its members did was to send to the prison for the men whom they supposed they had so securely confined. Judge of their surprise, however, when the officers returned, and said, "The prison truly found we shut with all safety, and the keepers standing without before the doors; but when we had opened, we found no man within." They were amazed, and as they were wondering whereunto the thing would grow, another came and said, "Behold, the men whom ye put in prison are standing in the Temple, and teaching the people." This was defiance indeed! not to be endured a moment longer; so the captain and officers went and brought them before the Council; using no violence, however, for the double reason that none was needed, and that the people, if it had been offered, might have attempted a rescue.

When the apostles were set before the Sanhedrim, the high-priest began the proceedings against them by putting a question and making an accusation. He said, "Did not we straitly command you that ye should not teach in this name? And, behold, ye have filled Jerusalem with your doctrine, and intend to bring this man's blood upon us."

Mark how contemptuously he alludes to Jesus, contriving all the while to avoid the mention of his name, as if, forsooth, the mere pronunciation of it would pollute his lips. "This name;" "this man's blood;" "your doctrine." He would not contribute to the preservation of the name of Jesus by condescending even to utter it; and now all that is known about him is, that he had the hardihood to resist the Lord's apostles.

Observe, also, the admission which he makes as to the progress of the Christian faith: "Ye have filled Jerusalem with your doctrine." There may be some rhetorical exaggeration in this mode of stating the case; but still it indicates that already the new society had become formidable in the eyes of the priesthood, and that it was continuing to make great advances.

Observe, once more, the indications of conscience in the words, "Ye intend to bring this man's blood upon us." Peter had, indeed, used very strong and pointed language on that subject. He had not scrupled to charge the leaders of the people with being the crucifiers of Jesus, and at an earlier date the members of the Council would neither have hesitated nor blushed to own the deed. They deemed it at the time a fine stroke of policy, and congratulated themselves that thereby they had got rid of a troublesome adversary. But now that the followers of the Nazarene were becoming so numerous, now that so much was said about the resurrection of Jesus, and so many miracles were wrought by his followers, they began to feel uneasy, and wished to repudiate all connection with his crucifixion, or at least to exonerate themselves from all blame for his death.

But Peter was ready with his reply. He gave utterance to the determination of himself and his fellow apostles in words which at the same time assert the important principle of liberty of conscience. He said, "We ought to obey God rather than men." The rulers of the people laid one set of commands upon them. God gave them injunctions of an opposite character, and they chose to obey God, and to take the consequences at the hands of men. Thus their conduct here at once explains and limits the principles which they have elsewhere laid down as to obedience to civil government. When Paul, writing to the Romans, says, "Let every soul be subject to the higher powers,"* we must not forget that he was himself imprisoned for refusing to comply with the demands of civil rulers; and when Peter says, "Submit yourselves to every ordinance of man for the Lord's sake; whether it be to the king, as supreme; or unto governors,"† we must bear in mind that it was he who uttered this noble protest, "We ought to obey God rather than men." It is evident, therefore, that there are limits within which civil governments may be obeyed, and ought to be obeyed, but beyond which they have no jurisdiction. It is right to obey them when that which they enjoin is within the sphere of government as such, and when it has been constitutionally enacted; but if that which they command is in opposition to the word of God, and within a province to which their power does not extend, we ought to follow the example of the apostles here, and disobey them, cheerfully taking the consequences. God alone is Lord of the conscience; and if any earthly usurper should attempt to invade that sacred territory, he is to be resisted "even unto blood." This is the meaning of the stand here taken by Peter; and the battle commenced that day has gone on through the centuries,

> "Bequeath'd from bleeding sire to son,
> Though baffled oft, is ever won;"

so that now we see this principle recognized and acted upon by a larger multitude than ever before upon the earth; and when

---

* Rom. xiii, 1. † 1 Peter ii., 13.

we honour the memories of those heroes to whom the world owes that religious freedom which is the crown and glory of civil liberty, let not the Apostle Peter be forgotten!

But it might have been objected to the apostle, that he was wrong in supposing that God had given them such commands, and so he proceeds to justify his confidence by alleging that God had raised up Jesus, whom they had slain, and that he had exalted him "with his right hand to be a prince and a Saviour, for to give repentance to Israel, and the remission of sins." And lest they should suppose that all this was imaginary, he affirms that it was attested, first, by the evidence of their own senses; and, second, by the Holy Ghost, who had been given by the ascended Jesus to all them that obeyed him, and by whose power their miracles had been wrought, and their characters had been formed. "The whole remonstrance is," as Alford has said, "a perfect model of concise and ready eloquence, and of unanswerable logical coherence: and a notable fulfilment of the promise, 'It shall be given you in that same hour what ye shall speak.'"*

Thus, for the fourth time, we have Peter connecting the Church of the present on the earth with the ascended Christ, as receiving from him not only such miraculous gifts as those with which the early Christians were endowed, but also the more valuable spiritual blessings of repentance, forgiveness, and holienss of life. Nothing is more remarkable to the student of this early history than the fact that Peter constantly insists upon the connection between the crucifixion of Christ, on the one hand, and his resurrection and ascension on the other; and that he traces the gift of the Holy Spirit back through the exaltation to the crucifixion. This is the Petrine Gospel, as clearly as the doctrine of justification by faith is the Pauline. The one met the condition of the Jewish mind, just as the other was especially adapted to the Gentile; but both are true, and both

---

* Matt. x., 19. Alford, *in loco*.

were held alike by Peter and Paul. Still, the fact that each dwelt more upon the one than upon the other is suggestive, as hinting to us that while we must never shun to declare to men all the counsel of God, there are times and places when the presentation of one aspect of truth is more important than that of another.

The reply of Peter exasperated the members of the Council. They were indeed "cut to the heart," but the sorrow was not "after a godly sort." It was "the sorrow of the world;" and in their rage they consulted together to put them all to death. But before they came to their decision they were softened down by the moderate counsels of one of their own number. This was Gamaliel, the son of Simon, and the celebrated teacher of the Apostle Paul. According to Dr. Ginsburg, the modern Jewish scholar, "the fragments which have Gamaliel's name attached to them" prove "that he was endowed with great intellectual powers, a fondness for study, and for definitely settling every point of difficulty, refined taste, and good judgment; that he was humane, anxious to ameliorate the condition of the helpless. a strict Pharisee, yet liberal-minded, and averse to persecute those who differed from him."* He did not belong to the sect of the Sadducees, who were the chief movers in the present attempt to silence the apostles; but the estimation in which he was held by all the people secured for him an attentive hearing. He recommended his colleagues to be cautious, and to wait a while before they took any violent measures. It might be that the new movement was of God; and if so, they could not put it down, no matter what they did. But if, on the other hand, it were not of God, it would very soon die out of itself; as in two other instances to which he referred, and which were still fresh in their recollection, had actually been the case. Their wisest course, therefore, was to let the men alone; and as at the moment it did not seem to the Sadducees that they had

---

* Alexander's "Kitto," *sub voce* GAMALIEL.

any pretext strong enough for taking cruel measures, they agreed to follow this advice. So, when they had ordered the apostles to be beaten with rods, they let them go; but the treatment which they had received did not damp the ardour of their zeal, for " they departed from the presence of the Council rejoicing that they were counted worthy to suffer shame for his name; and daily in the Temple, and from house to house, they ceased not to teach and to preach Jesus Christ."

In this speech of Gamaliel there are two things which seem to call for special remark. The first is, that there is an apparent discrepancy between him and Josephus as to the insurrection of Theudas. A person of that name is spoken of by the Jewish historian as having headed an insurrection; but, then, the date of his rising was some years subsequent to that of the events which we have now been reviewing. Hence, many would infer that the account given in the Acts is erroneous. But that is far from being a just conclusion; for, apart altogether from the consideration of the question of Luke's inspiration, Josephus was just as likely to be wrong as he was. Nay, the history of Josephus, as Alford remarks, "teems with inaccuracies;" so that we have no right to argue that, because he says one thing and Luke another, therefore Luke must be wrong. Moreover, Josephus himself, speaking of a time which might very well accord to that referred to here, says, "Now at this time there were ten thousand other disorders in Judea, which were like tumults, because a great number put themselves into a warlike posture, either out of hopes of gain to themselves or out of enmity to the Jews."* Once more, the name Theudas was by no means uncommon; and it may very well have been that a person called by it may have been the leader of one of those tumults to which, in the passage which I have just quoted, the historian has referred. The case of Judas is referred to by Josephus, and has occasioned no difficulty; and we need not linger a single moment upon it.

---

* " Antiquities," 17, 10, 4.

But we cannot pass Gamaliel's advice in silence. It is hardly necessary to say that he was speaking his own opinion, and that his words are not an authoritative statement. For it is not the fact that human inventions in religious matters always come immediately to naught. The case of Mohammedanism, which has held its ground for nearly twelve centuries, is one in point; and when we remember that, we cannot give unqualified assent to the rabbi's assertion.

Neither, again, is it invariably the fact that truth will hold its ground in the face of error and opposition. The seat of the Seven Churches of Asia is now almost entirely a Mohammedan district, and the Reformation was almost completely trodden out both in Italy and Spain. I admit, indeed, that as a broad law characterizing the administration of the Divine government from the beginning to the end, it will hold good; for, when we look thus at history, we can fully indorse the words of our own poet:

> "Truth crushed to earth shall rise again :
> The eternal years of God are hers;
> But Error, wounded, writhes with pain,
> And dies among his worshippers."

But as applied to individual cases within even such a range as the life-time of a man, it fails. Immediate success is thus not an infallible evidence of truth, neither is the absence of such success a sure indication of error. Therefore, in settling the matter of the soul's allegiance, we have to do with other, and more important, elements than that. We must determine whether the claims put forth in the Gospel are convincing on such evidence as Peter put forth then; and, having made the decision, we must act "in scorn of consequence." Gamaliel's words have been often quoted as if they had been almost inspired. But, indeed, they are far from being universally true; and they read to me more like the saying of a man who wanted an excuse for doing nothing, than like the utterance of an earnest inquirer after truth.

But what shall we say of his advice: "Refrain from these men, and let them alone?" That was wise; but it was so just because it is always wise to leave religious questions untouched either by civil enactment or magisterial interference. If a cause is right, you cannot ultimately kill it by persecution; if it is wrong, you will by persecution help to keep it alive, for you give its adherents the glory of martyrdom. But whether right or wrong, so long as a man's devotion to his religion does not interfere with the civil rights and liberties of others, he is to be let alone. His conscience is a sacred thing, and he has a right to say to all civil governments, "Hands off! that is for my God, and not for you." But that was precisely what Peter said; and so, rightly viewed, the world owes far more to the ringing notes of Peter than to the timid, cautious, Micawber-like policy which was advocated by Gamaliel.

In reviewing the section of sacred history over which we have passed, let us learn, in the first place, to keep the conscience for Christ. All through I have been remembering the words of John Bunyan: when condemned to three months' imprisonment for preaching the Gospel, and told that if he did not then promise to abstain from the course which he had been pursuing he must be banished from the realm, he nobly replied, "I am at a point with you; if I were out of prison again to-day, I would preach the Gospel again to-morrow, by the help of God." Nor can I forget the noble army of those who, all through the centuries, have sought to obey God, even at the forfeit of their liberties and lives.

But that is not the department in which our danger lies. What we need to-day is to keep conscience for God in the ordinary affairs of life commonly called secular. Let us see to it, then, that in the shop as well as in the Church, on the exchange as well as in the ecclesiastical assembly, we act out the dictates of conscience as enlightened by the Word and Spirit of God. Say not, in the cant phrase of multitudes, that you "cannot afford to keep a conscience." Cannot afford to keep a conscience! What! is it then come to this? Shall this divine faculty be weighed in the balance with silver and gold? and is the fear that you may lose profits to keep you from doing that which you know and feel to be your duty? What is gold compared with the assurance that you have done that which God would have you? What will whole mines of wealth and whole burnt-offerings of human applause avail if, after all, you are despised by yourself, and your conscience upbraids you with meanness and corruption. Rather would I enjoy a crust, in the consciousness of unfaltering allegiance to my God, than roll in affluence, with remorse gnawing at my heart; and he may well embrace the darkness of the dungeon, or the death of the scaffold, who is only sure of having a good God, a good conscience, and a good cause. Whatever, then, thy conscience, enlightened by God's Word, lays down, be sure thou follow it; for if thou canst not answer for thy conduct at the bar of conscience, how wilt thou answer for it at the bar of God?

But we may learn, in the second place, that while contending for conscience' sake we may expect to be assisted by God. In the case before us, he sent his angel to open the prison doors for his servants, and sustained them in giving their testimony before the Council. Nor are these solitary instances of his favour. As we shall see, Peter was similarly delivered from the fury of Herod at a later day; and we know how Paul and Silas were at length brought out of the Philippian dungeon. These were miraculous instances, no doubt, but things almost as wonderful have occurred in God's ordinary providence.

I have already alluded to John Bunyan. Take the following incident from his life by Offor, prefixed to the collected edition of his works: "He had at times, while a prisoner, an extraordinary degree of liberty: like Joseph in Egypt, some of his jailers committed all to his hands. There can be little doubt but that he went from the prison to preach in the villages or woods, and at one time went to London to visit his admiring friends; but this coming to the ears of the justices, the humane jailer had well-nigh lost his place, and for some time he was not permitted to look out at the door. When this had worn off, he had again the opportunity of visiting his Church and preaching by stealth. It is said that many of the Baptist congregations in Bedfordshire owe their origin to his midnight preaching. Upon one occasion, having been permitted to go out and visit his family, with whom he intended to spend the night, long before morning he felt so uneasy that at a very late hour he went back to the prison. Information was given to a neighbouring clerical magistrate that there was strong suspicion of Bunyan having broken prison. At midnight he sent a messenger to the jail, that he might be a witness against the merciful keeper. On his arrival he demanded, 'Are all the prisoners safe?' The answer was 'Yes.'—'Is John Bunyan safe?' 'Yes.'—'Let me see him.' He was called up and confronted with the astonished witness, and all passed off well. His kind-hearted jailer said to him, 'You may go out when you will, for you know much better when to return than I can tell you.'"* We do not call that a miracle, yet who shall dare to say that an angel had nothing to do with it? And in any case when we are suffering for our adhesion to God, we may be sure that somehow he will come near us with his help. If in no other way, we may rely upon it that he will fill our hearts with joy, so that his gladness will be our strength.

It has been remarked of the era of the Reformation in Europe, and of the Covenant in Scotland, that those who suffered for conscience' sake were invariably full of exalted assurance as to their present acceptance with God and their future glory in heaven. No doubts, or fears, or misgivings were permitted to disturb them. So true it is that "God stayeth his rough wind in the day of his east wind." If he requires us to endure in one way, he will give us enjoyment in another.

---

* "Works of John Bunyan," by George Offor, vol. iii., lix.

So let us adhere to him at every sacrifice. He will be for us, if we will be for him. And in the end, whatever may happen, we shall be "more than conquerors through him that loved us." Give us but the assurance of his favour, and of eternal glory with himself at last, and what can be put into comparison with that? Who would not rather be the despised apostle shivering in the cold, dark, damp Mammertine, yet able to say, "I know whom I have believed, and am persuaded that he is able to keep what I have committed to him against that day; henceforth there is laid up for me a crown of righteousness"—than the imperial Nero on his throne, hated by his contemporaries, and gibbeted for ever on the page of history as the monster of monarchs? For earthly glory and for heavenly immortality, for peace within and for blessedness above, the only specific is loyalty to conscience and to God. Come, then, raise with me again the shout of high resolve and holy consecration: "We ought to obey God rather than men;" and, by his grace, we will! we will!

XVII.

SIMON MAGUS.

ACTS viii., 5-25

SINCE the second appearance of the apostles before the Council, many events fraught with important results have occurred in the infant society.

As, perhaps, might have been foreseen, the distribution of the benevolent fund by men who had so many other and more exacting matters to attend to, led to dissatisfaction on the part of some who supposed that, because they were Jews of foreign birth, they had been neglected. This difficulty was met in the wisest manner by the apostles, who embraced the opportunity to secure the election of seven men who should have it for their special business to look after the "daily ministration." Nor was the Church itself lacking in prudence in the matter; for as the complaint had come from the Hellenistic Jews, the brethren selected men who, if we may judge from their names, were all Hellenists, under whose administration of the fund the confidence of the aggrieved party would be restored.

But though the special duty of the deacons was to attend to the "serving of tables," they were not debarred from preaching the Gospel; and one of their number, Stephen by name, became very energetic and successful in his discussions with the members of several foreign synagogues in Jerusalem. So far as we can gather from the record, he was the first of the Christian converts who had any clear anticipation of the facts that Christianity was to supersede Judaism, and to spread over the earth, including in it Gentiles on equal terms with Jews. These opinions he brought out in the course of his disputations, fortifying them with so much argument taken from the Old Testament itself, that his opponents "were not able to resist the wisdom and the spirit with which he spake."

But in setting forth such views he roused all Jewish exclusiveness against him; and, as the result, he was brought before the Council, whence, after he had made an address replete with argument put forth under the guise of history, he was taken out and stoned to death.

His was a brief, bright record; and we think of him now as of a young soldier, the first to fall on some great battle-day when truth and freedom are hanging on the issue. He was a hero before he was a martyr, but the sanctity of the cause in which he suffered has embalmed his history, so that to-day his name and fame are as familiar as they were to those who had seen his face and listened to his words.

On that memorable day, a youth was present named Saul of Tarsus, who was in himself an impersonation of the fury of the persecution, and in his history an illustration of the indestructibility of truth. He was about the last man there who would have been supposed to have any leanings to the new religion; yet before long he became a convert, and, taking up the mantle of the ascended Stephen, he received a commission "to preach among the Gentiles the unsearchable riches of Christ." Not yet, however, had he been confronted by the Lord in the way. He was now "breathing out threatenings and slaughter against the disciples of the Lord;" and if you multiply his fury a thousand-fold or more, you will understand how it became necessary for all the prominent members of the new society to leave Jerusalem for the time. The Master himself had said to the first evangelists, "When they persecute you in one city, flee ye into another;" so they were scattered abroad, and wherever they went they preached the Word. Till this time, indeed, they had restricted their ministrations to the Holy City; and it does not appear that they would have thought of going elsewhere, had they not been driven out by persecution. Thus good is made to come out of evil; and not seldom God uses the cruelties of the ungodly as a scourge of small cords wherewith to chastise his own people, and send them forth to the performance of neglected work.

One of those thus driven from the Holy City was Philip, the deacon, whose labours are specially particularized because they prepared the way for the admission of Gentiles into the Church. He found a refuge in Samaria among that peculiar people who were neither Jews nor Gentiles, but occupied a middle position, and dwelt in an isolation which was owing as much perhaps to their own self-conceit as to their neighbours' arrogance. They were the descendants of those colonists from Babylon, Cuthah, Hamath, Ava, and Sepharvaim, whom the King of Assyria planted in the land of Israel when he carried the ten tribes into captivity.*

At their first settlement these idolators worshipped their own divinities, but afterward, on account of a plague of lions, they procured a Jewish priest to teach them, as they said, "the manner of the God of the land;" and under his guidance they added to their other religious services the worship of Jehovah. As the sacred chronicler has put it, "they feared Jehovah, and served their own gods." They received, perhaps from their priestly teacher, a copy of the law of Moses, and that was the only part of the Old Testament Scriptures which they recognized. They had built a temple on Mount Gerizim, in which they offered sacrifices; and though they observed the same festivals as did the Jews, and expected the same Messiah, yet from the date when Nehemiah rejected their offer of alliance at the rebuilding of the wall of Jerusalem, they had been at constant feud with their neighbours. But as the Lord Jesus himself, a few years before the events which we are now rehearsing, had preached to the inhabitants of Sychar, Philip felt

---

* 2 Kings xvii., 24-34.

warranted in proclaiming the Gospel to the people of the place in which he was. Some, indeed, have supposed that the city visited by him at this time was the same as that in which our Lord had spent two memorable and successful days. But though the expression is indefinite, and may mean any city of Samaria, the probability is that the capital city is intended. In any case, the labours of Philip were attended with signal results; for "the people with one accord gave heed to his words," and what with the gladness of those who had found salvation for their souls, and the gratitude of those whose bodily diseases had been healed by his miracles, "there was great joy in that city."

Among those who professed to be converted to the faith, and received baptism at his hands, was one who belonged to a class of men who were signally, nay, even shamefully, prevalent in that strange transition age, in which so many elements were seething. As Neander has admirably put it, "A lively, but indefinite, obscure excitement of the religious feeling always exposes men to a variety of dangerous delusions. This was the case with the Samaritans. As at that time, in other parts of the East, a similar indefinite longing after a new communication from heaven—an ominous restlessness in the minds of men such as generally precedes great changes in the history of mankind—was diffused abroad, so this indistinct anxiety did not fail to lead astray and to deceive many who were not rightly prepared for it, while they adopted a false method of allaying it. A mixture of unconscious self-deception and intentional falsehood moved certain Goëtæ, who with mystical ideas proceeding from an amalgamation of Jewish, Oriental, and Grecian elements, boasted of a special connection with the invisible world, and by taking advantage of the occult powers of nature, and by various arts of conjuration, excited the astonishment of credulous people, and obtained credit for their boastful pretensions. To this class of men belonged a Jewish or Samaritan Goës named Simon who, by his extraordinary magical powers, so fascinated the people, that they said that he must be more than man; that he was the great power which emanated from the invisible God by which was brought forth the universe, now appearing on earth in a bodily form."*

Before Philip had made his appearance in Samaria, this man had obtained a very large following. But as he who digs deepest gets the water from the spring, so he who deals with the undermost necessities of humanity must always in the long run have the allegiance of men. We cannot wonder, therefore, that the people laid aside the superficialities of Simon for the satisfying truths which Philip taught them; and it is quite in keeping with the nature of such a man as Simon was that when he saw himself deserted he followed the multitude to see what he could make thereby.

Such was the condition of things in Samaria when the apostles, hearing of Philip's work, sent Peter and John to visit the new converts, not, as I judge, because they were in any doubt of the propriety of the course which Philip had pursued, but rather in order that these two might bestow upon the Samaritan disciples the miraculous gifts of the Holy Ghost, and so make them equal in privilege to the brethren in Jerusalem.

It is to be remembered that in so speaking we refer exclusively to the extraordinary operations of the Holy Ghost, consisting in gifts of healing, prophecy, and the like, and not at all to the ordinary workings of his grace; for without these, conversion would have been impossible. But these were altogether independent of the presence of the apostles, and were enjoyed by every believer; while the miraculous endowments were bestowed only by the laying-on of the hands of the apostles. When, therefore, our Episcopalian brethren refer to this incident in primitive Church history in support of their service of confirmation, as if it had here received the sanction of apostolic

---

* Neander's "Planting and Training," vol. i., pp. 57, 58.

authority, they are confounding two things which are entirely distinct. It may be right and proper to have some special observances connected with the reception of young converts into the membership of the Church, and each society of believers is at liberty, under the guidance of the Holy Ghost, to make its own form for that purpose; but to claim apostolic authority for the laying on of episcopal hands on such occasions seems to me both unwarranted and unwise, since it was in their case invariably accompanied with the communication of the extraordinary gifts of the Holy Ghost. We have apostolic authority for leaving each Church to its own choice on all such matters; and so no particular form should be exclusively set up, for in reference to all these things, "The Church of Christ is the freest society in the world."

In the case before us, the result of the laying-on of the apostles' hands was that the individuals thus distinguished became possessed of the power of working miracles in some form or other. It does not appear that Simon received the gift; but the fact that Peter and John were able to communicate such energy to others awoke his astonishment and envy. He had never really perceived the spirituality of the Gospel. He had gone in with the new movement merely to follow the multitude, and see what he could make for himself. In his eyes all religious teachers were alike impostors; for he measured them all by his own standard. Perhaps in his past life he had purchased the power to perform many a trick from poor practitioners in the magical art, even as now a professor of legerdemain will pay a high price for initiation into the mystery of some new feat. And so, thinking that Peter stood on the same plane with himself, and was only a more accomplished sorcerer than he was, he offered him money, saying, "Give me also this power, that on whomsoever I lay hands, he may receive the Holy Ghost."

The proposal was in the highest degree dishonouring to God. It put the operations of the Holy Ghost on a level with the deceptions of men; it proposed to make merchandize of that which was the richest gift of the Divine goodness; it wanted to turn to individual aggrandisement that special blessing which God had bestowed upon the Church to assist its progress in the world. Therefore Peter was utterly shocked by the blasphemy of the man, and exclaimed, with holy indignation, "Thy money perish with thee, because thou hast thought that the gift of God may be purchased with money." Then, using this opportunity as an occasion for leading the man to a full knowledge of himself, he gave him to understand that, as his action indicated, he had no real interest in Christ or his salvation. He used great fervour of speech, saying, "Thou hast neither part nor lot in this matter: for thy heart is not right in the sight of God;" and, again, "I perceive that thou art in the gall of bitterness, and in the bond of iniquity." But as he might not yet be beyond all hope, he urged him to repent of his wickedness, and pray God, if perhaps "the thought of thine heart may be forgiven thee." This so terrified the sorcerer that he cried, "Pray ye to the Lord for me, that none of these things which ye have spoken come upon me;" and with that appeal he disappears from the sacred page, and we hear of him in Scripture no more. But he is by Neander supposed to be the same person who, some ten or fifteen years after this date, is found in the company of Felix, the Roman procurator, and by whose immoral and deceitful practices Drusilla, the sister of Agrippa, was enticed away from her own husband, Azizus, and induced to become the paramour of Felix. Irenæus, one of the earliest fathers of the Church, has written of him in this manner: "This man was honoured by many as a god, and taught that it was he who had appeared among the Jews as the Son, among the Samaritans as the Father, and among other nations as the Holy Ghost; and that he was the most sublime virtue, or Father of all, by whatever name he was known among men. Having brought from the city of Tyre an infamous woman, called Helena, he carried her about with him, affirming that she was the first conception of his mind, the mother of all beings, by whom in the beginning he formed angels and archangels. He persuaded those who believed in him and this woman that they might live as they pleased, and so 'his followers led flagitious lives, practised magic, and adored the images of Simon and Helena.'"* If all this be true, then there was no real repentance exercised by him, and so he passes away with the doom of the blasphemer upon him, leaving a name which lives only in the designation of the vilest traffic which the Church of Christ has ever seen, namely, the buying and selling of the sacred office of the cure of souls.

In reviewing this interesting chapter of primitive Church history, one or two practical reflections are suggested to us.

We are reminded, for one thing, that when God's people neglect their duty, he finds means of stirring them up to its performance. Before his ascension, the Lord said to his disciples, "Ye shall be witnesses unto me, both in Jerusalem and in all Judea, and in Samaria, and unto the uttermost parts of the earth." But up to this time there is no record of any attempt to carry the Gospel outside of Jerusalem. True, the apostles and first preachers of the cross would come in contact with many strangers at the three great annual festivals observed in the Holy City; but still that was not a full obedience of the Lord's command; and it does not appear that in these first years they had formed any plan for the carrying-on of missionary operations outside of Jerusalem. But just then the persecution arose about Stephen; and, as the storm separates the seed from its parent stem, and carries it far away to other localities, so the assaults of the enemies of the faith were made the means of spreading it in other places. We cannot but admire in all this the wisdom of the Lord; and yet there is here also a lesson which ought never to be forgotten by the members

---

* Iren. contra Hæres., lib. i., cap. xx., quoted by Dick, in "Lectures on the Acts," p. 144.

of the Christian Church. Neglect of duty will surely bring some sort of punishment in its train ; and as the Church is designed to be aggressive, we may rely upon it, that when either home or foreign missionary effort is abated by it, calamity of some sort is at hand. Either a persecution will arise, as in this instance, which will scatter Christians to their work; or internal dissensions will make their appearance, and the society which should be the abode of peace will be rent asunder by strife and debate; or worldliness will come in like a flood, and sweep away its members into open ungodliness ; or in some other manner "the candlestick will be removed out of its place." The safety and happiness of the Church depend thus, under God, on its efficiency as an aggressive force upon the world. Stagnation is death. The physical philosopher tells us that heat is only a form of motion ; and the warmth of Christian love is only one of the forms of Christian activity. The pool is very soon corrupt, and becomes the home of noisy frogs ; but the river filters itself into purity as it flows, and sings the while a sweet song in the ear of God. So the church that is doing nothing in the missionary enterprise, either for those who dwell in the streets and lanes beside it, or for those in other lands who are sitting in the region and shadow of death, will, ere long, be full of croakers, and all connected with it will become callous and selfish ; while that which is constantly at work for Christ and for the world will be a centre of happiness for its members and a source of joy to all around. Aggression on the world is the safety-valve of the Church ; and when that is closed up, then look out for an explosion !

We are reminded, again, that the reception of the gospel invariably produces joy. What words are these, "There was great joy in that city !" Nor is this a solitary instance in which such terms are employed. Last Lord's day evening we saw that the disciples actually rejoiced that they were counted worthy to suffer shame for Jesus' name ; and if you glance down the chapter from which our theme for to-night has been taken, you will find it recorded of the Ethiopian treasurer, that, after he had been baptized by Philip, "he went his way rejoicing." So, again, we read that "the fruit of the spirit is joy;"* and Paul prays for his Roman friends that the God of hope might fill them "with all joy and peace in believing."† The Gospel thus produces joy. I know that a different impression is prevalent. It is supposed by many that religion is a melancholy thing, and that faith in Jesus Christ has a tendency to make men gloomy, morose, and sad.

Now, there are two ways of accounting for this erroneous view of the matter. It is due, in some, to the fact that all they know about religion is conviction of sin. When they think upon the subject at all, they are immediately impressed with their guilt; they are filled with fear at the mention of God; and trembling gets hold upon them when they hear about the final judgment. But that is not the full Christian experience; for the belief of the Gospel allays all these fears, and gives peace to the troubled soul. Hence, they who call Christianity a melancholy thing are judging of it only from those workings of conscience which reveal the necessity for salvation, and which the acceptance of the Lord Jesus as a Saviour entirely removes. And the view they take is refuted by the recorded experiences of some of its most eminent disciples. What, for example, can be more genial and joyous than the home-life of Martin Luther, as it comes out in his table-talk? What an abode of happiness was the house of Thomas Chalmers! And who that ever heard Thomas Guthrie laugh could doubt the genuineness of his joy? The mention of that last name reminds me of the fact that the autobiography of Dr. Guthrie came into my hands at the same time as that of John Stuart Mill. The one was the sunniest, cheeriest, mirthfullest memoir I ever read; the other was the darkest, saddest, and most dismal work it has ever been my lot to peruse. To me they were

---

* Gal. v., 22. † Rom. xv., 13.

typical instances. Let the one stand as an illustration of the fact that "true piety is cheerful as the day;" let the other indicate how cold and dark the world of atheism must be

But another reason for the impression that the Gospel is a melancholy thing, is to be found in the fact that many of its disciples misrepresent it, and are morose and moody. They go about almost as if it were a sin to laugh, and when they do allow themselves to give way to mirth, they only "grin horribly a ghastly smile." They will always play the part of the mummy at the feast table, and generally they make an opportunity for remarking that "we never read of the Saviour laughing." Now, all that is to caricature Christianity. The Gospel makes men earnest, but never miserable; and there are few things which do more to attract disciples than the manifestation of cheerfulness. "The joy of the Lord" is the Christian's strength, and when that joy is seen by others it commends the Gospel to their acceptance. Why, then, should we not be joyous? Who can better afford to be cheerful than he whose sins are forgiven, and who has the assurance that He who sits upon the throne of heaven is his elder brother? "You seem a happy man," said one to Duncan Matheson, the Scottish evangelist, as he sat singing in a railway-carriage. "Yes," was the reply, "I cannot be but happy; I am safe for time, and safe for eternity." This introduction led to further conversation, which ended in Matheson's being called to preach at the residence of the gentleman who had thus accosted him, and it is the testimony of his biographer that his cheerfulness was often more powerful to win souls than were words of persuasive eloquence.* Friends, let not the lesson be lost upon us: if we wish to be happy, let us become Christians; and if we become Christians, let us be happy Christians, that so our very cheerfulness may be a power in the hands of the Holy Spirit for attracting souls to Christ.

We are reminded by this history, further, that in all times of

---

* "Life and Labours of Duncan Matheson," by the Rev. John Macpherson, p. 305.

religious interest we may expect to meet with cases of hypocrisy. Every revival has its Simon Magus; yet sad as such a fact is, that does not dishonour the work as a whole. You are familiar with the saying that "hypocrisy is the homage which vice renders to virtue;" and if the genuine money had not a certain value, there would be no counterfeiters. So the appearance of a hypocrite in connection with such a work of grace as this at Samaria is only an incidental corroboration of the genuineness of the movement. Now this ought to comfort us when cases of hypocrisy come before us. They are sad, exceedingly; yet they are only the shadows cast by the greatness of the Christian character as a whole; and when we hear of such cases as that which occurred the other day at Boston, when one who had been a Methodist clergyman for years absconded, after committing a series of the most terrible forgeries, let us not think the worse of Christianity because of them. The Christian religion rests on Christ, not on any professed disciple of his; and when such a catastrophe occurs, do not suppose that the foundation of the Church is giving way. The only thing which is sinking is the foundation on which the man's deception stood. That is all! He was always resting on the sand, and the flood of covetousness has swept him away. Had he been building on the rock, it would have been otherwise.

Neither let us imagine that, because a revival has developed a few hypocrisies, therefore it is all a sham. After the flood you will see a few dry sticks left high and dry upon the branches of the trees that line the river's bank; yet it would be a mistake to judge of the effects of the flood by them. These were only the incidental accompaniments of it; but the fertilizing influences that came from it, and the purifying effect it had upon the city through which it ran, are things which cannot be so easily discovered. Yet they are none the less real because of that. When, therefore, our honoured brethren begin their work for God in this city* to-morrow,

---

* The reference here is to the work of Mr. Moody and Mr. Sankey in the Hippodrome.

let us not go into it hunting for hypocrites, but rather desirous by every means in our power to turn their visit to the fullest possible account for Jesus and his cause.

Finally, we are reminded by this history that they who mock at the mercy of God by their hypocrisy in such seasons of privilege are in special danger of becoming aggravated sinners. What a dreadful after history was that of Simon Magus! and how deeply suggestive it is of the fact that it is an awful thing for a man to come into direct and immediate contact with Christ and his salvation! Either he accepts that salvation, and passes on to happiness and glory, or he rejects it, and descends to still deeper degradation than he had ever before touched. The Ethiopian treasurer, after Philip preached Christ to him, "went on his way rejoicing;" but the young man who came to Jesus, and refused to do as he commanded, "went away sorrowful." Ah! the pungency of that sorrow! A new element of bitterness had dropped into his heart, because a new sort of guilt had been incurred by him. So, here, Simon became a more miserable and abandoned wretch than ever. He asked Peter's prayers indeed, but he did not apparently pray for himself; and thus he is here in the ancient narrative held up for a warning to the Church in every age. Let the hypocrites among us learn the lesson for themselves. It is a fearful thing to make merchandise of religion; and if you are giving money to the Church only that she may cover you with respectability and give you a fairer platform for the prosecution of your worldly calling, you are repeating in another form the guilt of Simon here, and will perhaps at last make as dreadful and as disastrous a shipwreck as he did. Remember this: baptism will not save you, for Simon Magus was baptized; a profession of Christian discipleship will not save you, for Simon Magus made such a profession; an interested astonishment at the preaching of the Word and its effects will not save you, for Simon Magus "wondered beholding the miracles and signs which were done." Nothing will save you but that regeneration, that change of heart, which Christ alone can produce by his Holy Spirit. Rest in nothing short of that; and let the story of this ancient sorcerer only give greater emphasis to your prayer, "Create in me a clean heart, O God, and renew a right spirit within me."

XVIII.

ENEAS AND DORCAS.
ACTS ix., 32-42.

BETWEEN the interview with Simon Magus and the incidents now to be considered by us, the sacred historian puts the record of the conversion of Saul, who was afterward called Paul. That event occurred in the neighbourhood of Damascus, from which city the new convert went to Arabia, whence, after spending probably some eighteen months, he returned to Damascus. There he began to labour with so much enthusiasm that the Jews took counsel to slay him, and so, escaping by night from the city, he came again to Jerusalem. But, remembering his former bitterness against them, the brethren there were afraid of him, imagining that his profession of discipleship was a ruse for the purpose of entrapping them into some new snare. By the kind offices of Barnabas, however, he was introduced to the apostles; and when he began to labour among the Grecians, disputing with them after the manner of Stephen, they sought to get rid of him as they had done of the protomartyr. But God had more work for him to do in the world, and he received a commission to depart from the city, with the assurance that he would be sent among the Gentiles. So he went to Tarsus, there to wait upon and watch for the directions of God's providence.

Thus, for the first time, Peter and Paul met and took counsel together. We learn from Paul's letter to the Galatians that his sojourn in Jerusalem on this occasion lasted only fifteen days.* But it was long enough to give each an admiration of the other, and to establish a cordial understanding between them. At first, indeed, Peter might be reserved to one who had been so pronounced an adversary, and so fierce a persecutor of the faith. But his was not a nature to harbour suspicion; and when he saw what Paul really was, he would give him all his heart. He would hear the wondrous story of Paul's conversion, and, as seems likely also, the account of his appointment to the apostleship, and of the revelations which he had received directly and immediately from the Lord, while Paul would learn of Peter's position in the Church, and of the work which had been spreading through Judea and Samaria. We wonder if at this time either of these men had any idea of the magnitude of the work in which they were both engaged, or of the great things which they were both to do and to suffer for Christ's name's sake. This, at least, we do know, that the world around them was altogether unconscious of their pre-eminence. How true it is, that the greatest ones that have ever lived were hardly recognized at all by their contemporaries! At Jerusalem, in those days, if it had been asked whose name was most likely to be remembered in history, some would have specified Gamaliel, and some perhaps would have named Annas, the high-priest; but now the one is principally remembered as the early instructor of Paul, and the other as the persecutor of Peter. So, to-day, the men who will live in history are not to be sought for in our senates, or among those whose names are at present most loudly trumpeted by the heralds of fame. It will turn out at last that they have been obscurely toiling in the midst of us, hardly acknowledged by the leaders of society, and accounted, perhaps, even by those who knew them, fanatical and foolish.

Immediately after mentioning the fact that Saul had retired to Tarsus, the historian says, "Then had the churches rest throughout all Judea, Galilee, and Samaria, and were edified:

---

* Gal. i., 18.

and walking in the fear of the Lord, and in the comfort of the Holy Ghost, were multiplied;" and it has been supposed by some that the cessation of persecution was caused by the conversion of Saul. That, however, is to give Paul a prominence which did not belong to him. His conversion had really occurred two years before; and if it had been the cause of the churches' rest, the description of it would have been connected with his first departure from Jerusalem. The true account of the matter seems to be that the Jews were at this time so much engrossed with other affairs, that they had no leisure to persecute the followers of Jesus. For we have come now to about the date A.D. 39, which puts us in the reign of Caius Cæsar, commonly called Caligula; and Josephus tells us that he had claimed divine honours, and had ordered Petronius to set up his statue in the Temple of Jerusalem. This naturally raised a terrible commotion, not only in the city, but throughout the land; and in their anxiety to keep the holy place from defilement, the people lost for the moment all interest in the movements of the disciples of Christ. But when, through the intercession of Herod Agrippa, the order of Caligula had been rescinded, and Claudius had succeeded to the imperial throne, we shall see that the persecution broke out anew.

Meanwhile, however, there was an interval of tranquillity, and a change of circumstances brought with it for Peter a change of work. While the storm is raging, the mariner's chief attention is given to the safety of the ship, and the post of the officer is on the deck; but when the wind has gone down, he can go below and make minute examination of the cargo and the hull, and do any thing which may be needed in the hold. So while persecution was hot at Jerusalem Peter's place was at Jerusalem; but when an interval of relief was enjoyed, he took the opportunity of making an apostolic visitation of the different churches which had been founded in Palestine.

We have no account of the planting of these churches. We cannot tell whether they were all founded by such missionary journeys as that of Philip to Samaria, or whether they owed their beginning to the labours of some earnest believers, who, having been converted at Jerusalem on the occasion of some festival, returned to their places of abode, bearing with them the good seed of the Word. All we know is, that churches were already in existence in each of the three districts into which Palestine was divided.

Now let us pause a moment to take in the full significance of such a fact. Recollect that we stand at about the year 39 or 40 of the Christian era; but as Christ was born, as all are now agreed, four years before the commencement of the era which has been called by his name, and as his crucifixion occurred when he was thirty-three years of age, this would make his death fall in the year A.D. 29. We are here, therefore, at a point ten years subsequent to the death and resurrection of Christ, and the descent of the Holy Spirit. In that decade thousands were converted at Jerusalem, and these churches in Galilee, Samaria, and Judea came into existence.

Now, if we were right in inferring from the statement of the historian which we considered in our last lecture, that the disciples in Jerusalem had largely neglected missionary work outside of that city, until by persecution they were driven to perform it, then it will follow that the greater part of this progress was made in about three years. For seven years the efforts of the apostles centred in Jerusalem; for the next three years many of the disciples went everywhere preaching the Word, and as the result behold these churches! Here, then, in the very neighbourhood where the facts to which they testified were said to have occurred, the first and greatest successes of the preachers of the Gospel were achieved. In the very locality where their falsehoods, if they had been falsehoods, could have been most easily detected, they made their first converts, and that not by twos or threes, but by thousands. Nay, more; in the face of bitterest opposition and fiercest persecution, these successes were achieved by men who had no world-power at their command, and who were unlearned and ignorant. How shall we account for all this on any other supposition than that the Gospel is true? Some tell us, indeed, that these beautiful biographies which we call the Gospels are mainly mythical and legendary, and that they were created by the churches in the first days of their devotion. But what created the churches? Everybody admits that the churches existed before the books of the New Testament were written; but what created the churches? What but the truth of those well-attested facts that Jesus died and rose again from the dead?

In the course of his journeyings throughout all quarters, Peter came to Lydda. This was a town situated within the limits of the tribe of Ephraim, about nine miles east of Joppa, and on the road between that sea-port and Jerusalem. It was called in Hebrew Lod, or Lud; and a few years subsequent to the date of our narrative it was burned by Gallus on his march against Jerusalem, but it must have been speedily rebuilt, for we find it under the name of Diospolis in the reigns of Severus and Caracalla. In the sixth century it was the seat of a bishopric; and here, according to tradition, that George was born of whom the mythical story of the dragon is told, and who is styled the patron saint of England. The town is now in ruins, and the tomb of St. George is shown, among its attractions, to the traveller; but to me the place would be a thousand-fold more interesting from its association with this visit of the Apostle Peter.

We are not told how long the apostle abode in Lydda, nor are any particulars of his interviews with the members of the Church there preserved for us. The evangelist narrates only one outstanding miracle which was wrought through his instrumentality. He found in the city a poor paralytic named Eneas, who had been for eight years suffering from the palsy, and he raised him from his couch. The history is exceedingly brief, and many points concerning which we should have liked information are left in darkness. Thus we could have wished to ask, whether this man was a Christian before Peter's visit—whether he had himself requested to be healed—how Peter was brought into contact with him—and what, generally, were the surroundings of the miracle? But all such enquiries are vain. We know only that Eneas had lain in helplessness for eight years. Eight years ! Ah ! how much we have to be thankful for in continued health and strength, and how little we think of these blessings until we have lost them ! What weary days and nights he must have had ! And as they told him of the lame man who had been healed at the gate of the Temple, and of the sick ones who had been cured as the shadow of Peter fell on them, while he was passing on the street, how he must have longed to see the great apostle ! But now Peter had come to his own chamber, and as his eyes rested on the loving face of the man of God, he felt, that now, indeed, he was about to be delivered, not by the death he had so long been anticipating, but by the return of that health which he had lost so many years before. Peter said to him, " Eneas, Jesus Christ maketh thee whole." What simple words are these ! yet who can tell what the feelings of Eneas were as he listened ! He knew that strength was passing into him. He felt a tingling life in those limbs which had been paralyzed so long; a strange sensation ran along his nerves; and ere Peter had finished the command, " Arise, and make thy bed," he was able to obey it, and rose at once to fold up his couch. A wonder ! and yet not a wonder. A wonder when we look at Peter, the human instrument; but no wonder at all when we think of Jesus Christ, the Divine agent. It is divine power that works in daily order, and divine choice can alter that order in an individual instance. Hence, let but the Deity of Jesus Christ be granted, and the whole matter is explained.

So felt, and so reasoned, the inhabitants of the town, and of the entire district of Saron that lay between it and Joppa ; for when they saw the man whom Christ had healed, they turned unto the Lord. They were convinced of his Divinity and

Messiahship, and they received as the Gospel to themselves, taking them only in a spiritual sense, the words which Peter spake to Eneas, "Jesus Christ maketh thee whole." Ho! sinner, I say the same to thee to-night. Paralyzed as thou art by sin; unable to help thyself; feeling thyself impotent in the grasp of thine own lusts, this is my message unto thee, "Jesus Christ maketh thee whole." Arise, then! Shake off thy weakness, snap asunder the bonds by which thy sins have held thee fast, and walk forth in the health of soul which Jesus only can confer. All that is needed on thy part is the believing ear and the willing heart. With these, thou mayst be delivered now; without these thou canst be delivered never.

While the apostle abode at Lydda, a message came to him from the brethren at Joppa desiring his immediate presence there. This place, now called Jaffa, is one of the oldest towns in Asia, and is situated on a sandy promontory jutting out into the Mediterranean between Cesarea and Gaza, and at a distance of thirty miles north-west of Jerusalem. Three of its sides are washed by the sea. It was, and still is, the chief port of Judea, and at one time and another has had considerable commercial importance. The modern city is surrounded by a wall, and has from four to five thousand inhabitants. One of its houses is still pointed out as that of Simon the tanner; and whether we accept the statement or not, the fact that on a house-top somewhere in that city the apostle ascended to pray, and saw that remarkable vision which not only reconciled him to the admission of Gentiles into the Church, but also brought him to feel that the glory of God was to be pre-eminently promoted thereby, gives this city an interest to us Gentiles which is second only to that belonging to the place in which Saul of Tarsus was converted to the faith.

The occasion of Peter's summons to Joppa at this time was the death of a disciple who was greatly beloved for her character and kindness. Her name was, in the Syro-Chaldaic tongue, Tabitha, and in the Greek, Dorcas, both meaning "gazelle;"

and, so far as appears, she was either a widow or an unmarried woman, who devoted her energies to the service of Christ in helping the poor and needy. She is described as being "full of good works and alms-deeds which she did." Observe, it is said, "good works," and not simply "good words." We are told, indeed, that "Good words are worth much, and cost little;" but there are some good words that are worth very little indeed. There is among many a saying, "Be ye warmed, and be ye filled," while those things which are needful for the body are not given, and it is in such cases abundantly plain that the expressions are worthless. There was no such hypocrisy, however, about Dorcas. It is particularly noted that she was "full of good works." Let those among us who may be in danger of letting our sympathy evaporate in empty phrases take a lesson from that statement, and henceforth speak principally in actions; for that only is true compassion which exerts itself for the relief of others; and,

"A man of words, and not of deeds,
Is like a garden full of weeds."

It is added that Dorcas was "full of alms-deeds which she did;" and, from the description which is here given, we discover that hers was not the cheap kindness of giving money merely, but that she actually wrought with her own hands for the help of the needy. It is important to note that fact, because in these days there are many who look upon the giving of a subscription to some society as all that is required of them; while there are others who, because they cannot give such a donation, imagine that they can do nothing at all. Now, so far as the record here goes, Dorcas may have been herself a comparatively poor woman. But whether she was or not, the important thing to be observed is, that she did not give her money in order to buy herself off from the obligation to work for the destitute. But she gave both her money and her work. No doubt societies are very useful things. Indeed, we could never get on, in grappling with the evils of our age, without them, but they have certainly special dangers connected with them, and against these we ought always to be on our guard. Even such an one as Thomas Carlyle, many years ago, in one of his suggestive essays, pointed out that we were in danger of being contracted and injured by what he called "machinery" in benevolence. We have associations of every sort, working like moral machines, for the bringing about of certain results; and by subscribing to these we too frequently seek to compound, as it were, for doing nothing in the way of personal service.

I admit, of course, that individual effort cannot do everything. And every one can see that by combination many together, may accomplish more than the same number of persons, working separately, could perform. But, in the carrying on of societies, the benevolent person is too commonly cut off from coming into actual contact and living sympathy with the sufferer who is relieved. A cold, perhaps also sometimes a gruff official takes the place of a generous benefactor.

Now this evil tells both on the giver and on the receiver. The giver is deprived, to a large extent, of the reflex influence that would come back into his own soul from the knowledge of him whom he relieves; and the receiver feels none of that holy and elevating power which stirs his heart at the touch of the giver's hand, and which is valued by him a thousand times more, as, indeed, it is a thousand times better for him, than the gift itself. Hence, while I would not interfere with the working of associations which, in a large city like this, are positive necessities, I would have each Christian, as far as possible, select for himself some one particular corner, however small—no matter though it should contain only one family—for whose benefit he specially works and prays. It is one of the drawbacks to congregational usefulness that we can generally, at least in ordinary times, get money more easily than we can get workers. And there are some reasons for this which must be pronounced valid, and, to a good degree, satisfactory. Thus, in these days, men's energies are largely drained by business, and little time or strength is left after working hours for personal benevolent exertions. But that I can regard only as a great misfortune to the individuals themselves, while it seems to me to be a source of weakness in the Church; for the fellowship of giving and receiving is one of the greatest agencies in knitting men together, and one of the strongest levers for raising the fallen from their degradation.

No matter, therefore, how small the area you undertake may be, I would have you select some special department to which you give not money merely, but yourselves, and in which you seek to labour for the welfare, both temporal and spiritual, of others. Suppose every Christian here were to select but one person, and to say, by the help of God, without taking anything from my subscriptions to good and useful societies, I will do my utmost that this person shall know through me the power of the Gospel, and be saved through my instrumentality from temporal suffering and eternal ruin; how much good might result both to ourselves and to them?

It is just here, I think, that the example of Dorcas is most needed to-day. We do not wish less energy in the work of associations and societies, but, along with that, we do require more individual exertion; and wherever that has been put forth the results have been the happiest possible.

A week or two ago, on the evening before the day of prayer for colleges, the Christian students of Princeton College pledged themselves at a prayer-meeting to each other and to God, that each of them would speak to some one on the next day about his soul's welfare; and out of that, taken in connection with other converging influences, has sprung one of the most genuine and extensive revivals with which that institution has ever been blessed. Let us, both in administering temporal relief and in seeking to benefit men's souls, proceed on a similar principle, and who may estimate the effects that shall be produced?

But I must not forget the history before me. This excellent woman died, and the usual preparations for the funeral were made; but hoping, perhaps, that she might be given back to them, the mourners sent for Peter, who, when he came, saw a very singular sight. There, in the upper chamber of Dorcas's house, was a company of weeping widows, speaking the praises of their benefactress, and showing the coats and garments which she had made for them. They did not ask that she should be raised from the dead; but their sending for him and their tears were even more powerful entreaties than their words would have been; so, putting them all forth, and kneeling down by the body, he prayed; then, turning to the corpse, he said, "Tabitha, arise!" and her soul came to her again. Then, taking her with him, he presented her alive to her friends, and turned their mourning into joy.

Here was a miracle; yet, in the manner of its performance by Peter, much more like the miracles of Elijah and Elisha than those of Christ; for he, like these ancient prophets, was a servant, while Jesus was the Lord from heaven. Not in his own name, or in his own power, was this great work accomplished. It was wrought by Christ at his entreaty, and it resulted in a great spiritual revival; for as at Lydda, so now at Joppa many believed in the Lord.

I have dwelt so much already on the practical bearing of this narrative, and have had so frequent occasion throughout these discourses to refer to the miracles of Christ and his apostles, that I need not now advert to either of these matters. But as in this chapter, for the first time, we come upon one of the most significant names of the Christian disciples, it may be well to conclude our present lecture with a brief consideration of that.

When Ananias was commanded by God to visit Saul at Damascus, he said, " I have heard by many of this man, how much evil he hath done to thy saints at Jerusalem." When Peter went on his apostolic tour throughout all quarters, he came down also to the saints at Lydda. And when he had raised Dorcas from the dead, "he called the saints and widows, and presented her alive."* Now, these are the first occasions on which this term was employed to designate the disciples of Christ; and the very enumeration of them may serve to correct the mischievous impressions which men have received regarding it. By some it is exclusively employed to designate the apostles and evangelists. They always say St. Paul, but they never think of saying St. Abraham or St. Moses. Others confer it only on those who have a place in the Romish calendar, in which truthful history is obliged confess that we may find the names alike of the worthiest and of the vilest of our race; while others still use it in a cynical and contemptuous fashion, to describe those whose religiousness wears a crabbed, gnarled, and repulsive form. Now, coming upon it here, where it first occurs in the history of the Church, we learn to rectify all such opinions.

Its primary significance is—individuals set apart to the service of God: and as only those who had been ceremoniously purified were, under the Jewish law, thus set apart to God's service, the term came to have associated with it the idea of purity. Thus it means persons consecrated to, and purified for, the service of God. Now, this consecration was, on the one side of it, the voluntary dedication of the individuals themselves, but, on the other, the anointing of them by God with his Holy Spirit. Therefore, combining these two things, we may define saints as those who, purified by God's spirit, have dedicated themselves to God's service; and, as thus explained, the name is appropriate to all true believers who are seeking to walk in holiness and love. There is no Scriptural warrant for restricting it exclusively to any persons as a title of special honour, distinguishing them from all other members of the body of Christ. Paul, in writing to the Christians at Rome, addresses them as "called to be saints;" and he speaks to the Corinthians as "to them that are sanctified in Christ Jesus,

---

* Acts ix., 13, 32, 41.

called to be saints." So he begins his epistles to the Ephesians, Philippians, and Colossians thus: "To the saints which are at Ephesus;" "To all the saints in Christ Jesus which are at Philippi;" and "To the saints and faithful brethren in Christ which are at Colosse." Every one, therefore, who has been regenerated by the power of the Holy Ghost, who is washed from his sins by the blood of Christ, and who has consecrated himself to the service of the Lord, is a "saint."

And, as we see from the narrative before me, taken in connection with the passages to which I have referred, their sainthood is to be manifested, not by forsaking the world for a conventual life, but by staying in it, in the places where God has put them, and seeking to benefit those who are around them. Here was Dorcas among her widows doing a work for Christ, and she was a saint indeed. So, in after-days, there were saints in Cæsar's household and in the Roman army; men who, by their earnest piety, were as pleasing to the Lord Jesus in their own callings as either Paul or Peter was in his. This is the kind of sainthood which we need to-day. Show me the man who spurns from him every bribe to do evil as an insult offered, not merely to himself, but to his Lord, and who turns away from it in memory of the Redeemer's cross; show me the merchant, who, out of regard to Jesus, is willing to lose money rather than do a dishonest act; show me the mechanic who works on at his bench, making every article with care and conscience, because he is making it for Christ; show me the politician who will forfeit even the prizes of his party rather than do what he knows to be against the will of God; show me the woman who will brave the scorn of fashion, and the ridicule of society, rather than yield to customs which disgrace her womanhood, and dishonour her Lord; and in each of these I will show you a saint indeed. Yea, wherever a disciple of Jesus is not ashamed to own and obey his Lord, though an unbelieving world should taunt him as a Methodist, you have saintliness of the truest type. Courage, then, my hearers:

there is hope for you that you may win the honour of this name. You may already be nobler saints than any in the purest calendar, for there is a holiness in labour done for Christ; there is a saintliness in the wearing of a constant cheerfulness, when that is felt to be the reflection of the Saviour's smile; there is a halo, brighter than ever artist painted, round a mother's patient love for the children whom she has consecrated in baptism unto the Lord; there is a canonization, more real than ever pope decreed, in the father's faithful toil as, week in, week out, he goes about his round of labour that he may support his family, and bring them up in the nurture and admonition of the Lord. And, haply, in the day when God makes up his jewels, it may be found that out of the ranks of our modern and ordinary life, commonplace as men may call it, there have arisen more Christian heroes than in the time when the disciples sought refuge in the Catacombs, or when martyrs burned at the stake. It is an easy thing, comparatively, to die for Christ, but it is a hard thing, and a noble thing, to live for him. Such a life is the highest sainthood, and to that I incite you now.

> "We need not bid, for cloistered cell,
> Our neighbours and the world farewell :
> The trivial round, the common task,
> Will give us all we ought to ask—
> Room to deny ourselves, a road
> To bring us daily nearer God."

Follow that road; it is the way of holiness; "The unclean shall not walk there; and the wayfaring man though a fool, shall not err therein."

XIX.

CORNELIUS.

Acts x.

THE city of Cesarea was situated on the coast of the Mediterranean Sea, about thirty miles north of Joppa. It was built by Herod the Great, about twenty-two years before the birth of Christ, and named by him after his imperial patron. It was the civil and military capital of Judea so long as it remained a Roman province; and it had a certain pre-eminence belonging to it as the residence of the procurator. Its population was mainly Gentile, though some thousands of Jews dwelt within its walls. At this time it was garrisoned by soldiers, most of whom were native Syrians; but there was one cohort composed of volunteers from Italy, and over a division of that there was a certain centurion named Cornelius, whose character is very pleasingly sketched by the sacred historian. He belonged to an illustrious Roman clan, which had given to the State some of its ablest and most distinguished men; but greater than the glory of Sulla and the Scipios, who had made the Cornelian family everywhere renowned, is that which is conferred on this centurion when it is said that "he was a devout man, and one that feared God with all his house, which gave much alms to the people, and prayed to God always."

These words have been understood by many as equivalent to a declaration that Cornelius was a proselyte to the Jewish religion. But that opinion seems to me to be erroneous; for had he been all that is usually implied in that term, no hesitation would have been felt by Peter, or any one of the disciples, about receiving him into the Christian Church. Among the converts on the day of Pentecost were both Jews and proselytes; and that Cornelius belonged to neither of these classes is evident from the manner in which James refers to him in his address at the Council at Jerusalem, in which these words occur: "Simon hath declared how God at first did visit the Gentiles, to take out of them a people for his name."* We understand, therefore, that he was still uncircumcised, and that, though he had a good report among all the nation of the Jews,† he had not as yet, formally and finally, identified himself with them.

There were, at that time, among both the Greeks and Romans, many thoughtful men, who had become weary of the hollowness and worthlessness of their old religions, and to that class this devout soldier belonged. He had outgrown the superstitions of idolatry and polytheism. He had perhaps made himself familiar with the Greek translation of the Old Testament Scriptures, and had certainly become convinced of the unity and spirituality of God, and of the fact that Jehovah was the hearer of prayer. The great principles underlying the writings of Moses and the prophets had been accepted by him, but he had not yet seen his way to become a proselyte. Perhaps he might have become one if he had never heard of Jesus; but, as it seems to me, when he had come so far in the investigation of these momentous matters as to believe in God, and was about to entertain the question whether he should submit in all respects to the law of Moses, and become virtually a Jew, he heard of the death and resurrection of Jesus; and, being a genuine truth-seeker, he determined to wait for light regarding him before he should take any decisive step. There was, as he could not but see, a division of opinion among the Jews themselves regarding Jesus; and therefore he would not commit himself to Judaism until he had made up his mind about the facts, of which, as appears clearly from Peter's discourse, he had already

---

* Acts xv., 14.   † Acts xv., 22.

heard. Thus he stood outside of Judaism, while yet he was indebted to the Jewish Scriptures for his knowledge of the true God.

If this be a correct description of his position, then it will enable us to understand the special object which he had in view in his fasting and prayer. His four days' devotion must have had a purpose, and it is most natural to suppose that it was connected with a spiritual struggle through which he was passing. There had come to him that question which, in one form or other, confronts every one who even hears about Christ: "What wilt thou do with Jesus who is called Christ?" and in his anxiety as to the answer which he should give, he cried most earnestly to God for light. As Neander has said, "He had probably heard very various opinions respecting Christianity; from many zealous Jews, judgments altogether condemnatory; from others, sentiments which led him to expect that in the new doctrine he would at last find what he had so long been seeking: thus a conflict would naturally arise in his mind which would impel him to seek illumination from God on a question that so anxiously occupied his thoughts."*

Nor did he seek in vain; for, as he prayed, he saw, in a vision, "an angel of God coming in to him, and saying unto him, Thy prayers and thine alms are come up for a memorial before God. And now send men to Joppa, and call for one Simon, whose surname is Peter: he lodgeth with one Simon a tanner, whose house is by the sea-side: he shall tell thee what thou oughtest to do." He was too much in earnest either to doubt concerning the character of this communication, or to delay acting upon it; so he sent two of his servants and a soldier, who was like-minded with himself, to find Peter and bring him to his house.

They started from Cesarea in the evening, and, having rested by the way, it was noon of the next day before they arrived at

---

* Neander's "Planting and Training," vol. i., p. 69.

Joppa. But God had gone before them, and was even then preparing his servant for their appearance. Peter had retired to the flat roof of the house in which he lodged for the purpose of enjoying a season of devotion; and as he was engaged in prayer he became very hungry, and desired food to be made ready for him; but while the servants were preparing it, he fell into a trance, in which he saw, three times repeated, a very singular vision. A great sheet was let down to him from the open heaven, "wherein were all manner of four-footed beasts of the earth, and wild beasts and creeping things, and fowls of the air." As it came down to him, he heard a voice saying to him, "Arise, Peter; slay and eat." But the strong convictions of the apostle remonstrated against such a command, and he replied, "Not so, Lord; for I have never eaten anything that is common or unclean;" whereupon the voice answered, "What God has cleansed, that call thou not common."

The meaning of this is apparent to us in a moment. It was a symbolical revelation of the fact that the restrictions of the Mosaic law were now removed; and that the distinction between Jew and Gentile, out of which these grew, and for the maintenance of which they were designed, was now abolished. It indicated that now "creation itself had been purified, and rendered clean for our use by the satisfaction of Christ,"* and that men of all nations were now to be dealt with in the same manner for salvation.

Peter, indeed, did not see all that just at the moment; but while he was pondering on the vision, and wondering what it meant, he was helped to a clearer comprehension of it by the arrival of the servants of Cornelius, and by the message which they brought. They told him of the vision which had come to their master; and that gave him a key to the interpretation of the communication that had come to himself. So, putting the two together, he determined to go with the

---

* Alford, "Commentary" *in loco.*

men to Cesarea. But, knowing how jaded they were with their journey, he lodged them for the night, and set out with them the next day.

As we learn from the statement made by him afterward at Jerusalem,* he took with him six brethren from Joppa; and it is not difficult to account for such a precaution. His own extraordinary vision, taken in connection with the narrative told by the servants of the centurion, convinced him that some important event in the history of the Church was about to happen, and he desired that Jewish witnesses should be present, to give a faithful report of every thing that might occur. He wished also that they should take part with him in the performance of any duty that might develop its obligation at the moment. And so we see that, impulsive and impetuous as Peter was by nature, he was not by any means destitute of prudence; for in this instance his conduct was worthy both of praise and imitation.

The party arrived at Cesarea on the following morning; and when Peter reached the house of Cornelius, he found a considerable assembly, composed of the kinsmen and friends of the centurion. As he entered, the Roman officer met him, and fell down before him; not to pay him divine homage, for Cornelius knew better than to do that, but to show him respect according to the custom of the country. Yet, knowing how likely his acceptance of any such honour was to be misunderstood, Peter said unto him, "Stand up; I myself also am a man:" an expression which showed also that he had already learned the great lesson of the vision on the house-top, which was the equality of men in the sight of God.

When he came into the chamber where the household and friends of Cornelius were assembled, he thought it needful to explain how he, a Jew, came to be in such close contact with the Gentiles, and gave his interpretation of the Divine revela-

---

* Acts xi., 12.

tion which had been made to him in these emphatic words: "God hath showed me that I should not call any man common or unclean." Then, referring to his prompt response to the invitation which he had received, he asked the centurion why he had sent for him. In reply, Cornelius detailed those particulars with which we are already familiar, and concluded his narrative with these earnest words, which reveal his sense of the importance of the occasion: "Now therefore are we all here present before God, to hear all things that are commanded thee of God." In response to this appeal, Peter delivered to them a sermon quite as remarkable as any of those which are recorded in this wonderful history. He began with a reiteration of the great doctrine which had been revealed to him in the vision at Joppa: "Of a truth I perceive that God is no respecter of persons; but in every nation he that feareth him, and worketh righteousness, is accepted with him."

Yet let us not misunderstand these words; for through the oversight of the circumstances in which they were uttered many have drawn from them inferences which they do not warrant. They do not imply that the persons in regard to whom they are used are already saved, for Cornelius was one of them; and in the next chapter we read that when the angel commanded him to send for Peter, he said, "Who shall tell thee words whereby thou and all thy house shall be saved."* Up till that moment, therefore, Cornelius and his friends were unsaved. Hence the acceptance here does not denote salvation. What it does mean is virtually the same thing as the apostle had already expressed when he said, "God hath showed me that I should not call any man common or unclean."

Alford's note on the passage is exceedingly clear and valuable, and no words of mine could give the true interpretation so forcibly. He says: "The question which recent events

---

* Acts xi., 14.

had solved in Peter's mind was that of the admissibility of men of all nations into the Church of Christ. In this sense only had he received any information as to the acceptableness of men of all nations before God. He saw that in every nation men who seek after God, who receive his witness of himself, without which he has left no man, and humbly follow his will as they know it, these have no extraneous hindrance, such as uncircumcision, placed in their way to Christ, but are capable of being admitted into God's Church, though Gentiles, and as Gentiles. That only such are spoken of is agreeable to the nature of the case; for men who do not fear God and work righteousness are out of the question, not being likely to seek such admission. It is clearly unreasonable to suppose Peter to have meant that each heathen's natural light and moral purity would render him acceptable in the sight of God; for if so, why should he have proceeded to preach Christ to Cornelius, or indeed anywhere at all? And it is equally unreasonable to find any verbal or doctrinal difficulty in the phrase 'worketh righteousness,' or to suppose that righteousness must be taken in its forensic sense, and therefore that he alludes to the state of men after becoming believers. He speaks popularly, and certainly not without reference to the character he had heard of Cornelius, which consisted of these very two parts—he feared God and abounded in good works."

Thus, then, the doctrine of this verse is, that mere external things, such as parentage, nationality, and the like, are neither any recommendation of a man to God, nor any barrier in his way to God. The restrictions of the Mosaic institute were at an end; and in Christ Jesus there was to be "neither circumcision nor uncircumcision, barbarian, Scythian, bond nor free." Hence this passage has little or nothing to do with the question as to the possibility of the salvation of the heathen without the knowledge of the Gospel; and as to that of the possibility of the salvation of a man in a Christian land who is not a believer in Jesus Christ, but is living in morality and benevolence, it is decisive against it; for Cornelius accepted the Saviour when he was set before him; and if he had not done so, he would have been himself rejected.

Let no hearer of the Gospel, therefore, who is disbelieving Christ attempt to shelter himself behind this saying of Peter. As to the heathen, we may well leave them in the hands of God, believing that "the Judge of all the earth shall do right;" but as to ourselves, if, having heard the Gospel, we reject the Saviour, this will be "the condemnation that light is come into the world, and we have loved the darkness rather than the light, because our deeds are evil." Responsibility is according to privilege; the heathen will not be condemned for rejecting a Saviour of whom they have never heard, for they who have sinned without law shall also perish without law; but if we refuse this great salvation, our guilt will be greater than that of the inhabitants of Sodom, and our doom will be more terrible than that of Gomorrah.

After this introduction, Peter goes on to rehearse the Gospel to his audience. He takes it for granted that they had heard the reports which had been circulated far and wide about Jesus of Nazareth, and he proceeds to give a more formal account of the mission and work of the Lord. He begins with a reference to his old master, John, and tells of the baptism of Jesus, at which, by the descending Spirit, he was specially and abundantly anointed for his great work as the prophet, priest, and king of his people. He repeats the beautiful story of his beneficent life, and dwells especially upon his casting out of devils from them that were possessed, as a proof of the fact that God was with him. Then he brings himself and his brother apostles forward as witnesses, who spoke not from hearsay, but concerning things which came under their own observation. He refers to the crucifixion of Jesus by the Jews, to his resurrection from the dead, to the fact that he was seen of many after that event, and that he himself was one of those who did eat and drink with him. Then, without any special allusion to his ascension into heaven, he speaks of the command which had been given to the disciples "to preach unto the people, and to testify that it is he which was ordained of God to be the judge of quick and dead," and concludes with the declaration "that through his name whosoever believeth in him shall receive remission of sins."

It is interesting to compare the discourse thus epitomized with that which he delivered on Pentecost, and to observe that, with incidental variations, arising from the different circumstances in which they were delivered, there is yet virtual identity. In the Jerusalem sermon, which was addressed to Jews, there is copious reference to the Old Testament Scriptures; in this, while there are one or two allusions to the prophets, there are no formal quotations from them. In that, his hearers were directly charged with the guilt of the crucifixion; in this, he does not seem to connect his audience with that dreadful crime, but simply says, "whom they slew, and hanged upon a tree." In that, the conclusion was essentially Jewish: "Let all the house of Israel know assuredly that God hath made this same Jesus, whom ye have crucified, both Lord and Christ"; in this, the conclusion embraces humanity in its ample sweep, and emphasizes that glorious "whosoever," which is the sinner's encouragement in every Gospel invitation; but in both the personal Saviour is the great central figure. He set him before men's eyes, and directed them to believe in him for forgiveness and holiness. In spite of the temptation which on both occasions might have enticed him to put himself forward, he studiously placed himself behind his Master, and claimed only to be a witness-bearer to his majesty, his benevolence, and his grace.

While he was yet speaking, and indeed, as it appears, just as he was in the act of repeating the gracious invitation to which I have referred, the Holy Ghost miraculously descended on all them that heard the Word. It is not said in what form he came; but as, in the account which Peter gave at Jerusalem, he said, "The Holy Ghost fell on them as on us at the beginning;" and as the effects following on the descent were similar to those witnessed on the day of Pentecost, "they spake with tongues, and magnified God," I think it probable that here also there were "cloven tongues like as of fire."

This miraculous endowment of Cornelius and his friends with the Holy Ghost served three purposes; it certified the truth of Peter's words; it proved to Peter and to those who were with him the genuineness of the faith of the Gentile converts; and as it was bestowed through no apostolic intervention, but directly and immediately by the Lord, it indicated his will that they who had received it should be then and there admitted to the membership of the Church. Thus, at least, Peter understood it; for he said, "Can any man forbid water, that these should be baptized which have received the Holy Ghost as well as we?" So he commanded them to be baptized in the name of the Lord. He did not administer the ordinance himself, but left it, as seems probable, to the brethren who accompanied him to do that act, believing with Paul, "that Christ had sent him not to baptize, but to preach the Gospel."

This was the Pentecost of the Gentiles; and so it was brought about that Peter opened the door of the Church for their admission according as the Lord had promised him. In many respects he was the most unlikely among the apostles for the performance of such a work; but, by the discipline of God's Holy Spirit, he was brought to see that no man was common or unclean; and when he beheld the descent of the Holy Ghost on Cornelius and his friends, he felt that to resist their admission into the Church would be "to fight against God."* So he cheerfully acquiesced; and, far from counting it a disagreeable duty, or from being eager to get away from the Gentiles, he consented to their prayer that he should tarry with them certain days.

---

* Acts xi., 17.

Thus the infant Church, under the guidance of its Lord, took a new departure, and entered upon that world-wide mission in which it is still engaged. At Cesarea, first, its preachers found out fully that its field was the world, and the churches of the Gentiles are the noble fruits of Peter's obedience to the heavenly vision.

Many interesting and important lessons are suggested by this striking narrative, but I can mention only one or two.

We may learn, then, in the first place, that the way to get light is to act up to that which we have, and pray for more. Cornelius was seeking after God. He had not yet found Christ, but he had found something, and "whereto he had attained he walked by that rule." He had discovered that God was one, that he was spiritual, that he was the hearer of prayer, and that he had enjoined upon men holiness and benevolence. So he acted upon these principles out of regard to God's will, and waited upon him in earnest prayer that he might know yet more concerning him. Then God sent directions to him, in the following of which he was led to fuller understanding of the truth, and to salvation through Christ.

Now, this is a uniform law of God's procedure. It is recognized by the Psalmist when he says, "Unto the upright there ariseth light in the darkness;"* and it is repeatedly referred to by our Lord himself as when he says, "Unto everyone that hath shall be given;"† and "If any man will do his will, he shall know of the doctrine, whether it be of God."‡ If, therefore, anyone here should be in a spiritual struggle, longing for light, and eagerly anxious to know what he must do, let me ask him to define clearly to himself what he does see and believe, and let me beseech him to act up to that; for as he does so, light will break upon his path, and in some way or other direction will be given him.

Those who have read the memoir of Frederick Robertson will remember how he stayed himself up with this principle

---

* Psa. cxii., 4.   † Matt. xxv., 29.   ‡ John vii., 17.

during that dark wrestle with doubt and disbelief which he had in his journey through the Tyrol. Everything else went from him, but he could hold by this : " It is always right to do right ;" and in the acting out of that he regained his hold of Christ. So let the seekers and the tempted among us follow his example, and cry mightily to God. He will guide us into the truth. Not now, indeed, by miracle as he led Cornelius; but we may rely upon it that if we are but earnest in our search, and faithful in our effort to act up to what we do know, he will, in some way or other, open up our way before us, making crooked things straight and rough places smooth. Here are his own assurances : " If from thence thou shalt seek the Lord thy God, thou shalt find him, if thou seek him with all thy heart and with all thy soul;"* "If any of you lack wisdom, let him ask of God, that giveth to all men liberally, and upbraideth not; and it shall be given him. But let him ask in faith, nothing wavering : for he that wavereth is like a wave of the sea driven with the wind and tossed."†

We may learn, in the second place, that in all spiritual matters we should be prompt. Cornelius lost no time in sending messengers for Peter. He was in earnest, and the sooner he could find rest for his soul, the better. Nay, after Peter came, he took in all he said while he was yet speaking, and so received the Holy Ghost. Let every inquirer imitate him in this:

> " To-day is yours ; to-morrow never yet
> On any human being rose or set."

Therefore do at once that which is needed to secure your soul's welfare. When Moses asked Pharaoh when he should entreat the Lord to remove the frogs that were croaking through all the palace, and leaping on his very couches, he said, "To-morrow!" and you marvel at his folly. You think that if you had been in his circumstances you would have said, " The sooner the better." But beware lest, in censuring him, you do

---

* Deut. iv., 29.   † James i., 5-6.

not condemn yourself; for when we press upon your attention the importance of spiritual and eternal things, and ask you to get rid of your sins, you say to us, "Yes, yes; you are speaking the truth, and I will attend to it soon, some time, to-morrow;" and when the morrow comes, the cry is still "To-morrow!" and when a death-bed comes, "to-morrow" is—in hell! Oh! be not so foolish. "To-day if ye will hear his voice, harden not your hearts." You do not need to send to Joppa in order to have the truth proclaimed to you. Nay, "The word is nigh thee, even in thy mouth, and in thy heart: that is, the word of faith, which we preach; that if thou shalt confess with thy mouth the Lord Jesus, and shalt believe in thine heart that God hath raised him from the dead, thou shalt be saved."* Linger not a moment longer, therefore, but "believe and live."

But the promptitude of Peter is as remarkable as that of Cornelius, and we who have to deal with men about their souls should take a lesson from his example. He went with the men "without gainsaying, as soon as he was sent for." So we ought to be willing, at any sacrifice of personal convenience, to help a sinner to salvation through Christ.

Many years ago, in connection with an effort which was made to reach the non-church-going population of Liverpool, I preached to an enormous audience in a circus. It required from me a great physical effort, so that when my discourse was finished I was myself completely prostrated. While I was in that condition, and before I had left the place, a person came up wishing to speak with me about the way of life. I made an appointment with him to meet me the next morning. But he never came. And so I have written down that as one of the lost opportunities of my life. I had not then fully learned the lesson which the Master taught me by the well of Sychar, and I cannot look back upon my error without emotion. Had I spent a few minutes with that man, he might haply have been

---

* Rom. x., 8, 9.

brought to Christ. The memory of that incident has been a spur to me in later years; and I have told it now, that all of us who, in the providence of God, may have an opportunity of dealing with an inquiring sinner, may use promptitude. "The king's business requireth haste." Now—alike for preacher and hearer—is the accepted time.

We may learn here, thirdly, that preachers and hearers are prepared for each other by God. Cornelius is led in a peculiar manner to send for Peter; Peter is fitted in a manner equally peculiar for going to Cornelius; and when they come together the result is a blessing. Now, it is precisely so yet with ordinary ministers and hearers—with this difference, that in our days the preparation is effected by the usual means of God's providence, and not by miracle. The preacher is led through a special spiritual history; he is guided to the choice of a particular subject, which his experience leads him to treat in a distinctive manner, and he is led to preach it in a place which perhaps is at a considerable distance from his stated field of labour. The hearer, again, is brought through certain circumstances, say of trial, temporal distress, bereavement, or spiritual perplexity; he is led on a certain day to a certain place of worship; he can give no precise reason why on that day he went to that place, but there he met the message which God intended for him. It seems to him, as he listens, that the preacher must somehow have known his past life, and is at the moment in possession of his innermost secrets; and speaking thus to his circumstances, he is blessed in his conversion.

This is no uncommon history. I have known many such cases in my own experience; and so firm is my faith in what I may call the forerunning grace of the Spirit and the particular providence of God, that I never preach to any audience, small or great, without the conviction that I am sent with a special word for someone there. Nay, more, I am impressed with the belief that God makes the moods and feelings and the personal and domestic history of the preacher a means of preparing him to benefit his people; and I try to think, when I am in joy or in sorrow, in despondency or in light, that God has sent me on ahead of my people, that I may be able the better to guide them in prosperity, and in adversity may "comfort them with the comfort wherewith we ourselves have been comforted of God." Jehovah gives the preacher visions now, not by "trances" upon the house-top, but through discipline and trial. Tears are often the telescopes through which he gives them a sight of the invisible; and their best sermons are those which he has written first upon their own hearts by the sharp "stylus" of affliction.

When Ezekiel was bereaved of his wife, it was that he might be made a sign to the people among whom he prophesied; and the personal history of the preacher prepares him to speak a word in season to them that are weary. But if this be so with him, the circumstances of the hearers ought to prepare them also for some helpful message through the pulpit; and every week you should be on the outlook for it, for such expectant hearers are never disappointed. If there were more audiences like that in the household of Cornelius, saying, "We are all here present before God to hear all things that are commanded thee of God," there would be more preachers like Peter. Model hearers will make model ministers. Ah, at how many points our histories touch each other! and while we are unconscious of the providence that is thus over us all, how God is working out his gracious purpose in us all! This subject ought to give new importance to the pulpit in your regard; and I am sure that it has given me new confidence and inspiration as a preacher of the cross. I am not drawing, day by day, my bow at a venture. I do not see, indeed, where the arrow is to find its mark; but the Holy Spirit is to me as the old prophet was to Israel's king,* for his hands are upon my hands; and as the bowstring twangs, he cries, "The arrow of the Lord's

---

* 2 Kings xiii., 17.

deliverance." Faithful preaching is never in vain; and the history of Cornelius sends me away to-night with a new interpretation of the poet's lyric:

> "I shot an arrow into the air:
> It fell to earth I knew not where;
> For so swiftly it flew, the sight
> Could not follow it in its flight.
>
> "I breathed a song into the air:
> It fell to earth I knew not where;
> For who has sight so keen and strong
> That it can follow the flight of song?
>
> "Long, long afterward, in an oak,
> I found the arrow still unbroke;
> And the song, from beginning to end,
> I found again in the heart of a friend."

No sermon preached for Christ misses its mark. Let the ministers among us take comfort at the thought, and labour on. We shall meet the fruits of our discourses in the better land.

XX.

PETER PRAYED OUT OF PRISON.
Acts xii.

THE proceedings of Peter in the household of Cornelius were heard of by the members of the Church of Jerusalem with surprise, and on his return to the Holy City the apostle was put on his defence for going in to men that were uncircumcised and eating with them. In reply he gave a simple narrative of all that had occurred, and called upon the six brethren who had accompanied him to Cesarea to confirm his statements; and the result was that his adversaries "held their peace, and glorified God, saying, Then hath God also to the Gentiles granted repentance unto life."

Shortly after this, tidings were brought to the members of the mother Church that certain of those who had left Jerusalem in consequence of the persecution in which Stephen suffered had gone to Antioch, and preached the Gospel to the Gentiles there; and Barnabas was sent as a special commissioner to examine into the matter and report. He found that a great number had believed and turned unto the Lord, and the sight of their decision and earnestness filled his heart with joy; while at the same time the success of the preachers among them gave him such an impression regarding the hopefulness of the field in their city, that he went at once to Tarsus, and brought Paul thence to labour with him in Antioch.

Here for a whole year these noble men continued their ministry, isolated in a great degree from the brethren in Judea, yet so interested in their welfare that at a time of famine they carried to the saints in Jerusalem a liberal contribution for their relief. But they did not remain long in the city which was so dear to them both, for just then a fresh persecution, organized and prosecuted by Herod the king, broke out against the Christians there.

This monarch was distinguished by the unscrupulous cruelty which characterized all the members of the family to which he belonged; and after a chequered career, remarkable for intrigue, cunning, and sycophancy, he was now upon the throne of Judea. He was the grandson of that Herod the Great who caused the murder of the infants at Bethlehem; the brother of that Herodias who instigated the execution of John the Baptist; and the father of that Agrippa before whom Paul afterward made his noble defence at Cesarea. He is commonly known in history as Herod Agrippa I.; and a brief epitome of his life up to this closing incident of his career may help to give you some idea of his personal character, as well as of the lawlessness and corruption of the age in which he lived.

Fleeing from Palestine to escape the rage of his grandfather, he spent the greater part of his youth in Rome; but by a course of reckless extravagance, he reduced himself to such poverty that he was obliged, in the year 23, to return to Judea. After living there in great penury for three years, he revisited Rome, and through the influence of his mother, Bernice, he was kindly received by the Emperor Tiberius, and became the friend of Caius Caligula, the heir-apparent, and afterward the occupant, of the imperial throne. Happening, in conversation, to express a wish that his friend were emperor, one who overheard his words repeated them to Tiberius, who threw him into prison and kept him there in chains; but when Caligula reached the throne, he was set at liberty and loaded with honours. The new emperor gave him a golden chain equal in weight to the iron one by which he had been bound, and conferred upon him, with the title of king, the two tetrarchies of Palestine, which happened at that time to be vacant. By his prudent management, he prevailed upon the emperor not to insist upon his impious demand to have his statue set up in the Temple of Jerusalem; and, true to his policy of worshipping the rising sun, after the murder of Caligula, in the plotting of which some suppose he had a share, he secured the favour of his successor Claudius, who confirmed the grants of the former emperor, and added to them the sovereignty of Judea and Samaria, thereby making him ruler of the whole territory over which his grandfather had held sway.

At the date of the events in this chapter he was in the fifty-fourth year of his age; and though he had offended the stricter Jews by his introduction of Roman customs, yet by his success in procuring the revocation of the odious edict of Caligula, and by seeking in every way to propitiate the favour of the people, he was very popular among his subjects. Josephus* has thus described him: "This king was by nature very beneficent and liberal in his gifts; and being very ambitious to oblige people with such large donations, he made himself very illustrious by the many expensive presents which he bestowed. He took delight in giving, and rejoiced in living with good reputation. . . . . Accordingly, he loved to live continually at Jerusalem, and was exactly careful in the observance of the laws of his country. He therefore kept himself entirely pure; nor did any day pass over his head without its appointed sacrifice."

The sacred and profane historians are thus in perfect accord regarding this man. The master passion of his soul, in the view of both, was to please the people. His ruling principle was love of display, for the purpose of obtaining the admiration and the good opinion of the multitude. This made him, among Jews, an exact and even scrupulous Jew; and it was only natural that his pious zeal should show itself in seeking to extirpate the Christians; while again, seeing how grateful this was to the feelings of those with whom he came into contact, he was thereby encouraged to prosecute the work of intolerance

---

* "Antiquities," 19, 7, 1.

with increasing energy. How mixed the motives which operate in the human heart! and in how many is an apparent zeal for some religious cause only the outcome of personal vanity and the desire to secure the favour of the multitude! Not such assistance nor such defenders does the truth require; for he who is its Lord has said to all his followers, "Put up the sword into its scabbard."

The principal victim of Herod's persecution was the Apostle James. We know nothing more of this early martyr than what has been told us in the sacred narrative. He was the son of Zebedee and Salome, and the brother of John. He was one of the three most favoured disciples, and was present at the raising of Jairus's daughter, and on the Mount of Transfiguration. He was, besides, one of those who were taken farthest with Jesus into the Garden of Gethsemane. Along with John, he was so distinguished for zeal and energy in the Master's cause, that he called them Boanerges ("sons of thunder"). And as it is the loftiest towers that are first struck by the lightning, and the tallest trees that feel most the fury of the blast, it is probable that by eminence, ability, and success he stood so prominently forward among the Christians as to attract the attention and provoke the enmity of their opponents. For him and John his mother had asked from the Redeemer the highest posts of honour in his kingdom; and though he said that she knew not what she asked, he promised that they should drink of his cup, and be baptized with his baptism.

In different forms this cup was presented to them. John lived to be the last witness-bearer of the apostles, and passed through many fiery trials; but James, in his early ministry— for it was yet no more than thirteen years since the crucifixion —followed Jesus, through the fire of martyrdom, to the throne of glory. Perhaps, as he was being led forth to be beheaded by the sword, there might come back upon him the memory of the Lord's answer to his mother's request, and with that the feeling that he was entering into the fellowship of his

Redeemer's sufferings preparatory to the sharing with him of his glory. We cannot tell, but we may be sure that he who sustained Stephen in that hour

> "When, from a happy place,
> God's glory smote him on the face,"

would not forsake James; and, though little or nothing is here said of his departure, we are not, on that account, to think that his bearing would be less worthy of a Christian apostle than that of Paul in after-days. His dying words are not recorded, nor is his courage dwelt upon. It is taken as a thing of course that he glorified Christ in both; and yonder he is one of the foremost leaders in that "noble army of martyrs" who praise the Lord continually.

Encouraged by the effect produced on the minds of the Jews by the killing of James, and wishing still further to secure their applause, Herod apprehended Peter, and put him in prison until the Passover should be over, intending then to make a grand public spectacle of his execution. What was a human life or two to him, compared with his darling popularity? That he might not be foiled in his plans, he watched his victim very closely. Not only was he put in prison, but sixteen soldiers were appointed to keep guard over him day and night, four and four by turns. Two were in the dungeon with him, one being chained to him on each side; one was at the door of his dungeon, and one was at the prison door itself: and all these precautions were taken over and above the ordinary safeguards of the place.

One might have thought it was a waste of resources thus to set soldiers beside a poor defenceless man. What had he done that he should be so guarded? Was he some murderous Barabbas, or some powerful partisan? or had he behind him some unscrupulous associates, who would resort to violence and set him free? Nothing of the kind. He was an unlettered man, who preached "Jesus and the resurrection." But there were some about Herod who could tell of this same Peter that once before he had got out of prison they knew not how; and so he would be sure that there would be no second deliverance. Vain man! Did he think himself a match for God? Did he imagine that, if it was God's will to set his servant free, his bolts and bars and sentinels would matter anything? Very likely he did not think of Jehovah in the matter at all; but in the end he was constrained to confess that Providence was stronger than his prison. For some days, indeed, nothing occurred to disturb his equanimity. It was the very night before the coming spectacle. It was probably the last watch of the night; all arrangements had been made; and he was, perhaps, by anticipation congratulating himself on the splendour of the show which the morrow was to usher in, when, all silently and divinely, his prisoner was taken out of his hands.

How this was accomplished is minutely told us in the narrative. The brethren of the Church were unceasing and earnest in their prayers on Peter's behalf. The ear of Herod was denied them; and even though they could have obtained access to him, there was little hope of moving him from his determination; but they made supplication unto God. Beautiful exceedingly is this trait in the character of these simple-hearted ones. They were not anxious for their own safety merely, but tenderly attached to Peter, who had been so identified with the early history of the Church, and who, by his zeal and affection, had endeared himself to them all. Therefore they brought his case to Jesus. Nay, seeing days of darkness settling down upon the spiritual society of which they were members, and knowing how valuable the son of Jonas was as a counsellor and leader, they were anxious for the future of the Church. "Their hearts trembled for the ark of God;" and to God, its omnipotent protector and sure defence, they made their appeal. We know not how they shaped their supplications, or what it was precisely that they asked; but we may conjecture that they earnestly besought either that he might be delivered, or that he might be sustained and strengthened so to die as to demonstrate to every beholder the beauty and power of that truth which he had so earnestly proclaimed. Nay, the very remembrance of that former deliverance, the report of which, perhaps, made Herod guard the prison so securely, would make them more earnest and believing in their prayers. They had no misgivings as to God's willingness to hear or ability to help; and so they agreed to meet each other at the throne of grace, and make united supplication for the much-loved apostle; for had they not this as their warrant: "If any two of you shall agree on earth touching anything, ye shall ask the Father in my name, and it shall be given you?"

And what, meanwhile, of Peter? The sacred historian is silent concerning his prison exercises; but we cannot doubt that he, too, would commit his cause to his Redeemer, and would calmly and peacefully wait the issue. The next day, so far as he knew, was to see his public execution; but he would sleep as usual. So, unbinding his girdle, and throwing off his upper garment, and loosing his sandals, he lay down to rest. We may not argue too much from this, indeed, for many of the vilest malefactors have slept soundly on the eve of their death; yet if an eloquent historian and a brilliant artist have both singled out the "Last Sleep of Argyle" as a beautiful and touching illustration of the calm composure which a peaceful conscience gives, even in the most appalling circumstances, we may surely be excused for remarking on the deep slumber of Peter here. On the one hand, we may see in it the evidence of his spiritual tranquillity, and, on the other, we may view it as a signal instance of the benignity of him who "giveth his beloved sleep." And who would not prefer the rest of the apostle, though his couch was in a prison, and his hands were manacled, to that of Herod in his palace, surrounded with all the luxuries of rank and wealth? Better far the clanking chains that bind the limbs than those more insidious bonds that fetter the soul.

But not long now was Peter to be fettered; for, all unchallenged by the sentinels, the angel of the Lord entered the cell, and awoke the apostle while yet his keepers slept. He bade him rise up quickly, and, as he rose, the chains fell from his hands. He commanded him to gird himself, and bind on his sandals—for when God works there is no undue haste; and then, asking him to cast his upper garment round him, he said, "Follow me." Scarcely knowing whether he were "in the body or out of the body," and hardly believing that he was not in a trance, the apostle accompanied him. They passed in safety the other two guards who had been so warily posted; and when they came to the outer gate of iron that opened into the city, lo! it swung back of itself before them, and they stood upon the street! Then all need of miracle was over, and the angelic messenger departed, leaving Peter in a state of bewilderment. But soon he came to see how it had been, and acknowledging God's care over him, he turned his steps to the house of Mary, whose son, John Mark, was already known in the Church. There, all untimely as was the hour, many were assembled in earnest prayer. The portress came to the gate as he knocked, and, recognizing his well-known voice, she ran to tell the news that he was there, instead of opening the gate, as a sensible girl should have done. The friends would not believe her words. They insisted that she had seen an apparition like the apostle, or that she had been visited by his guardian angel; for Jesus had declared that every one of his dear ones has a guardian angel before God's face; and they believed—whether rightly or wrongly, the historian does not tell us—that such ministering spirits may occasionally appear in the likeness of him whom it is their office to attend.

In their controversy about this matter, one wonders that none of them should have thought of going directly to the gate and making personal investigation; but the circumstances were so unusual that we may well excuse the flutter into which they were put. Meanwhile the knocking continued; and when at length the gate was opened, there, in reality, was Peter, and they were astonished. They had been praying for his deliverance, and when the answer came they were surprised. Alas! it has been often so since. Our faith is so feeble that when an answer to our supplications comes, it takes us by surprise; whereas, if we were really believing, the wonder would be that an answer should not come.

The appearance of Peter was the occasion of much inquiry among them all. Many of them were speaking at once, and a kind of confusion ensued; but with a presence of mind greater than that of any in the meeting, Peter realized the danger in which he stood, and so, proclaiming silence by the beckoning of his hand, he told them all that God had done for him, and commanded them to inform the members of the Church in general, and in particular James (usually called the Less, and sometimes denominated the Lord's brother), of his deliverance. Thereafter he departed to seek safety by prudent concealment.

In the morning great consternation was felt when it was known that the prisoner had escaped; and Herod, in his wrath, caused the keepers to be put to death. His fine scheme of a public execution had been frustrated, but his proud heart had not been humbled; for he went immediately to Cesarea, and, as we know from Josephus, began to hold a great festival in honour of Claudius. Either it was the celebration of the emperor's birthday, or the observance of the games known as the "Quinquennalia," or fifth-year exhibition; or, as is most likely, a special festival to mark the triumphant return of Claudius from Great Britain, where he had conquered some of the native princes. During these games, he publicly received a deputation from the inhabitants of Tyre and Sidon, with whom he had been at variance. It does not appear that there had been any actual war; but as the people in Sidonia depended almost entirely on Palestine for their supplies of food, it was very inconvenient to have any rupture of any sort with the king; so, having, probably by a handsome gift, secured the good offices of Blastus, the chamberlain, they obtained a reconciliation, and in their fulsome adulation used words of blasphemy, which Herod knew were altogether inappropriate to him, but which he did not put from him. In the midst of all this pomp, he was smitten with a deadly disease in the bowels, and in five days he was no more.

The history of Josephus is here so interesting, and so tends not only to confirm, but also to illustrate, the narrative before me, that I shall transcribe it entirely. You will observe, as I do so, how characteristic it is of divine inspiration that Luke makes no mention of the ill-omened owl, which is so prominent in the story of the Jew: "Now, when Agrippa had reigned three years over all Judea, he came to the city Cesarea, which was formerly called Strato's tower; and there he exhibited shows in honour of Cesar, upon his being informed that there was a certain festival celebrated to make vows for his safety. At which festival a great multitude was gotten together of the principal persons and such as were of dignity through his province. On the second day of the shows, he put on a garment of silver tissue, and of a texture truly wonderful, and came into the theatre early in the morning. The silver of his garment, being illuminated by the fresh reflection of the sun's rays upon it, shone out after a surprising manner, and was so resplendent as to spread a horror over those that looked intently upon him. Presently his flatterers cried out, one from one place, and another from another (though not for his good), that he was a god; and they added, 'Be thou merciful to us; for although we have hitherto reverenced thee only as a man, yet shall we henceforth own thee as superior to mortal nature.' Upon this the king did neither rebuke them nor reject their impious flattery. But as he presently afterward looked up, he saw an owl sitting on a certain rope over his head, and immediately understood that this bird was the messenger of evil tidings, as it had once been the messenger of good tidings to him, and fell into the deepest sorrow. A severe pain also arose in his belly, and began in a most violent manner. He therefore looked upon his friends, and said, 'I whom you call a god am commanded presently to depart this life. While Providence thus reproves the lying words you just now said to me, and I, who was by you called immortal, am immediately to be hurried away by death. But I am bound to accept of what Providence allots, as it pleases God; for we have by no means lived ill, but in a splendid and happy manner.' When he had said this, his pain became violent. Accordingly, he was carried into his palace; and when he had been quite worn out by the pain, in five days he departed this life."* Thus far Josephus. Luke, as himself a medical man, tells us the nature of his disease: "He was eaten of worms;" and with deep suggestiveness, after this proof of the transient glory of earthly greatness, he adds, "but the word of God grew and multiplied."

And now, having given such amplification and explication as seemed needful to the full understanding of the history, I close by enforcing one or two practical inferences.

Let us learn, in the first place, the true unity of the Christian Church. The Apostle Paul has told us that when one member of the body suffers, all the members suffer with it, and here we see how the assault that was made on Peter affected all the saints in Jerusalem. They knew that the Church did not rest on him, but was founded on the Lord Jesus Christ. They believed also that even if Peter had been put to death at this time, God could and would have raised up another who should enter into his labours, and carry on the work with which the son of Jonas was identified. Yet they could not contemplate his removal from them without dismay. He had been a leader among them. They had been accustomed to rely on his judgment. They had learned to love him for the frankness of his nature and the generous impulses of his heart; and they could hardly conceive what the Church would be like without him.

---

* Josephus, "Antiquities," 19, 8, 2.

They felt regarding him as Luther felt regarding Melanchthon on that memorable occasion when, with amazing boldness, the great Reformer told the Lord that he could not do without his Philip, and must have him by his side. And so they had in him not an interest of benevolence alone, but one of identity. They were afflicted in his affliction, and Peter's extremity was their extremity. Indeed, so far as appears, the concern throughout was felt by them rather than by him. He was, we may suppose, like Paul, in that strange dilemma—not knowing what to choose; having a desire to depart and to be with Christ, yet willing to remain in the flesh for their sakes. But they were deeply moved.

Now, all this illustrates the unity of the Church of Christ. Let one child in the home be smitten with disease, and all the members of the family are deeply affected. Let some public-spirited patriot be stricken by some terrible calamity, and the whole nation feels the blow. But even more keenly than in such cases as these the Christian feels the affliction of a brother in the Lord; and if the troubled one be eminent as a leader in the sacramental host, the feeling is proportionately intense.

There is nothing which merges relationship into identity so thoroughly as the Gospel. In Christ we are all one; and so each feels the other's woe. But then, on the other hand, Christ feels with us all; for "in all our afflictions he is afflicted, and the angel of his presence saves us." This is the true brotherhood. Better than all secret badges, or mystic grasps, or talismanic pass-words, is this "union in Christ;" for it opens every Christian's heart to us, and gives each believer a personal interest in our welfare. The Church of Christ ought to be the most helpful and loving society in the world; and if it were what it ought to be, there would be no clamouring or craving among men for some other association to meet their needs. If you wish to keep your neighbour from stealing the water from your spring, you must dig deeper than he; and if we would do away with the necessity for all mystic associations, we must make the Church of Christ more like its divine ideal than it is now among us.

Let us learn, in the second place, the power of earnest, believing, and united prayer. Observe this statement made by the historian: "Prayer was made without ceasing of the Church unto God for him;" and then mark how the answer came. It was long delayed. The last night had arrived. The hearts of the suppliants might be beginning to fail, yet they continued their petitioning, and lo! at the darkest hour the dawn began to break! Now here is an example for us. We are not warranted to expect such answers as that which in those days of miracle was vouchsafed to the Church of Jerusalem; yet I do not hesitate to say that God would sooner work a miracle like that here described than suffer his faithfulness to fail, or let his cause be permanently put back. For the resources of the universe are at his command, and it is equally easy for him to answer prayer through the ordinary operations of his providence, or through the bringing of new causes into operation.

What we have to remember is that he is the hearer of prayer. We do not thoroughly believe that, else there would be more definiteness, directness, and what I may call business-like purpose in our petitions. We do not receive, because we do not ask. Is it not the fact that when we have concluded our devotions, it would often puzzle us to tell what we have been praying for? And then when we have asked for certain things, we have become discouraged because we have not had an immediate answer. Have we forgotten the story of the Syrophenician woman? or the injunction of the Lord that we are to "knock that it may be opened unto us?" Why are we thus disheartened? and why are God's answers thus delayed? It may be because, in our pride of heart, we are desirous of sharing in the glory of the answer. Have you marked these words in the doxology to the Lord's Prayer, "for thine is the glory?" Ah! when we are willing that all the glory shall go to God, the blessing is not far from our hands. Or, again, it may be because God wishes to develop patience in us, or to bring our faith to some such height as that of her to whom he said, "Oh, woman, great is thy faith!" But, in any case, if we were more definite in our petitions, and more continuous in our prayers, we should see more frequently the results for which we long. The philosophy and the discussions of our times have made us feel almost as if we needed to apologise for offering prayer; and so even the Church has been weakened by the materialism of the age. But all that is the merest folly; for if we believe that God is—or, to put it in another form, that there is a God —then he can help his creatures when they call upon him.

They tell us of the fixed laws of nature; but who dares maintain that He who fixed these laws cannot use them for the purpose of answering his people's prayers? There are postal laws in this country; but are the facilities for answering letters through these laws open to all but those members of Parliament who have made them? The very thought is absurd. And yet men who are using the laws of nature every day to help their fellows when they call on them—like medical men, for example —will deny to the God who made these laws the liberty which they are daily exercising for themselves. Nay, more; may not God, as in this case before us, sometimes send an answer to his servant, as I may say, by the hand of an angelic express? If I do not put a letter in the pillar at the street corner, may I not in my chamber telegraph for a message-boy, and send him on with an immediate answer? and am I breaking the postal laws when I do that? Nay, I am only bringing a new cause into operation for the producing of a new effect. I may send my little liveried telegraph messenger, but God may not send his angel! Oh, brethren! when one thinks of the learned nonsense that has been written on this subject, it is hard to speak regarding it in terms of moderation. But argument will not answer it. Nothing will put a stop to it save the earnest prayerfulness of Christ's own people. Give us a few John Knoxes in the Church concerning whom men will say, "We fear their prayers more than armed antagonists," and then we shall hear no more of prayer-gauges, and be able to defy all the objections of philosophy. The Church of Jerusalem prayed Peter out of prison. Let that fact sustain us while we supplicate for those who are spiritually imprisoned, that they may be set free.

Let us learn, in the third place, that while earthly glory fades, the word of the Lord endureth for ever. See how soon Herod disappears. Like a foambell on the stream, he dazzled men's eyes for a moment with the reflection of the sunlight; and then like it, too, he burst and disappeared. The shouting of the idolatrous crowd could not keep away retribution from his door. No Roman sentinel could turn back from his palace gate that pale horse which bore the rider whose name is Death. He went to his own place. But all his efforts to retard the progress of the Gospel were in vain, for "the word of God grew and multiplied."

Even as a policy, persecution is a mistake; for it always haloes with a certain glory the cause of those who suffer. Therefore, though the Gospel had been false, the course of Herod regarding it was, in the parlance of Talleyrand, "worse than a crime—a blunder." But being true, the antagonism of the king brought it only into greater prominence, and turned the hearts of the people to its acceptance.

Trial matures the Christian, and brings into greater conspicuousness the graces of patience, fortitude, faith, and forgiveness of injuries; so that they who look upon the confessor in the court, or the martyr at the stake, are moved to think of him in whose strength alone, and for whose sake alone, these characteristics are manifested. Thus it has come that the blood of the martyrs is the seed of the Church. This has been the case in all ages. The death of Stephen had its glorious outcome in the conversion of Paul; and in the early days of the Scottish Reformation it was said that the smoke of Patrick Hamilton infected all on whom it blew. So, in the present day, the sources of that great religious movement which has changed the whole face of the island of Madagascar are to be found in the persecutions with which the first Christians there were assailed. It is another application of the Saviour's words, "Except a corn of wheat fall into the ground and die, it abideth alone; but if it die, it bringeth forth much fruit." There are worse things than persecution for Christ's sake, and among these is that supple conformity to the world, that easy indifference, which bends to every influence, and has no principle of resistance in it. That way lies the danger of the Church of to-day; and it would not suffer from a storm if only the chaff were to be thereby separated from the wheat. Indeed it never really suffers from persecution, for the true Church is as indestructible as Christ, and "the gates of hell shall not prevail against it."

I cannot allow myself to conclude this discourse without bringing before you a little poem by a gifted Presbyterian minister of England,* now in heaven, which in the most exquisite manner uses the apostolic narrative to illustrate the death of the Christian, and to administer consolation to the bereaved. Never since I first saw it have I been able to read this chapter without recalling its exquisite lines to memory; and I am sure that many among you will thank me for bringing them to your notice. They are as follows:

> "The apostle slept; a light shone in the prison;
> An angel touched his side;
> 'Arise!' he said, and quickly he hath risen.
> His fettered arms untied.
>
> "The watchers saw no light at midnight gleaming,
> They heard no sound of feet;
> The gates fly open, and the saint, still dreaming,
> Stands free upon the street.

---

* The Rev. J. D. Burns, of Hampstead, London.

"So when the Christian's eyelid droops and closes,
    In nature's parting strife,
A friendly angel stands where he reposes,
    To wake him up to life.

"He gives a gentle blow, and so releases
    The spirit from its clay;
From sin's temptations and from life's distresses
    He bids it come away.

"It rises up, and from its darksome mansion
    It takes its silent flight;
And feels its freedom in the large expansion
    Of heavenly air and light.

"Behind, it hears Time's iron gates close faintly;
    It is now far from them;
For it has reached the city of the saintly—
    The new Jerusalem.

"A voice is heard on earth of kinsfolk weeping
    The loss of one they love;
But he is gone where the redeemed are keeping
    A festival above.

"The mourners throng the ways, and from the steeple
    The funeral-bell tolls slow;
But on the golden streets the holy people
    Are passing to and fro;

"And saying, as they meet, 'Rejoice! another,
    Long waited for, is come:'
The Saviour's heart is glad, a younger brother
    Hath reached the Father's home."

XXI.

PETER WITHSTOOD BY PAUL AT ANTIOCH.
GALATIANS ii., 11-21.

AFTER the escape of Peter from the prison at Jerusalem, he does not appear again in the apostolic narrative until the meeting of the council which was held for the settlement of the circumcision controversy. That discussion had originated at Antioch, whither certain Jews had gone from Jerusalem, and where they had insisted that conformity to the law of Moses was essential to salvation even through Christ. Paul and Barnabas, who were in Antioch at the time, and who saw the gravity of the crisis, affecting, as it did, the great doctrine of justification by faith, and the hope of the Gentile nations, met these strangers with uncompromising opposition. But as they came from the Holy City, and might seem, therefore, to be acting under the sanction of the mother Church, it was determined that certain delegates should accompany Barnabas and Paul to Jerusalem, to submit the whole question to the apostles and elders there.

When the assembly was convened, there was at first considerable discussion; but at length Peter gave the weight of his influence in favour of the fullest freedom to the Gentile believers. He rehearsed again the incidents which in his own experience had happened before and after his preaching in the household of Cornelius, and characterized the law of Moses as a yoke which neither they nor their fathers had been able to bear.

He was followed by Barnabas and Paul, who "declared what miracles and wonders God had wrought among the

Gentiles by them." And then James came forward with a compromise, which, after the sweeping statements of Peter, the assembly was now quite ready to accept. He was careful, however, in the outset, to declare his perfect agreement in principle with Peter, and expressed his conviction that God had prepared for himself a people from among the Gentiles. These statements he fortified by an appeal to the prophecy of Amos, which must have had great weight with those who were willing to be taught out of the Scriptures. He could not think, therefore, of compelling the Gentiles to submit to circumcision, for that would have been to give up the principle which he had first assented to; but he counselled, not as a matter of absolute duty, but as a thing expedient in the circumstances, that they should abstain from those practices which were particularly offensive to a scrupulous Jew, namely, from eating meat offered to idols, from blood, from strangled animals, and from fornication. This advice met with general acceptance, and on its being reduced to writing, it was sent to Antioch by the hands of Judas Barsabas and Silas.

Thus far, therefore, Peter and Paul were in absolute harmony. The apostle of the Gentiles could not have wished for a broader assertion of the abrogation of the law of Moses than that which had been made by the apostle of the circumcision; and though they might have preferred a decree which would have been more sweeping in its terms, they were both willing, for the sake of weaker brethren, to sacrifice liberty for peace.

But not long after this amicable settlement of the question at Jerusalem, Peter himself seems to have visited Antioch, and then it was that he was guilty of such vacillation as constrained Paul to withstand him to the face.

The only account which we have of the circumstances is that which Paul has given in the Epistle to the Galatians, and from that it appears that at first Peter mingled freely with the Gentiles, even eating with them, and going out and in among them, just as he would have done if they had been Jews. But after a time, some scrupulous believers from Jerusalem made their appearance at Antioch, and then, from fear of offending them, he "withdrew and separated himself." The effect of such conduct in such a man was very pernicious, for the Jewish members of the Antioch Church followed his example, and even Barnabas also was carried away by what Paul has called their dissimulation. We can readily understand the case. Peter had not changed his principles. Had any one asked him, even at that moment, whether circumcision were necessary to salvation, he would have answered, without the least degree of hesitation, No. But the men from Jerusalem got round him, and wrought upon his fears. They represented, perhaps, that a great outcry would be made against his conduct by his friends in the Holy City; that the course which he was taking would create controversy, and develop antagonism; that it would seriously interfere with his future comfort, and mar his after-usefulness; and that if he had any regard whatever for his own happiness, he should at once retrace his steps. So, by confining his attention to that view of the case, and carefully shutting out every other consideration, they effected their purpose; and, after they had succeeded with him, it was easy to bring over Barnabas, for even his failings leaned in the direction of amiability; and if it could be shown to him that the course suggested would be agreeable to his old friends at Jerusalem, then he would be moved to take it.

But there was another side to all this, and that Paul, from his intense interest in the Gentiles, was the first to see. It was a change of conduct which in the circumstances would be held as resulting from a change of conviction. But Paul knew that neither Peter nor Barnabas had altered his opinion on the main question. Therefore, in assuming this attitude toward the Gentiles they were guilty of dissimulation; that is to say, they appeared to be what they really were not. While Peter believed as he had always done since his visit to Cornelius, his refusal now to eat with the Gentiles was virtually also a refusal to regard them as brethren, a confirmation of the prejudice against them as unclean, and a violation of the compromise agreed upon at Jerusalem.

His error was not one of doctrine, but of practice; and so they are entirely at fault here who bring up this difference between the apostles as if it disproved the inspiration of either or of both. Inspiration is one thing, sanctification is another. Both, indeed, are the effects of the work of the Holy Spirit in the soul. In the one he employs the powers of the mind for the communication of truth to others; in the other he operates in the formation of the character of the individual himself. There may be inspiration without sanctification, as in the case of such a one as Balaam; and there may be sanctification without inspiration, as in the experience of believers among ourselves.

In respect of inspiration, the two apostles were upon an equality; and the sermons and epistles of Peter are in perfect harmony with the discourses and letters of Paul. But in respect of sanctification, they were different. Each had his own distinctive excellencies, and each his own characteristic defects. In Peter there was a generous impulsiveness, which sometimes made him the first in noble daring; and occasionally, as in the instance before us, led him to act with flagrant inconsistency. In Paul there was a sensitiveness of conscience, which while, as in this case, it moved him to stand up for the right, did sometimes border upon a sternness that was in danger of breaking the bruised reed and quenching the smoking flax. They were both imperfectly sanctified men, and one may see at a glance that the conduct of Peter here is quite in keeping with the disposition which he so frequently manifested while the Saviour was on the earth. As Lightfoot has well said. "It is at least no surprise that he who at one moment declared himself ready to lay down his life for his Lord's sake, and even drew his sword in defence of his Master, and the next betrayed him with a thrice-repeated denial, should have acted in this case as we infer he acted from the combined accounts of Luke and Paul. There is the same impulsive courage, followed by the same shrinking timidity. And though Paul's narrative stops short of the last scene in this drama, it would not be rash to conclude that it ended as the other had ended; that the revulsion of feeling was as sudden and complete; and that again he went out and wept bitterly, having denied his Lord in the person of these Gentile converts."*

It scarcely belongs to a series of discourses on the life and character of Peter to take cognizance of the procedure of Paul at this trying time; yet we cannot present a complete account of the case without including his protest. He felt that something ought to be done to counteract the evil which otherwise would result from the conduct of Peter; and nothing could have been better than the course which he adopted. He went directly to his friend, and publicly exposed the inconsistency of which publicly he had been guilty. He knew that Peter's deepest convictions were already on his side. He wished to make his appeal from Peter in a panic to Peter calm and rational. And in making that appeal he was sure that Peter had a generous affection for himself, and a genuine loyalty to the Lord Jesus, and was deeply interested in the promotion of the Gospel among the Gentiles as well as among the Jews.

This explains both the frankness and the fidelity of his address; which presents the finest possible combination of firmness with delicacy, and faithfulness with affection. It would well repay the most minute consideration; but I must be content with setting before you the substance of the argument which it contains, in the shape of an expansion of his words. It is something like the following:

If you who are a Jew by birth, and therefore have been brought up under the law of Moses, feel yourself at liberty to

---

* "St. Paul's Epistle to the Galatians," by J. B. Lightfoot, D.D., p. 128.

disregard its prohibitions, and to live, as you were doing a little while ago, after the manner of the Gentiles, it is absurd in you to oblige the Gentiles to conform to all the requirements of the Jewish law. You do not, indeed, insist on that in so many words; but still the natural inference from your present withdrawal from the Gentile Christians is, that you have now come to believe that circumcision is essential to salvation. For this is not a case of conforming to the wishes of a weak brother; it is a complying with the demands of those who say, "Except ye be circumcised after the manner of Moses, ye cannot be saved." Now observe how your conduct affects the fundamental principles of the Gospel. We who are Jews, having become convinced that we could not be justified by the works of the law, have sought salvation through faith in Christ; but if in so doing we are, after all, found to be transgressors, because we have willfully neglected the law as an appointed means of salvation, then it must follow that Christ, who taught us to neglect it in that relation, has been to us the minister of sin. That is a conclusion from which, of course, you will shrink with horror; still, you must be prepared to face it, or you must admit that by your present conduct you have made yourself a transgressor. There is transgression somewhere. If you were wrong before in eating with the Gentiles, then, as you did that under the direct command of the Lord given to you in a vision, he was to you the minister of sin. But if you were right before, then you are wrong now, and you are yourself the transgressor. There is no other alternative; and I know you so well that, when the matter is put before you in this way, there will be no hesitation in your mind as to the course you should adopt. Indeed, the simple truth is, that as a believer in Christ I have now no more to do with the law of Moses for my justification. Through the law itself, that is to say, through having its requirements satisfied, and its curse endured by Christ for me, I died to the law: not, however, that I might live a lawless life, but rather that I might live wholly to God. Nay, such is my union to the Redeemer that I am crucified with him, and it is no longer I that live, but he that liveth in me; for the life that I live in the flesh I live by the faith of the Son of God, who loved me and gave himself for me. Hence I do not make the grace of God unnecessary; as I should certainly do if I were to go back to the law for salvation; for if it were possible to obtain righteousness by the law, then there was no necessity for the death of Christ.

There is nothing said as to how Peter received this admonition; but, from what we know of his character and temperament, we may conclude that he frankly owned his error, so that the Gospel might not be hindered; and we are sure that the affair left no poison of bitterness behind it, for long afterwards Peter writes of the apostle of the Gentiles as "our beloved brother Paul."

Two different sets of lessons may be drawn from this subject, according as we look at Peter's procedure or at Paul's; and it will give completeness to our treatment of it, if we set them both briefly and pointedly before you.

Looking, then, at Peter's conduct, we may learn that it is never safe to act from one-sided views of things. The strangers from Jerusalem so buzzed about our apostle that they gave him no time to think all round the subject. They filled his ears with their forebodings of panic, and so moved his heart with the thought of the storm which they alleged he would have to meet on his return to the Holy City, that he became alarmed and hastily decided to take his place among them. I do not know whether in planning their campaign at Antioch these Jews took Peter's temperament into consideration, but impulsive men are ever open to just such management; and they who care to descend to work upon their fears are generally sure to win them over in the end. I do not mean to convey the impression that Peter was always willowy and pliant in his nature. We know otherwise. We saw him in the Council stand bravely before the rulers, and shall never forget his ringing words of unwavering decision, "We ought to obey God rather than men." So it will not do to call him a coward. Neither, from an incident like this, should we be warranted to style him a traitor. The truth seems to be that he was stricken with panic, as when he was trying to walk upon the waters, and when he was set upon by the maid-servant and the lackeys of the high-priest.

He was afraid, first of all, to stand out against these Jews, who had come to Antioch; and finding him in that mood, they frightened him still farther, by conjuring up before his imagination a terrible ordeal through which he would have to pass when he went back to Jerusalem, and so he yielded. But he took no note of the injury which he was doing to the Gospel, of the sorrow which he was inflicting upon Paul, or of the dishonour which he was doing to Christ. "Truly the fear of man bringeth a snare." We are never safe so long as we contemplate any course of conduct simply and only in the light of the opinions of our fellow-men. We have to view it as in the sight of God; and it was because Peter neglected to do that on this occasion that he fell so grievously.

It is worthy of remark in this connection that when Christ himself was set upon by Satan, he lifted the enticements which the adversary put before him up above all merely human considerations, and put them in the light of God. To the first he answered, "Man shall not live by bread alone, but by every word that proceedeth out of the mouth of God." In the second he replied, "Thou shalt not tempt the Lord thy God;" and he met the third with these words, "Thou shalt worship the Lord thy God, and him only shalt thou serve."

Now, in all this we are taught that our only safeguard is to go to God for the solution of every question of conduct. Truly has the Psalmist said, "In thy light shall we see light clearly." And when we are doing that which is right in the sight of God, we need not be afraid of men. Peter knew that perfectly; for as we saw when he was before the Council, he lifted the whole question in debate above the sphere of earthly tribunals, and said: "Whether it be right in the sight of God to hearken unto you more than unto God, judge ye." But doing is different from knowing, and the fact that even such a one as Peter failed to carry out a principle which he had himself so fully enunciated ought to be a warning to us.

Let us not take counsel too largely with flesh and blood. Whether we act from a regard to the good-will of men, or from the fear of giving men offence, or with the view of making them feel that we are cold and distant to them, we are equally at fault. The first thing we ought always to seek is to please God. The determining elements, at all times of hesitancy, ought to be these: "What will the Lord Jesus Christ have me to do? How will my conduct either way affect the Gospel of Christ? What is the right in the case as between God and my conscience? And when we have these answered, let us go forward, no matter who may be displeased, or what predictions of strife and storm and suffering the petrels of alarm may utter. Who were these Jews that Peter should have feared them so? Had not God twice over delivered him from prison, and was he not able to protect him still? Ah! what a firm hold nature has upon a man! He who drew his sword in the presence of the Roman band could not stand the banter of a silly girl. He who patiently endured persecution at the hands of Herod fears these Jewish members of the Christian Church. Yet let us not condemn him overmuch, for if we look within we may find a Peter in each breast among us.

Looking again at Peter's bearing here, we may learn that when we are withstood for being in the wrong we should take it meekly, and retrace our steps as speedily as possible. I believe that Paul's appeal was not in vain. He was too noble to include in a letter to the Galatians anything which might seem to humiliate his brethren; but from what we know of Peter on other occasions, we may conclude that he was as willing to confess his fault as he had been rash and inconsiderate in its commission. Indeed, the careful student of his epistles will discover that in this very matter he is in them perfectly at one with Paul. In the letter to the Galatians, the one apostle has said, "Ye have been called unto liberty: only use not your liberty for an occasion to the flesh, but by love serve one another;" and in his first epistle the other has these words: "As free, and not using your liberty for a cloak of maliciousness, but as the servants of God." We infer, therefore, that he accepted Paul's rebuke in the spirit of meekness. Very evidently he did not believe in his own infallibility; and he was far from resenting the course which Paul had pursued. Now, in all this there was a magnanimity which was worthy of all praise. So far as appears, he did not become excited, and exclaim against Paul for presuming to think that he could be wrong; but he did a far more difficult and more noble thing: he acknowledged his fault, and did his best to undo its evil consequences. Now, here was a triumph of grace. It may seem a paradox to say it, but there are few things to test a man's real Christianity more than his bearing when he is found fault with for that which is actually blameworthy. It is easy to guard against giving offence, but it is a harder matter to keep from taking offence in such a case as this, and to say, with the Psalmist, "Let the righteous smite me, it shall be a kindness; and let him reprove me, it shall be an excellent oil, which shall not break my head."

We all assent to Solomon's proverb, "Open rebuke is better than secret love:" but when the rebuke comes, most of us, on the whole, would prefer the love; and too frequently we are disposed to resent the faithfulness of the brother, even though he should hint only in the most delicate manner that we have been in the wrong. We all have our faults; and when the statement is made in that general fashion, we can all assent to it; only when we do we are thinking of other people's faults rather than our own! We cry out against the dogma of papal infallibility; but each of us has far too much faith in that of personal infallibility; for our tempers are roused, and our hearts are estranged, by any expostulation with us for error or inconsistency. How many permanent alienations and pernicious schisms might have been prevented, if there had been on the one side the manly frankness of Paul, and on the other the ingenuous honesty and meekness of Peter, as they come out in this transaction.

But now, turning to Paul's part in this controversy, we may learn from that, first, that before we withstand a brother, we must be sure that he is to be blamed, and that the occasion is such as calls for our protest. Paul would not have cared to interfere with Peter in any trifling matter, nor would he have felt constrained to move in the case if any more charitable construction could have been put upon his conduct. No one ever had so full a comprehension of the doctrine of Christian liberty as Paul; and no one was ever more jealous of any unwarrantable interference with it than was Paul. Hence, if it had not been that the fundamental principle of the Gospel was at stake, he would not have said a word. In themselves considered, the things which Peter had done were indifferent; but by doing them, in the circumstances in which at Antioch he was placed, he had imperilled the freeness of salvation through Christ; and as that was dearer to Paul than friendship, or even life itself, he could not be silent. He practised his own charity, which "believeth all things;" and if he could have believed that Peter's conduct was right from any one point of view, he would have honoured him; but seeing no explanation of his procedure which was consistent with loyalty to the truth of the Gospel, he spoke out against it—in love, indeed, but with unmistakable condemnation. Now, let us withstand a brother only when we are thus constrained to do so by allegiance to the truth as it is in Jesus. If in any respects we cannot approve of his conduct, while yet it is susceptible of explanation in harmony with Christian principle, let us give him the benefit and be silent. But if the glory of the Gospel or the purity of the Church be endangered by his procedure, let us withstand him.

Nothing ought to be dearer to us than truth and purity; and if our brother is indulging in a liberty which compromises these, or if he is insisting on an intolerance which would make the gate of life narrower than Christ has left it, no influence whatever should prevent us from withstanding him; only let us be sure that he is doing either of these things before we cry out against him.

Again, we may learn from Paul's conduct that we must not be deterred from condemning wrong by the position of him who has done it. Peter was an apostle. He was, in fact, one of the pillars of the primitive Church; but Paul was not kept, by any consideration of these things, from protesting against his injudicious and unseemly vacillation. On the contrary, the very prominence of Peter made it all the more important that his inconsistency should be exposed and rectified. Had he been a mere private member of the Church, Paul might have been disposed to pass his conduct by with a mild remonstrance. But his very eminence as an apostle gave importance to his example, and made it certain that, if he remained uncondemned, great evil would result. Hence Paul took the course which he adopted. We may be sure that it cost him much to take the stand which he felt compelled to assume; but it would have cost him far more to take no notice of his brother's error. It was not, therefore, because he loved Peter less, but because he loved the Gospel more. Now, it is the same still. Evil in any man is dangerous, but it is far more so when it appears in the conduct of one who is a leader of the people; and, however painful it may be to oppose it, duty leaves no alternative in such a case. We ought, lovingly, indeed, but firmly and courageously, to withstand him. Great eminence may command our respect, but Christ and his truth are of more importance even than an apostle; and nothing whatever should be allowed by us as an excuse for dishonouring his name, or compromising the principles of his Gospel.

Finally, we may learn from Paul's conduct here that when we withstand a brother, it should be to his face. Paul did not go hither and thither among the elders and members of the Church of Antioch, speaking against Peter and complaining of his conduct, while, at the same time, he kept religious silence concerning it to Peter himself. He did not say behind Peter's back that which he was afraid to utter before his face; but he spoke out all that was in his heart openly, and to Peter himself. Now, in this also he has left us a valuable example. When we have any thing against a brother, let us say it to himself. Too often, alas! a contrary method is pursued, both in the Church and in the world, and men go round the whole circle of society, turning it into a great whispering-gallery, in which they defame the character of one who has no opportunity of vindicating his name. "It is very sad, isn't it? And you must not say that I spoke to you upon the subject; but he has done thus and so, and I feel greatly distressed;" and so it passes on from one to another, gathering as it goes, until a thing which might have been settled at first by a few kindly words assumes a very formidable appearance, and perhaps ends in the permanent estrangement of the persons more immediately concerned, while it produces discord and heart-burning in the whole community. If we have any thing to say of a brother, let us say it first to him. Let us say nothing in his absence that we should be afraid to utter in his presence. Nor does this law concern the speaker only; it has a bearing also on the hearer; and when any one comes with an evil report against his neighbour, let us refuse to listen to him, unless he can assure us that he has said all that he is going to utter to the person whom it most concerns. "Where no wood is, there the fire goeth out;" and if all to whom evil gossip is retailed were to shut their ears against it, on the principle which I have just enunciated, we should soon banish it from our homes. Who would harbour an assassin in his house? Yet the man who strikes at a neighbour's character in his absence is as bad as he who, with stealthy stiletto, stabs the unwary victim from behind. If we must withstand a brother, therefore, let us do it to his face.

XXII.

LETTERS AND LAST DAYS.

AFTER the incidents which occurred at Antioch, and which formed the subject of our last discourse, we have no account of Peter in the New Testament until we come to his first epistle. Paul, indeed, alludes to a party in the Church of Corinth, which called itself after Cephas; and we may almost infer from his words that Peter had been for some time in the city on the isthmus; for as he speaks of Cephas precisely as he does of himself and of Apollos, the presumption is that the faction had formed itself in connection with a personal visit. This is in some degree confirmed by the reference made by Paul in the same letter to Peter's custom of taking his wife with him in his apostolic journeys, which seems to intimate that he had been at Corinth accompanied by his partner. But though, in the divided state of the Corinthian Church, one section called itself after Cephas, it must not be supposed that, even if he did visit Corinth, he was in the least degree responsible for the doings of the schismatic party which used his name.

There is no evidence to show that the ritualistic party in the primitive churches received the slightest countenance from him, except on the one unfortunate occasion at Antioch, when, under the influence of panic, he was guilty of apparent vacillation. At all other times he spoke and acted in perfect harmony with his utterances at the Council of Jerusalem; and the manner in which Paul uniformly refers to him in his epistles to the Corinthians makes it absolutely certain that Peter was guiltless of doing or saying any thing to cause divisions among them.

When Peter wrote his first epistle (the genuineness of which, universally acknowledged in the ancient Church, has been fully sustained, after the most searching scrutiny by modern critics), he was at Babylon on the Euphrates. An attempt, indeed, has been made to prove that this term means Rome; but such a view is ludicrous in itself, and, for the Church in whose interests it is advanced, destructive. The dating of a serious letter is not an occasion on which one would naturally use an allegorical name. Moreover, it was not until long after the publication of the Apocalypse that the use of Babylon for Rome became intelligible even in an allegorical sense. While, again, if it be insisted on that by Babylon Peter actually meant Rome, then to Rome must belong the character and doom of the apocalyptic Babylon; so that whatever of prestige the Imperial City might claim from the presence of Peter in it when he wrote this letter is more than neutralized by the inferences which must be drawn from the assumption on which such a claim is based. There is, therefore, no good reason to doubt that when Peter sent forth this letter he was labouring in the well-known city of that name on the banks of the Euphrates.

This natural view of the case is confirmed, rather than otherwise, by the fact that in its decayed state, and long after the great majority of its other inhabitants had left it, Babylon continued to be the residence of many Jews; and though in the last years of Caligula there had been a persecution of the descendants of Abraham there, in consequence of which many had fled to Seleucia, yet in the twenty years which had elapsed between that date and the time of the writing of this letter we may conclude that their number had once more increased to such an extent as to make the place a most inviting field of labour for him who was pre-eminently the Apostle of the Circumcision.

From the letter itself we learn that Peter was at the moment associated with Mark, and that he employed Silvanus to carry it to the brethren to whom it is addressed. Now, these two facts are interesting from their bearing on the date of the epistle, and of the state of feeling between Peter and Paul.

In the first place, as to the date. When Paul wrote, during his first imprisonment, to the Colossians, he speaks of Mark as having been a comfort to him at Rome, and says, "If he come unto you, receive him." Now that implies that Mark was then projecting a journey into Asia. Again, in his second letter to Timothy (iv., 11), which was written by Paul during his second imprisonment, he says, "Take Mark and bring him with thee; for he is profitable to me for the ministry." Now, as Timothy was at this time in Asia, we have evidence that Mark had carried out his intention, and that in the interval between Paul's first and second imprisonment he had gone from Rome to the East. But here, in Peter's first epistle, he is found with the Apostle of the Circumcision at Babylon, and so, as the inference which is most natural in all the circumstances of the case, we conclude that his visit to Peter was made on the occasion of the journey into Asia, to which we have just referred, and thus we date this letter at some time between Paul's first and second imprisonment, that is, between the years 63 and 67 of our era.

But it is no less interesting to remark that these two friends who were with Peter when he wrote this letter stood high in the confidence of Paul. Mark, indeed, had been the occasion of a sharp contention between Paul and Barnabas; but subsequently, as we have just seen, he regained his place in the heart of the apostle, and he was one of those for whose presence he longed as he lay, weary and lonesome, in the Roman dungeon. Silvanus, whom we identify with the Silas of the Acts of the Apostles, had been with Paul in his second journey through Asia Minor into Macedonia. He shared his imprisonment at Philippi, and took part in his evangelistic work at Corinth; nay, so highly did Paul esteem him, that he associated him with himself in his epistles to the Thessalonians. He stood apparently next to Timothy and Luke in the affection and esteem of Paul; and it is not by any means improbable that this visit to Babylon was made by him at the suggestion of the Apostle of the Gentiles, for the purpose of obtaining from Peter some written exhortations which might be valuable to the believers scattered throughout Asia Minor.

Now, when we put all these things together, we have a beautiful evidence of the truth that these two apostles, in spite of the error committed by the one and the protest uttered by the other at Antioch, were still full of affection for each other, and were both characterized by loyalty to Christ. Peter, though labouring in a city chiefly inhabited by Jews, writes to brethren who were principally Gentiles; and in his letter there is no narrow exclusiveness, but rather the widest comprehension consistent with allegiance to Christ, and a spirit perfectly in harmony with the writings of his beloved brother Paul.

The character of the epistle is described by himself in these words: "I have written briefly, exhorting and testifying that this is the true grace of God wherein ye stand." The letter is thus an exhortation and a testimony, or a series of counsels, founded on and confirmed by experience. I know not whether, in writing it, the words of the Lord to him at the supper-table, "When thou art converted, strengthen thy brethren," were distinctly present to his memory; but the establishment of the brotherhood in time of trial was the great object which he had in view.

Those to whom it was addressed were passing through persecution, originating partly in their separation from the amusements and dissoluteness in which they had lived prior to their conversion; and they are exhorted to stand fast in their allegiance to Jesus and his truth. There is not in the letter the same logical unity and coherence which we find in the more important epistles of Paul, for the writer returns again and again to topics which he has already handled; but we have, throughout, the ardour which we have seen so frequently in the conduct of its author, while as the result, perhaps, of the mellowing influence of years, we have a tender and pathetic under-tone which moves the heart of every reader.

Two things about it impress every careful student. These are, first, the frequent references which its author makes to the sufferings of Christ; and, second, the repeated allusions which he makes to the future glory of the believer. We have not forgotten how, after his noble confession of the Lord's Messiahship, when he heard the first plain reference to the Master's death, he made rash and unbelieving reply: "Be it far from thee, Lord; this shall not be unto thee." But now the richest consolation administered by him to the Christian in trial is that he is following in the wake of the Lord Jesus, and soon to be a partaker in his glory. The pith of his epistle may be given in these two verses (iv., 12, 13): "Beloved, think it not strange concerning the fiery trial which is to try you, as though some strange thing happened unto you; but rejoice, inasmuch as ye are partakers of Christ's sufferings; that, when his glory shall be revealed, ye may be glad also with exceeding joy." Yet while speaking directly of the example which Christ, while suffering, left us, "that we should follow his steps," he is careful also to give prominence to the sacrificial character of his death, declaring, as he does, that we "were redeemed with the precious blood of Christ;" that "Christ suffered for us;" that "he bare our sins in his own body on the tree;" that he "once suffered for sins, the just for the unjust, that he might bring us to God;" and that "he hath suffered for us in the flesh."

Equally remarkable is the frequency of his references to the future life. As one has well said, "Peter, indeed, might be called the apostle of hope. Doctrine and consolation alike assume this form. The 'inheritance' is future, but its heirs are begotten to a 'living hope' (i., 3, 4). Their tried faith is found unto glory 'at the appearance of Jesus Christ' (i., 7). The 'end' of their faith is 'salvation' (i., 9); and they are to 'hope to the end for the grace that is to be brought unto them at the revelation of Jesus Christ' (i., 13). Their ruling emotion is, therefore, 'the hope that is in them' (iii., 15); so much lying over in reserve for them in the future, their time here is only a 'sojourning' (i., 17); they were merely 'strangers and pilgrims' (ii., 17); nay, 'the end of all things is at hand' (iv., 7). Suffering was now, but joy was to come when 'his glory shall be revealed' (v., 1)."*

From these two characteristics, which are so strikingly apparent in it, this epistle is, perhaps, the richest treasure of consolation to those who are in trouble, which the sacred canon contains. It comes, warm and living, from the apostle's heart, and bears on its style the marks of that disposition which was so prominent in himself. It is vivid, clear, earnest, having occasionally transitions so striking and rapid as to remind us of the impulsiveness of him who passed off so frequently at some tangent of association, and surprised us so often with the singularity of his sayings. We feel throughout that we are dealing with one whose theme is not a thing out of and apart from himself, but who is reading to us a chapter of his own experience, and telling us how, amidst manifold trials, he was sustained by turning in faith to the cross, and in hope to the crown.

There are some books of the Bible, like the sweet pastoral of Ruth, and the cheerful letter of Paul to the Philippians, which should be read in the bright sunshine of a cloudless day; there are others that are meant for the darkness, and of these, to use one of its own terms, this letter of Peter is one of the most "precious." One sees not the phosphorescence of the wave save in the night; and the true glory of this noble letter comes out most brightly in the suffering of the sick-chamber or the experience of the troubled. It is a light in the carriage-roof, whereby the Christian pilgrim may be cheered as he passes through the tunnels of his life-journey. In the open daylight,

---

* Alexander's "Kitto," article PETER, FIRST EPISTLE OF.

he may be unconscious of its value; but in the darkness it reveals itself by its unwelcome lustre, and is prized accordingly.

Concerning the genuineness and canonical authority of the second epistle, more serious questions have been raised than concerning those of any other book in the New Testament. It would be quite out of place for me to enter upon the full consideration of these here, involving as they do the testimony of the early fathers; the absence of this letter from some of the ancient versions of the New Testament; the difference in style between it and the first epistle; and the singular resemblance which a portion of one of its chapters bears to the Epistle of Jude. We have to admit that doubts were entertained regarding it even in primitive times, and that it was not formally admitted into the canon until the close of the fourth century; and it has to be confessed, also, that in modern days many of the most renowned critics have decided against it.

Yet, after having read all that I could lay my hands on regarding it, I am disposed to agree with those who believe that it belongs of right to the canon of Scripture. For this is not a case like that of the Epistle to the Hebrews, which is simply anonymous. Its author claims to be Simon Peter, and we must therefore either regard the epistle as a deliberate forgery, or accept it as the work of the great apostle. Moreover, even if we give full weight to all the objections which have been advanced against it, there are sundry personal allusions which tell largely in its favour; for the writer refers to the scene on the Mount of Transfiguration, and in doing so employs language which, to one acquainted with the original, has some subtle links of association with the conversation of the three glorified ones on that occasion, that could hardly have been fabricated. Besides, we have the immense improbability that one who had the spiritual insight that could perceive the truths expressed in that letter, and the courage to enforce the exhortations to truth and righteousness which it contains, should be himself a lying impostor seeking to palm himself off for that which he was not.

The truth is, that there are but two alternatives here. Either the author of this treatise has perpetrated a fraud, and is guilty of forgery, in using the name of Peter; or he was the apostle himself, and we have in it the latest production that came from his pen. And the whole question may be dismissed in the following calm and unbiassed sentences from the pen of one of the contributors to Smith's "Dictionary of the Bible:" "If it were a question now to be decided upon for the first time, upon the external or internal evidences still accessible, it may be admitted that it would be far more difficult to maintain this than any other document in the New Testament; but the judgment of the early Church is not to be reversed without far stronger arguments than have been adduced, more especially as the epistle is entirely free from objections which might be brought, with more show of reason, against others, now all but universally received; inculcating no new doctrine, bearing on no controversies of postapostolic origin, supporting no hierarchical innovations, but simple, earnest, devout, practical—full of the characteristic graces of the apostle, who, as we believe, bequeathed this last proof of faith and hope to the Church."[*]

We have nothing to guide us in fixing the date at which this epistle was written; but from the reference made in it to his former letter, it seems to have been designed for those to whom that had been addressed. Its general character is admonitory. It was evidently designed to warn its readers against falling from their steadfastness, and to exhort them to grow in grace and in the knowledge of the Lord Jesus Christ. After an enumeration of Christian privileges, and an injunction to make their calling and election sure by the performance of Christian duties, he touchingly alludes to his own approaching death, and, making a passing reference to the certain evidence which

---

[*] Smith's "Dictionary," vol. ii., p 810: *a*.

he possessed for the truth of the doctrines which he proclaimed, he guards them against being led away by false teachers, predicts the overthrow of all the opponents of Christian truth, and in connection with a prophecy of the second advent of Christ, and the destruction of the world by fire, he holds out the promise of new heavens and a new earth wherein dwelleth righteousness.

This gives him an opportunity, which he eagerly embraces, of bearing testimony to the harmony existing between himself and Paul, whose epistles are put by him on a level with the other Scriptures; and so the continued confidence of these two men in each other, which was a matter of inference from the former letter, is in this one plainly expressed.

The later events of Peter's life are involved in obscurity. Some would have us to believe that he lived at Rome for twenty years, and that he was the first bishop of the Church in that city. But there is not a word of that in the New Testament. That he was not there before the year 58, when Paul wrote his Epistle to the Romans, is, as nearly as possible, absolutely certain; and we may conclude with equal assurance that he was not there during Paul's first imprisonment. It is clear, moreover, that he did not found the Church of Rome; and that he never was, in any sense of the word, a bishop of that Church.

But whether he ever visited the city, and whether he suffered martyrdom in it, are questions which are not so easily solved. The evidence of his martyrdom is complete, though the story of his requesting to be crucified with his head downward, because it would be too much honour to be put to death precisely as his Lord was, seems to me to be apocryphal. Equally so is the legend found in Ambrose to this effect: When the Christians at Rome were assailed by persecution, anxious to preserve their teacher, they persuaded him to flee, a course which they had Scriptual warrant to recommend, and he to follow; but at the gate he met the Lord. "Lord, whither goest thou?" said Peter. "I go to Rome," was the answer, "there once more to be crucified." Peter well understood the meaning of the words, returned at once, and was crucified. The probability, in my mind, is, that some one had introduced into a discourse, for the purpose of illustration, and as a purely imaginary thing, such an interview between the Master and his apostle, and that, bye-and-bye, it was accepted as a fact.

The only reliable witness whom we can cite regarding Peter's last days is Clement of Rome, who was almost a contemporary, for he wrote about the year 96 or 97, not more than thirty years after Peter's death. The passage in which he refers to him and Paul is as follows: "But not to dwell upon ancient examples, let us come to the most recent spiritual heroes. Let us take the noble examples furnished in our own generation. Through envy and jealousy, the greatest and most righteous pillars have been persecuted and put to death. Let us set before our eyes the illustrious apostles. Peter, through unrighteous envy, endured not one or two, but numerous labours; and, when he at length suffered martyrdom, departed to the place of glory due to him. Owing to envy, Paul also obtained the crown of patient endurance, after being seven times thrown into captivity, compelled to flee, and stoned. After preaching both in the East and West, he gained the illustrious reputation due to his faith, having taught righteousness to the whole world, and come to the extreme limits of the West, and suffered martyrdom under the prefects. Thus was he removed from the world, and went into the holy place, having proved himself a striking example of patience.*

Within the last few weeks the announcement has been made that an almost complete manuscript of the Epistles of Clement has been discovered in the library of the Patriarchate of Jerusalem, and published at Constantinople by Bryennios, the Bishop of Serrae, in Macedonia. It promises to fill up many

---

* *Presbyterian Quarterly and Princeton Review* for April, 1876, p. 270.

of the gaps in the former manuscripts, and may cast new light upon the passage which I have now read. But taking it as we now have it, the following things are certain: (1) that both the apostles Peter and Paul suffered martyrdom; (2) that Paul was put to death at Rome; for, as Lipsius affirms, that is the sense now universally given to the words "the extreme limits of the West;" (3) that the place of Peter's martyrdom is not mentioned by Clement. The words referring to him are less definite than those employed concerning Paul. This seems evidence that Clement did not know so much concerning Peter's death as he did concerning Paul's. But if that were so, then it is almost conclusive proof that he was not put to death at Rome.

An article in the April number of the *Princeton Review* seeks, very opportunely for me, to give Dr. Lipsius's view on this controverted question, as that is elaborately stated and defended in a forthcoming book, and puts the result in these words: "At the close of the first and up to the beginning of the second century there was in Pauline circles, inside and outside of Rome, no knowledge of Peter's labours in that city; no knowledge of his martyrdom there under Nero."*

Now, I am aware that over against all this we have to put a well-nigh unbroken tradition to the effect that Peter did labour in his latest days at Rome, and was there sacrificed as a victim to Nero's cruelty. This is attested by Eusebius, Origen, and others; but it has to be remembered, on the other side, that such a tradition as that would be likely to be formed around the growing claims to supremacy put forth by the Church of Rome, and would be fostered by all who were in favour of supporting these.

Of course, we can see the question of Peter's residence at Rome and the primacy of the pope are two separate and entirely unconnected things; for though we should admit that

---

* *Presbyterian Quarterly and Princeton Review* for April, 1876, p. 272.

Peter had been Bishop of Rome all his Christian life, that does not by any means cover the assumption that the pope is his successor in the sense of possessing all that Peter as an apostle ever possessed, and of claiming more than Peter would have had the presumption to think of. But still, it is not by any means certain that he ever was at Rome, and facts may yet be brought to light to make it certain that he never was.

As the case stands it may cautiously be stated thus: it is certain that Peter suffered martyrdom; it is probable that his martyrdom was by crucifixion; it is probable that his martyrdom took place at Rome; but it is clear that he never was for any length of time resident in that city, and morally certain that he never was bishop of the Church there.

We cannot now attempt any analysis of the great apostle's character, but, reserving that for a concluding lecture, we shall content ourselves for the present with one or two practical inferences suggested by the ground over which we have come.

In the first place, we may learn that the great concern of the ministers of Christ ought to be to preserve and perpetuate the truth. Peter, in his first epistle, draws a striking contrast between the frailty of men and the permanence of the Word, saying, "All flesh is as grass, and all the glory of man as the flower of grass. The grass withereth, and the flower thereof falleth away: but the word of the Lord endureth for ever." Yet he did not forbear to use means for its conservation; for in his second letter he says, "I will endeavour that ye may be able after my decease to have these things always in remembrance;" and he proceeds to expose the deceitfulness of those false teachers who sought to lead them astray.

Now, we may learn a lesson for our times from this. God has given us in the truth a banner, not to be folded up and laid past, but to be displayed; and it is our duty to hold forth, and to hold fast, the Word of life. But we falter often in discharging that duty. Instead of boldly asserting the truth, we go about almost as if we felt that we should apologise for being Christians.

Under the guise of charity, we are becoming latitudinarian; and, lest we should provoke controversy, we are tempted timidly to hold our peace. But there are some things concerning which it is a sin to be silent; and among these I place all opinions that degrade either the person or the work of Christ.

Who so loving as the Apostle John, especially in his closing days? Yet it is he who has written these words: "If there come any unto you, and bring not this doctrine, receive him not into your house, neither bid him godspeed." Who so forbearing as Paul, who became all things to all men, that he might by all means save some? Yet when ritual observances were alleged by some to be indispensable to salvation, he gave place by subjection—no, not for an hour, but said, "If any man preach any other Gospel to you than that ye have received, let him be accursed." Who so liable to be influenced by others as Peter? And yet it is thus he characterizes those who would seduce professing Christians from the right way: "These are wells without water, clouds that are carried with a tempest; to whom the mist of darkness is reserved forever."

Let us imitate the holy boldness of these servants of God, and give prominence to the truth as it is in Jesus. Let us enthrone Christ in our hearts, that his truth may be continually on our lips. Let us give distinct and decided pre-eminence to Christ alike in our religious opinions and our religious teachings; and as the preaching which every age needs is the preaching of the Gospel, we shall see again the fact revealed that it is "the power of God unto salvation to every one that believeth."

We may learn, secondly, that the great secret of Christian peace and usefulness is the cultivation of holiness. In his first letter, Peter, quoting from one of the Psalms, says, "He that will love life, and see good days, let him refrain his tongue from evil, and his lips that they speak no guile: let him eschew evil, and do good; let him seek peace, and ensue it;" and in his second, after exhorting to the cultivation of the Christian graces, he adds, "If these things be in you, and abound, they make you that ye shall neither be barren nor unfruitful in the knowledge of our Lord Jesus Christ." Christianity is not a creed merely, though it is of immense importance that the creed be sound; neither is it an emotion merely, though wherever it is genuine there is sure to be emotion; but it is pre-eminently a character built upon the foundation of the Lord Jesus Christ, and after the pattern of his spotless life.

No one can read these letters of Peter without having that thought deeply imprinted upon his heart. To be happy, we must be holy. True Christian experience is not a mere effervescence of feeling, or a simple intellectual assent to a system of doctrine. It is CHARACTER-BUILDING; and only in the proportion in which we attain to the likeness of Christ can we be either happy or useful in the world. Let us leave off, then, all other considerations if we want to have joy; let us lay our faith on Christ, and then add to our faith courage, and knowledge, and temperance, and patience, and brotherly kindness, and love; for thereby alone can we make our "calling and election sure." And while thus we labour for our own comfort, we shall be at the same time working for the benefit of others, for the influence—call it rather the effluence —of character cannot be over-estimated. We are moulding others wherever we are, and then most of all when we are least conscious that we are doing so. And if we were in every respect to live according to the Gospel, we should be the noblest missionaries of the cross whom the world has ever seen.

Let us therefore resolve that, by the grace of God, we shall regulate ourselves by those principles which Christ enforced by his teaching and glorified by his example. In the family let us cultivate the graces of patience, forbearance, love, and self-sacrifice; in the social circle, let us manifest meekness and purity; in business pursuits, let us show that we are actuated by justice and integrity; yea, wherever we are, let us endeavour to have our conversation so worthy of the Gospel that men shall "take knowledge of us that we have been with Jesus." In vain are all other efforts for the evangelization of the people, if they be not accompanied by this godly living. To no purpose is our profession of attachment to Jesus if it be not confirmed by this holy character. We may not be able to speak or write for Jesus, and for the moment other walks of usefulness may seem closed against us; but we can all live for him; and the purer our characters, the happier will be our hearts, and the more useful our lives.

Finally, in contending for the truth and striving after holiness, we are to expect affliction. As long as we are on the earth, we shall have trials. These may come either in the providence of God, or as the result of the wickedness of our fellow-men; but, rightly borne, they will only purge our characters and enlarge our usefulness. What a rich catena of consolation may be formed out of these letters! And how can I better conclude than with a specimen, which may send you to the letters themselves for the rest: "Though now for a season, if need be, ye are in heaviness through manifold temptations, that the trial of your faith, being much more precious than of gold that perisheth, though it be tried with fire, might be found unto praise and honour and glory at the appearing of Jesus Christ;" "Wherefore gird up the loins of your mind, be sober, and hope to the end for the grace that is to be brought unto you at the revelation of Jesus Christ;" "Beloved, think it not strange concerning the fiery trial which is to try you, as though some strange thing happened unto you: but rejoice, insomuch as ye are partakers of Christ's sufferings; that, when his glory shall be revealed, ye may be glad also with exceeding joy;" "Wherefore let them that suffer according to the will of God commit the keeping of their souls to him in well doing, as unto a faithful Creator;" "An entrance shall be ministered unto you abundantly into the everlasting kingdom of our Lord and Saviour Jesus Christ;" "Account that the long suffering of our Lord is salvation;"

"Be diligent that ye may be found of him in peace, without spot and blameless;" God "hath begotten us again unto a lively hope by the resurrection of Jesus Christ from the dead, to an inheritance incorruptible and undefiled, and that fadeth not away, reserved in heaven for you, who are kept by the power of God through faith unto salvation ready to be revealed in the last time."

XXIII.

SIMON PETER A SERVANT AND AN APOSTLE OF CHRIST.

2 Peter i., 1.

THE study of a single biography, especially if it be that of a distinguished and earnest man, is apt to beget in us the disposition to imitate it. We are prone to make it the mould into which we determine to run ourselves; and character in us, instead of being developed from within, is repressed and regulated from without. We cut and shape it after the style of our model, as the old-fashioned gardener used to do with his trees and shrubs, instead of allowing it to spread out into its own individuality and pruning off mere excrescences, as the skilled botanist does with each plant under his care. That which ought to be natural is made artificial; the spontaneousness goes out of it, and character degenerates into caricature. Thus hero-worship becomes positively injurious; and, strange as it may seem, it tends, by the exclusiveness of its homage, to overlay and destroy the very things by which it was first evoked.

The echo is always more indistinct and shadowy than the voice; and he who tries to make himself into another man only mars himself, while he falls very far short of reaching the other's excellence. The highest merit of character, next after its moral and spiritual excellence, is individuality. This is true in all departments; but it is too often forgotten in the religious life. The poet, or painter, or philosopher who is simply and only an imitator has not risen to the highest greatness.

We crave in literature and art for originality. But in religious things men are apt to imagine that they must keep down their individuality, and squeeze themselves into the shape and pattern of certain excellent ones with whose histories they have become enamoured. It is not enough that they come to Christ, but they must get up the same precise experiences in coming to him that their model passed through. It is not sufficient that they should serve Christ; but their service, no matter what the times require of them, must take the same form as that of their models. What was proper and noble in the one becomes thus forced and exotic in the other; and so too frequently the happiness of the heart and the usefulness of the life are impaired.

Now, it seems to me that there is no better corrective to this evil than the analysis of the characters of the good men whose lives are given in the Word of God. In the great inner principles of faith in God and loyalty to him they were all alike; but in their individual features there is as much diversity among them as there is in the countenances of this audience. The heart-beat in man is the same in all races; but there is still a marked difference between the European and the red man; and so, though they are all alike in the great heart-throb of faith, there are yet clear distinctions between those whose histories are recorded here. Isaac, with his meditative and pensive spirit, is in many respects a contrast to the active and energetic Abraham. Moses, the man of God, is easily distinguishable even from one so nearly related to him as Aaron; and though, in many respects, they remind us of each other, Nehemiah had not the mystic fervour and keen-eyed insight of Daniel. So among the apostles, there were no two alike. John was the man of intuition, who took in things more by absorption than by reasoning. Thomas was the representative of independence, who would be satisfied on all subjects for himself. Philip was the plain matter-of-fact one, who never thought of a figurative sense in which words were to be understood, so long as he could cling to a literal one. Andrew was the usher among the twelve, finding his delight in leading

Y

friends and strangers alike to Jesus. And Peter was the outspoken, impulsive, irrepressible, who was first and fieriest in everything. They were all different; and yet the Holy Ghost, working in them all, turned their idiosyncrasies to good account in the service of their Master. He did not make each the fac-simile of the other, but he developed each into himself, only that self, purified, sublimated, and ennobled.

Now, the lesson of all this for us is, that we should not seek to repeat another in ourselves, but rather should endeavour, like all the twelve, to reduce the principles on which they acted to such practice as is demanded by our circumstances and our age. There is only one whom it is safe for us exclusively to imitate, and he was more than man. Yet, even in regard to him, we shall make egregious mistakes if we attempt to repeat his actions from without, instead of imbibing his spirit, and leaving that to manifest itself through us as occasion requires. Naturalness is indispensable to sincerity; and the development of principle from within is indispensable to naturalness. There ought to be no fashion in piety. In the matter of character as well as of party, no one should say, "I am of Paul," or "I am of Cephas;" but each should say, "I am of Christ:" meaning by that that he has adopted the principles of Christ, and is seeking to apply them every day to his circumstances and responsibilities.

When, therefore, we proceed, in this concluding discourse, to point out the distinctive features of Peter's disposition, you will understand that we are using him only as an aid in self-formation, and that we do not seek to induce you to merge your individuality in his. He was himself only saved and sanctified by Christ; and the great lesson of his career is that we should be ourselves only saved, and, if possible, still more highly sanctified than he was.

In analysing the character of Peter, I place first his transparent sincerity. You could read him at a glance. His heart was always in his countenance and on his lips. He could not be a hypocrite; and the only time he attempted to deceive, he made such bungling work of it that no one would believe his lie. What was in him, was sure in some way or other to come out. He had no diplomacy about him, and was as far as possible from believing that language was designed to conceal thought. Nay, rather, he thought aloud; and the result was, that while men sometimes admired him, and sometimes laughed at him, and sometimes blamed him, they always loved him. He always believed in taking the straight line. There was no cunning or duplicity about him. He could not have gone about like Judas, nourishing secret enmity in his heart, and seeking a favourable opportunity for its gratification. Neither did he seek honour by roundabout ways. In this respect he was superior even to James and John, who schemed, through their mother, for the highest places in the kingdom. He did nothing underhand. All about him was open and above board; and when he had heard about himself, he was eager also to know what should come to his friend.

Now, in all this there was much to admire, and not a little to desire; for, sooth to say, this simplicity of sincerity has gone largely out of fashion among us. Men isolate themselves by their reticence, and repel all advances by their reserve; they count it a merit to be inscrutable, and a silliness to be open and ingenuous. Scheming is the order of the day, and life is regarded as a game of whist, in which each one keeps his hand hidden from his neighbour. Frankness is the mark of inexperience, and the wearing of a mask is not by any means confined to the ball-room, but may be seen, perhaps more frequently, in the exchanges, and even in the Church.

Now, I am aware that frankness may be carried, as it was occasionally in Peter, too far. We cannot blame him for his words to the Lord regarding his death, or his answer to Jesus about the washing of his feet; while his language on the Mount of Transfiguration was strangely out of place. But still he was genuine; and I have no hesitation in saying that the mistake of an honest man is better than the hypocrisy of a dishonest one. The openness of Peter, though it was now and then foolish, and even sinful, was a far higher thing than the cautious and apparently blameless demeanour of Judas; though, of course, better than either is the well-balanced self-control of him who has learned that there is a time to speak and a time to be silent.

We need not, perhaps, like Peter, utter all we think or feel on every occasion; for not to say that we may often be wrong, there are many seasons and many subjects on which we are not called to speak at all. But it ought to be an invariable rule with us not to say anything which we do not think or feel. No matter what it may cost us; though we may lose profits by it; though for the moment we may lose friends, and forfeit the good opinion of those we love; though it may threaten to bring ruin upon us, yet it is above and beyond all things needful that we be sincere. The only disgraces that came on Peter were the results of his attempting a dishonest course; and we may be sure that how great soever the calamity may be with which our honesty threatens us, the degradation of insincerity will be lower and more debasing than any suffering. There is no ruin possible to a man save that of character, and insincerity always scuttles that. All may seem prosperous around; the sky above may be bright, the sea may be calm, the vessel may be well provisioned; but away down in the secret hold it is pierced through, and the water is rushing in which by-and-by will make the ship sink, all unrecorded, beneath the waves. I tell you, friends, I had rather have the outburst of an occasional storm the result of impetuous rashness, than a slow, remediless, and unwept foundering like that!

A second feature in the character of Peter was promptitude. He did at once what his hand found to do. He lost no time over deliberation, and never hesitated to say what he felt to be true, or to do what seemed to him to be right. When the Lord revealed himself to him in the miracle of the first draught of fishes, he cried out in a moment, "Depart from me; for I am a sinful man, O Lord." And though, on that occasion, his perception of a clear truth took rather an unfortunate way of expressing itself, yet it was the very same readiness that prompted him in other circumstances to say, "To whom shall we go? thou hast the words of eternal life; and we believe and are sure that thou art the Christ, the son of the living God."

So, again, when John hesitated to enter the sepulchre, Peter went in at once; and when he was sent for to come to Joppa without delay, in consequence of the death of Dorcas, he arose and returned with the messengers. In like manner, when the servants of Cornelius came for him, he responded to their invitation without gainsaying as soon as he was sent for. His habit thus was to act on the moment. It would have been better, indeed, if he had been occasionally more deliberate. He was apt to be zealous at the expense of prudence, and was guilty of speaking and acting, even in circumstances of importance, without due reflection. What he was going to see at all, he commonly saw at a glance; and he did not take time in all cases to look round a subject before he committed himself regarding it. This frequently brought him into inconsistencies and absurdities from which a little forethought would have saved him. Thus, if he had reflected for a little, he never would have presumed to rebuke his Master for his reference to his death, or to resist the washing of his feet, or to take out his sword and cut off the ear of Malchus. In fairness, however, it must be added that, if this feature of his character sometimes led him into errors, it prompted also to his speedy relinquishment of them when their nature was pointed out to him. If he did say, "Thou shalt never wash my feet," he was as ready to exclaim, when the significance of this act was explained to him, "Not my feet only, but my hands and my head;" the very extravagance of the recoil indicating how sincerely it was made. He did not anchor himself over his sayings, and stick to them, just to be consistent. But if he hastily uttered that which was wrong, he was as much in haste to retract it when he discovered what it really was. In this respect he was largely a contrast to his fellow-apostle Paul. The man of Tarsus was consistent throughout. He carefully examined his ground before he took it, but when he had taken it he was immovable. Peter, again, was quick in all his movements; and if he did sometimes step rashly in a marshy place, he sprung just as speedily out of it again.

But while all this must be frankly conceded, we must never lose sight of the fact that it was through this very promptitude to say out, and act upon, that which he saw at the moment, that he owed his position as the leader of the apostolic band on the day of Pentecost. For it was this that led him to utter his memorable confession at Cesarea Philippi, "Thou art the Christ, the son of the living God." Flesh and blood did not reveal that truth to him. It had been unveiled before him by his Father in heaven; but so soon as he saw it he said it, and the public utterance was a source of delight to the Lord.

We may moralize, if we choose, over Peter's impulsiveness, and bewail the absence of caution by which, on many occasions, he was characterized; but the fact remains, that the world has never owed very much to your prudent people, who are always afraid to do anything until they know assuredly that they are doing the right thing. If Luther had been a man of that temperament, there would have been no Reformation; and, for my part, I am almost ready to forgive Peter's mistakes, for the great blessings which his promptitude has secured for us. I would be far indeed from urging to precipitate action in any matter; and yet, if we could combine it with the wisdom of such a one as John, it would be well for most of us that we had Peter's promptitude.

The evil with many now is, not that they are in any doubt as to what they should do, but that they will not do it at once. Thus, in the matter of confessing Christ, there are probably very few among us who do not believe that he is the Saviour of the world, and are not trusting in him for our own deliverance; nay, there are, perhaps, not many among us who are not cherishing the purpose that, at some time, they will take a public stand under the leadership of Jesus; but they hesitate, deliberate, delay until at length the habit of procrastination is formed, and it is never done at all. I grant that a step should always be taken carefully, deliberately, and prayerfully; but we should not be always deliberating; and the example of Peter, with the honour that came upon him in consequence, is full of significance to those who are halting and irresolute. How much, also, is there in his readiness to go to the household of Dorcas or the abode of Cornelius, to instruct, if not indeed, to rebuke, the ministers of the Gospel! We postpone such calls too frequently to other and less important interests, and industriously fish in other less productive waters, when, if we were to repair to the chambers of the sick and the homes of the inquiring, we might be blessed in leading many to the Lord.

Peter's rule was evidently the same as that which the much-loved Payson had so frequently on his lips: "The man who wants me is the man I want;" and he sought to be a blessing to all who in any way needed or invoked his aid. Thus, without at all ignoring the evils that must result when promptitude degenerates into rashness, there are lessons from this aspect of Peter's character which are appropriate both to the occupant of the pulpit and the hearers in the pews. "Whatsoever thy hand findeth to do, do it with thy might; for there is no work, nor device, nor knowledge, nor wisdom in the grave whither thou goest."

Another element in Peter's character was his courage. We too frequently associate him with the denial of his Lord, and his vacillating conduct at Antioch, as if these were typical instances in his life. But, though it is undeniable that on both of these occasions he was seized with panic, we should do him great injustice if we were to suppose that they were normal or habitual with him. Now and then, after a day's terrific rain, there is a freshet in the river, which does a little damage, and spreads a little alarm; but that is not its usual condition. So these were freshets in Peter's history; and before one of them, at least, there was a night of such experiences as, on a nature like his, impulsive and sensitive and intense, might well produce a tendency to panic. Perhaps, also, if we fully knew the details concerning the other, we might see something in them which helped to explain the inconsistency which was so grieving to Paul. But, however that may have been, Peter was in the main a courageous man. If he did deny the Lord, do not let us forget that he was the only one of the twelve save John who had the courage to follow the Lord, after his apprehension, into the palace of the high-priest. Behold him, too, before the Council! There is no faltering in his speech, there is no quivering in his heart there. On the contrary, it was his boldness which, most of all, attracted the attention of his judges, and made them take knowledge of him that he had been with Jesus. And no one can accuse *him* of cowardice who was ready to die at the hands of Herod, and who actually gave up his life at last as a martyr for the truth as it is in Jesus.

Sometimes, indeed, his courage degenerated into rashness, as when, before fearful military odds, he drew the sword in defence of his Lord. But in general he was resolute and unbending. When he failed, it was because he trusted in himself; when he stood, it was because "he endured as seeing him who is invisible." So long as he thought of doing that which was right in the sight of God, he was inflexible and invincible; but when he counselled with flesh and blood, or had regard to the opinions or prejudices of men, he faltered, and fell back.

Now, we have here at once an example for imitation, and a beacon for warning. Our bearing before temptation will be like that of Peter before the Council, or like that of the same apostle before the damsel in the high-priest's hall, according as we are determined to do that which is right in the sight of God, or are trusting in our own strength, and glorifying in our own steadfastness. There is never any difficulty about determining what our duty is when we look at the matter as one between ourselves and God; and we shall always be enabled to perform that duty when we think of it as something laid upon us by Him who gave his life in our behalf. But when we hold parley with fashion, or interest, or earthly prudence, and allow the consideration of men's favour or antagonism to come into operation, immediately complication begins; and when we are in such a hesitating mood, even such a little thing as the banter of a silly girl, or the vague foreboding of some blind partisan, will be all that is needed to send us off in the wrong direction. When the balance is in equipoise, the slightest touch of an infant's hand upon the beam will send it down to its farthest limit. But when you put a weight into the scale, it is a harder thing to move it. So, if we would make ourselves immovably steadfast in the face of all temptation or threatening, we must weight ourselves down by confidence in God, and put him between us and the efforts of our assailants. When we do that, they will not stir us till they can cope with him.

I name only one other characteristic of Peter, namely, his *intensity*. There are some men so lymphatic in their temperament that they are moved by nothing. They hate enthusiasm, and cannot be made to alter their pace by any influence whatever. They must do everything with precision—slowly, orderly, without any emotion, or any manifestation of interest. And, not content with being such men themselves, each seems to carry about with him a portable fire-engine, with which he is prepared at once to extinguish every spark of enthusiasm that begins to glow in others. Peter was very far from being one of these. There was an ardour about him that radiated through everything which he said or did. His nature was pre-eminently incandescent. He was whole-hearted in all he undertook.

His opinions and actions were not separable from himself, but he sent himself after everything he said, and he "moved altogether when he moved at all." He seemed to be always at a white heat; and so when he was right, he was enthusiastically right; and when he was wrong, he was energetically wrong.

The hot-house brings forth weeds as luxuriantly as it develops flowers; and so a nature like Peter's leads to prominence in evil as well as pre-eminence in good. You see the same intensity in his denial as you do in his confession; but because the bent of his character was mainly toward Christ and holiness, his enthusiasm was most frequently manifested in his Master's service. What could be more touching than his expression of attachment to the Lord at the supper table, or his thrice-repeated answer to the Saviour's question on the shore of Gennesaret? And in the work of preaching the Gospel, there are no finer specimens of burning eloquence than his sermon on the day of Pentecost and his address before the Council. I could not put him higher in this respect than Paul, but he was at least on a level with him; and it is only because occasionally his courage gave way to panic, and his promptitude degenerated into rashness, that he was in any way morally inferior to the Apostle of the Gentiles. In one thing they were alike, namely, their ardent attachment to the Lord, and their jealousy of anything that infringed on his prerogative. Peter's reproof of Simon Magus stands side by side with Paul's trenchant address to Elymas, the sorcerer; and both are pervaded with that burning loyalty to the Holy Ghost for which they were remarkable.

But enthusiasm has its perils as well as its excellence. When the pendulum swings with all its weight to one side, there is always danger that it will go as heavily to the other; and so those who are gifted with intensity have need to be on their guard, lest they are borne by it in a wrong direction. "It is good to be zealously affected always in a good thing." Earnestness, in and of itself, is little; everything depends on the object in which it is enlisted. It is no mitigation of wrong to say that a man is sincerely wrong. It is no extenuation of evil to affirm that a man is earnestly in evil. The sincerity will make it all the more dangerous for himself, and the earnestness will render it all the more injurious to others. One is not the less really opposed to God because he is sincerely so, and the earnestness of his antagonism will lead him only to more aggravated sin.

Let us see to it, therefore, that we keep our intensity subordinate to conscience. It is always dangerous for a vessel to strike a rock; but if she be a steamship, with her engines going at full speed, the ruin will be tremendous. An ordinary carriage cannot be overturned without peril to its inmate; but the wrecking of an express train is something frightful. So when a man of intensity like David or like Peter goes into sin, the evil is terrible; and it behoves those who have such an ardent temperament to be peculiarly on their guard.

But I cannot conclude without making three inferences from our whole subject. The first is that a man's defects are frequently in the near neighbourhood of his excellencies. We have seen how Peter's promptitude occasionally leaned over into hastiness, and his courage sometimes degenerated into rashness; and if we take a wider range of inquiry, we may discover that good men are in most danger where they are usually strongest. I grant, indeed, that most of us have special weaknesses where we know we are most liable to fail: but, just because we know that, we are most watchful in regard to these. It is not so often considered, however, that we have all particular elements of strength, our knowledge of which leads to confidence in them; and that, again, is the precursor of a fall. In this way we account for the fact that some of the greatest saints who have ever lived have failed in their characteristic graces; and in Peter it was in those very elements of genuineness and courage which were his most marked excellencies that he fell, not once, but twice. So it is not safe to relax our watchfulness in any particular. "Let him that thinketh he standeth, take heed lest he fall;" and where we are commonly the strongest, let us post the wariest sentinel.

Again, we may learn that a man's usefulness often springs out of some recovery from sin. It is the high prerogative of God to bring good out of evil, and even the existence of sin has been the occasion of manifesting the mercy of Jehovah. So in the case of the individual believer, his very falls are turned by the Holy Spirit to good account in giving him an experience which enables him to be a benefit to others. Those who have been the victims of intemperance, and have been restored to themselves and to society by the grace of God, are thereby better fitted than other men for rescuing the drunkard; and their success in such Christ-like work is at least some consolation to them when they look back on the doleful past. In the same way, Peter's fall and restoration are the fountain from which has flowed the stream of his first epistle. That is, from first to last, a letter for the tried and tempted whom he seeks to comfort with the comfort wherewith he himself was comforted of God. Thus the fall of one Christian, when he is restored, may become the means of preventing others from yielding to temptation, or from sinking into despair; for he raises a beacon on the rock whereon he struck, and makes the navigation just so much the safer for those who shall come after him. Strengthen thy brethren, therefore, out of thine own experience; and if God have saved thee from peril, cry back a word of warning to those who are in danger, and send a message of cheer back to those who are in despondency.

Finally, we get a fresh glimpse into the Saviour's heart through his treatment of the son of Jonas. Is it not true, brethren, that God's revelations of himself to us come most strikingly and suggestively through his dealings with individual men? When we speak of him as the God of Abraham, we think of him especially in strengthening his people under severest trial. When we call him the God of Jacob, we have before us those two scenes at Bethel and Peniel, and we think of him as the God who heareth prayer. When we regard him as the Lord God of Elijah, we think of him as he who provideth for his own, aye, even when they lie under the juniper tree of discouragement and desertion of duty. And so the Lord Jesus has revealed himself to us through his dealings with his different disciples. As the Saviour of Thomas, he is brought before us as one who deals gently with the doubter, and leads him up to faith. As the Saviour of Paul, he is manifested to us as the sustainer of his servants in every form of trial and suffering. But as the Saviour of Peter, he is preeminently and emphatically the restorer of the penitent. What could be more touching in its tenderness than the fact that on the afternoon of the resurrection day the Lord Jesus had a private interview with his repentant servant, and kissed the past into forgetfulness? And is there not in this peculiar encouragement to the backslider to return to him? Is there one here who has denied the Lord—one who in business, or in domestic life, or in society, has repudiated the Saviour, whom in earlier days he sought to honour and promised to serve? Then let him learn from the history of that servant of God, whose life has been so long our theme, how freely Jesus will forgive those who return their allegiance to him. Come back, my friend, come back! He will not cast you out. He will put a new song into your mouth, and teach you to say, "He restoreth my soul: he leadeth me in the paths of righteousness for his name's sake." Take with you words, and say,

> "Jesus, let thy pitying eye
>   Call back a wandering sheep;
> False to thee, like Peter, I
>   Would fain, like Peter, weep.
>
> "Let me be by grace restored;
>   On me be all long-suffering shown:
> Turn and look upon me, Lord,
>   And melt my heart of stone;"

and soon the answer will come, "I will heal your backsliding; I will love you freely: for mine anger is turned away from you."

And so we take our leave of thee, thou generous, impulsive, wayward, impetuous, yet true-hearted man of God! We have come to know ourselves better through our acquaintance with thee, and even thy backsliding has shown us new depths of mercy in the heart of Christ. So, being converted, thou hast strengthened thy brethren, and we glorify God in thee. Thy very errors have brought thee closer to ourselves, and taught us at once our danger and our safety. Now hast thou ascended to the true Mount of Transfiguration, whereon thou dwellest in no frail "tabernacle" such as thou didst wish to rear on Hermon's summit, but in "an house not made with hands eternal in the heavens;" and when the chief Shepherd shall appear, may there be for us as for thee "a crown of glory that fadeth not away."

INDEX.

ALEXANDER, W. L., LL.D., edition of "Kitto's Cyclopædia," by, quoted from or referred to, 70, 223, 309.
Alford's "Commentary on the New Testament," quoted from or referred to, 108, 144, 222, 261, 263.
Ananias and Sapphira, sin of, 202—204 ; aggravations of their guilt, 204 ; punishment of, 206.
Andrew follows Jesus, 14 ; brings Peter to Jesus, 16, 20.
Antagonism to be expected by Christ's disciples, 187.
Antagonists of the apostles described, 182—184.
Apostasy, root of, 61 ; beginning of, 106.
Applause, human, fluctuating character of, 59 ; danger of, to the minister, 60.
Atonement, modern objections to, considered, 87—92.
Attitude of Christ to the inquirer, 17, 55 ; to the penitent, 133.

BABYLON, Peter at, 291.
Barnabas, liberality of, 202 ; at the Council of Jerusalem, 291 ; at Antioch, 291.
Beautiful Gate, lame man at the, 169.
Becket, Thomas à, Archbishop of Canterbury, reference to, 116.
Bethsaida described, 14, 15.
Biography, cautions in the study of, 320.
Bringing others to Christ, duty of, 20 ; methods of, 22 ; where to begin in, 23, 27.
Brown, John, of Haddington, description of, 41.
Bryant, W. C., quotation from, 225.
Bunyan, John, words of, 226 ; anecdote of, 228.
Burns, Rev. J. D., verses by, 289.

CARLYLE, Thomas, quoted from, 95, 210, 252.
Cesarea described, 258.
Cesarea Philippi described, 68.
Chalmers, Thomas, referred to, 27, 239.

Character-building the great end of Christianity, 317.

Christ receives Peter, 16; goes to Capernaum, 28; preaches from Peter's boat, 30; gives miraculous draught of fishes to Peter, 31; heals Peter's mother-in-law, 42; ordains the twelve, 42; hears of the death of the Baptist, 43; feeds the multitude, 44; sends his disciples across the lake, 44; walks upon the waters, 45; encourages Peter to do the same, 46; refuses to be made a king, 57; goes to Cesarea Philippi, 67; blesses Peter for his confession, 72; rebukes Peter for his aversion to the doctrine of a suffering Saviour, 85; takes Peter, James, and John up to the Mount, 96; keeps his last passover, 110; washes the feet of the disciples, 112; is denied by Peter, 113; death of, 139; resurrection of, 139; appears to the disciples, 140; and to Peter, 141.

Christians, remind on-lookers of Christ, 187; walk only after God's word, 190; have chosen fellowship with each other, 192.

Church, early Christian, relation of, to the Jewish, 167; female membership in, 216; early progress of, 246; unity of, 284.

Church in the house, importance of the, 24.

Clarkson and Wilberforce, anecdote of, 105.

Clement, testimony of, as to Peter's last days, 313.

Community of goods in early Church considered, 197—202.

Confession of Christ, the result of divine operation on the soul, 78; connected with the permanence of the Church, 80; and with its progress, 80.

Cornelius, character of, 258; vision of, 260; sends for Peter, 260; meets him with deference, 262; is received by baptism into the Church, 267.

Council, Jewish, described, 184; Peter's address before, 185; second appearance at, 219.

Courage, a characteristic of Peter, 327.

Cross, no kingdom without a, 92.

DANGER sometimes greatest where we are commonly strongest, 134; of one evil habit, 210; of one-sided views, 297.

Devotion needs seclusion, 104; sees new glory in Christ and in his word, 106; is not the whole of life, 107; furnishes support for duty and trial, 108.

Dick, Rev. John, D.D., quoted from, 237.

Difficulties of a speculative sort should not keep us from following Christ, 151.

Discipleship precedes apostleship, 32.

Distance from the Lord a precursor of denial, 128.

Dorcas, an illustration of practical beneficence, 251; raised to life by Peter, 254.

INDEX. 337

ELIJAH, the prototype of John the Baptist, 2; on the Mount with Christ, 99.
Eneas cured by Peter at Lydda, 250.
Experience, Christian, importance of, for steadfastness, 65.

FAIRBAIRN's "Imperial Bible Dictionary," quoted from, 17, 69.
Fidelity the truest kindness, 178, 300.
Finding Christ, meaning of, 18—20.
First Epistle of Peter, date of, 306; contents and characteristics of, 307.
Fishers of men, meaning of, 39—41.
Fishes, first miraculous draught of, 31; second miraculous draught of, 141; comparison of the one to the other, 142; meaning of both, 142.

GAMALIEL, character of, 223; advice of, 224, 225.
Gennesaret, Lake of, 29, 30; storm on, 45.
Gentiles received into the Church, 267.
Gift of tongues, 156; comparison of, with the phenomena in the Church of Corinth, 157, 158.
God's fullest revelations made through the histories of individual men, 333.
Gospel for the people, 218; Petrine, 222.
Guthrie, Rev. Dr. Thomas, contrasted with J. S. Mill, 239.

HAMILTON, Patrick, referred to, 288
Hanna, Rev. Dr. W., quoted from, 98.
Havelock, General, letter by, 190.
Hearers prepared for the preacher, 271.
Henry, Matthew, saying of, 106.
Herod Agrippa I., character of, 275; puts James to death, 277; imprisons Peter, 278; death of, 284.
High priest's accusation of Peter, 220.
Holiness essential to peace, 316.
Holy Spirit, baptism of the, 4, 9; gift of the, on Pentecost, 154—156; second baptism of the, 186; conferred on the Gentiles, 267.
Home the starting place of Christian work, 23—26.
House, description of an Oriental, 124.
Humility the spirit of martyrdom, 145.
Hypocrisy impossible with God, 211; a case of, does not prove a revival false, 241.

IMPRISONMENT of apostles, 184, 217; of Peter by Herod, 278
Inspiration different from sanctification, 294.
Intensity a characteristic of Peter, 329.

Z

JAMES, martyrdom of, by Herod, 277.
Jay, Rev. W., quoted from, 35.
John the Apostle, introduction of, to Jesus, 14 ; Gospel of, 137 ; runs with Peter to the sepulchre, 140 ; comparison of, with Peter, 168, 169.
John the Baptist, ministry of, 1, 13 ; preaching of, 3 ; baptism of, 4 ; points out Jesus to his followers, 5 ; humility of, 6 ; resemblance of, to Elijah, 6 ; a model of self-renunciation, 12.
Joppa described, 250 ; Peter's vision at, 261.
Josephus, Flavius, quoted from, 1, 224, 276, 283.
Joy the result of receiving the Gospel, 238.
Judas, beginning of apostasy of, 58 ; why chosen as an apostle, 62 ; explanation of treachery of, 63 ; remorse of, distinquished from repentance, 133.
Judea, condition of, when John the Baptist appeared, 1.

KEBLE, John, quoted from, 13, 257.
Keys, gift of, to Peter, 76—78.
Kingdom of Heaven, meaning of, 74 ; law of the, 92.

LAME man, the, at the Beautiful Gate of the Temple, 169.
Law of the kingdom, 92.
Laws of nature, in relation to miracles, 171 ; and to prayer, 287.
Leighton, Archbishop, saying of, 40.
Leighton, William, lines by, 54.
Liberty, relation of Peter's words to, 221.
Light increased to us when we use what we have, 268.
Lightfoot, Rev. J. R., D.D., quoted from, 295.
Lipsius, view of, on the question of Peter's visit to Rome, 314.
Longfellow, H. W., quoted from, 273.
Luther, Martin, referred to, 239.
Lydda described, 248.

MAMMON and God cannot be served at once, 209.
Matheson, Duncan, anecdote of, 240.
Mill, J. S., contrasted with Guthrie, 239.
Minister, the, must be absorbed in his work, 36 ; a fisher of men, 39—41 ; must be indifferent to applause for its own sake, 60
Ministry, faithful, effect of a, twofold, 207.
Miracle, definition of a, 171 ; possibility of a, 172 ; relation of, to the Gospel, 172 ; evidential value of a, 173.
Moffat, Robert, D.D., lines of, written in an album, 38.
Money not the most valuable thing, 177.

INDEX.

Moody, D. L., work of, referred to, 11, 241.
Moses on the Mount, 99.
Motive, true, to Christian work, 149.
Myers, F. W. H., quoted from, 7.

NEANDER, Augustus, quoted from, 9, 199, 234, 260.
Newton, John, anecdotes of, 36 ; saying of, 93.

OBJECTIONS to the doctrine of atonement considered, 87, 92.

PALAZZO, Rospigliosi, illustration from, 174.
Pastoral office, wide range of, 147.
Paul, first meeting of, with Peter, 244 ; at Antioch, 292 ; expostulation of, with Peter, 295 ; lessons from his conduct on that occasion, 301—303.
Pentecost, meaning of, 153 ; reasons for selecting day of, for the gift of the Holy Ghost, 154 ; meeting of the disciples on day of, 155 ; gift of tongues on, 155 ; Peter's sermon on day of, 159 ; connection of prayer with, blessings on, 163.
Perpetuity of the Word of God, 288.
Persecution, root of, 184 ; overruled for good of the Church, 237, 238 ; a blunder, 288.
Peter introduced to Christ by Andrew, 16, 20 ; lends his boat for a pulpit to Christ, 30 ; miraculous draught of fishes by, 31 ; effect of that miracle on, 31 ; called to apostleship, 31 ; first in all the lists of the Twelve, 43 ; walks on the water and begins to sink, 46 ; characteristics of, 46, 113, 114, 141, 147, 321—334 ; first confession of, 58 ; second confession of, 71 ; meaning of Christ's promises to, 72—78 ; rebuked by the Lord, 85 ; taken up to the holy mount, 96 ; washing of feet of, 112 ; consistent individuality of, in the New Testament, 113 ; denials of Christ by, 123—126 ; precursors of denials of, 127 ; sequel of denials of, 132 ; runs with John to the sepulchre, 140 ; receives a threefold commission, 143 ; sermon of, on Pentecost, 159 ; compared with John, 168 ; sermon of, at Solomon's Porch, 175 ; shadow of, 214, 215 ; before the council the second time, 221—223 ; reproves Simon Magus, 236 ; first meeting of, with Paul, 244 ; cures Eneas at Lydda, 250 ; raises Dorcas to life at Joppa, 254 ; vision of, at Joppa, 261 ; goes to Cornelius, 262 ; sermon of, in house of Cornelius, 265 ; promptitude of, 224, 269 ; imprisoned by Herod, 278 ; composure of, 280 ; released by an angel, 281 ; received by the disciples, 282 ; vacillation of, at Antioch, 292 ; reproved by Paul, 292 ; epistles of, 305 ; at Babylon, 305 ; did he visit Rome ? 312.
Philip the Deacon, preaching of, in Samaria, 232.
Pollock, Robert, saying of, 27 ; quoted from, 194.

Pope, the, not the successor of Peter, 77; washing of feet by the, 117; primacy of the, not connected with Peter, 214.

Porch, Solomon's, description of, 175; Peter's sermon in, 175, 176.

Practical beneficence illustrated by Dorcas, 251.

Prayer, Pentecost begun in, 163; the resource of Christians in trial, 194; offered by disciples for Peter's release, 279; power of, 286; relation of, to laws of nature, 287.

Preachers prepared by God for their hearers, 271.

Preaching, characteristics of Peter's, at Pentecost, 165, 166.

Pressensé, Edward de, quoted from, 6.

Prison, Peter's release from, an illustration of the Christian's death, 289.

Promptitude necessary in dealing with inquirers, 269; a characteristic of Peter, 324.

RASHNESS prepares the way for the denial of Christ, 127.

Renan's "Life of Jesus," quoted from, 138.

Repentance, as preached by John the Baptist, 3; preaching of, the prelude to revival, 8; genuine marks of, 133; connection of, with times of refreshing, 180.

Reproof to be received with meekness, 299.

Revival, begins in prayer, 163; shows itself first in the quickening of disciples, 164; accompanied by the preaching of the truth, 164.

Ritter's "Comparative Geography of Palestine," quoted from, 97.

Robertson, F. W., referred to, 268.

Robinson, Rev. Dr. Edward, quoted from, 68, 111.

Rogers, Henry, quoted from, 89.

SACRIFICIAL character of Christ's death, 11; importance of preaching the, 11; objections to be considered, 87—92.

Saints, Christians first called, 255.

Samaritans described, 232.

Sanctification distinct from inspiration, 294.

Schaff, Rev. Philip, D.D., quoted from, 199.

Scott, Thomas, story of, 22.

Second Epistle of Peter, genuineness of, 310

Self-confidence a precursor of denial, 126.

Self-denial, meaning of, as enforced by Christ, 93.

Self-knowledge, through the discovery of Christ, an element of ministerial power, 34.

Shadow of Peter, 214, 215.

Skepticism connected with the state of the Church, 10.

Simeon, Charles, anecdote of, 94.

INDEX.

Simon Magus, character of, 233, 236; request of, 235.
Sincerity, naturalness indispensable to, 322.
Smith's "Dictionary," quoted from, 311.
Speculative difficulties should not keep us from following Christ, 151
Spurgeon, C. H., referred to, 27.
Stanley, Dean, quoted from, 30, 68, 69.
Steadfastness, elements of, 64.
Stephen, preaching and martyrdom of, 230, 231.
Substitution, why impossible in human law, 90.

TABOR, Mount, not the scene of the Transfiguration, 97.
Thomson, Rev. W. M., D.D., quoted from, 45.
Tongues, gift of, 155.
Transfiguration, purpose of, as connected with Christ, 100; with Moses and Elijah, 100; with Peter, James, and John, 101.
Trench, Archbishop, quoted from, 21, 31, 48, 88, 97, 174.
Trial, often sent to prevent declension, 48; lightened by Christ's intercession, 50; removed by Christ's coming to us, 51; strength obtained for, in devotion, 108; to be expected in Christian experience, 318.

USEFULNESS of a man sometimes connected with his recovery from sin, 332.

WASHING of the disciples' feet by Jesus, meaning of, 116; lessons from, 119.
Wilberforce and Clarkson, ancedote of, 105.
Wisdom needed in the winning of souls, 170.
Wordsworth's "Commentary on the Greek New Testament," quoted from, 142.

THE END

www.ingramcontent.com/pod-product-compliance
Lightning Source LLC
Chambersburg PA
CBHW030319240426
43673CB00040B/1216